Publishing Plates

Publishing Plates

Stereotyping and Electrotyping in Nineteenth-Century US Print Culture

JEFFREY M. MAKALA

The Pennsylvania State University Press
University Park, Pennsylvania

Library of Congress Cataloging-in-Publication Data

Names: Makala, Jeffrey, author.
Title: Publishing plates : stereotyping and electrotyping in nineteenth-century US print culture / Jeffrey M. Makala.
Other titles: Penn State series in the history of the book.
Description: University Park, Pennsylvania : The Pennsylvania State University Press, [2023] | Series: The Penn State series in the history of the book | Includes bibliographical references and index.
Summary: "Explores stereotyping and electrotyping in U.S. literature and history. Examines how printers, typefounders, authors, and publishers managed the transition as new technologies displaced printing traditions of the early nineteenth century"—Provided by publisher.
Identifiers: LCCN 2022037231 | ISBN 9780271094038 (hardback) | ISBN 9780271094045 (paper)
Subjects: LCSH: Stereotyping (Printing)—United States—History—19th century. | Electrotyping—United States—History—19th century. | Printing industry—United States—History—19th century.
Classification: LCC Z252 .M35 2022 | DDC 686.2/314097309034—dc23/eng/20220818
LC record available at https://lccn.loc.gov/2022037231

Copyright © 2023 Jeffrey M. Makala
All rights reserved
Printed in the United States of America
Published by The Pennsylvania State University Press,
University Park, PA 16802–1003

The Pennsylvania State University Press is a member of the Association of University Presses.

It is the policy of The Pennsylvania State University Press to use acid-free paper. Publications on uncoated stock satisfy the minimum requirements of American National Standard for Information Sciences—Permanence of Paper for Printed Library Material, ANSI Z39.48–1992.

For Melissa, for everything

Why, sir, in this very city there is buried treasure, treasure under ground; not diamonds, not ingots, but treasure worth far more than any said to have been hidden by Captain Kidd. Genii, imprisoned in little boxes, that at the beck of the publisher start out with a power more potent than that of the spirit described in the Arabian tale.
—The Reverend E. H. Chapin, toast at the Association of American Publishers banquet, 27 September 1855

Were we required to characterise this age of ours by any single epithet, we should be tempted to call it, not an Heroical, Devotional, Philosophical, or Moral Age, but, above all others, the Mechanical Age. It is the Age of Machinery, in every outward and inward sense of that word; the age which, with its whole undivided might, forwards, teaches, and practices the great art of adapting means to ends.
—Thomas Carlyle, "Signs of the Times," 1829

Democracy not only infuses a taste for letters among the trading classes, but introduces a trading spirit into literature.
—Alexis de Tocqueville, *Democracy in America*, 1835

CONTENTS

List of Illustrations | viii
Acknowledgments | ix

Introduction | 1

1 The Development and Spread of Stereotyping in Europe and North America | 10

2 Mathew Carey and the Family Bible Marketplace | 41

3 The American Bible Society and the Possibilities of Large-Scale Printing | 68

4 Material Texts: Trade Sales, Reprinting, and the Book Trades | 102

5 Stereotyping in Language, Literature, and Material Culture | 129

Epilogue: Abraham Hart and Nineteenth-Century Changes in the Printing Trades | 147

Appendix A: First Uses of Stereotype Plates in the United States, by Date and Location | 153

Appendix B: "Directions for Repairing Plates," ca. 1820 | 156

Appendix C: Inventory of Stereotype Plates Belonging to the American Bible Society, 1829 | 158

Notes | 160
Bibliography | 175
Index | 188

ILLUSTRATIONS

1. Two electrotyped book plates | 14
2. Stereotype foundry, showing plaster being broken off a newly cast plate | 18
3. Stereotype foundry, showing casting and cleaning newly cast plates | 21
4. Casting box for making a plate | 22
5. Molding frame for making a plaster impression of type | 25
6. Stereotype block for raising a plate to type height | 26
7. The first book stereotyped in the United States | 47
8. Trade circular for Collins & Co.'s family quarto Bible, 1815, p. 1 | 53
9. Trade circular for Collins & Co.'s family quarto Bible, 1815, p. 2 | 54
10. Mathew Carey's Bible list, March 1816, p. 1 | 55
11. Mathew Carey's Bible list, March 1816, p. 2 | 56
12. "Adding plates to an electrotyping vat" | 136

ACKNOWLEDGMENTS

I would like especially to thank David S. Shields for his long-standing support, encouragement, and always excellent advice, especially in thinking about interdisciplinary scholarship. Paula Feldman, Gretchen Woertendyke, and Bobby Donaldson all provided crucial help and feedback over many years. Paula Feldman was, as always, an especially astute editor. Leon Jackson, Don Krummel, Mel McCombie, Joel Myerson, Patrick Scott, Laura Dassow Walls, and Michael Winship graciously provided direction at critical points.

Thanks also to Kate Adams, Emahunn Campbell, Cynthia Davis, Paul Erickson, David Gants, James N. Green, Zella Hilton, Brooke Palmieri, James L. W. West III, and to Patrick Alexander, Josie DiNovo, Ryan Peterson, Laura Reed-Morrisson, Alex Vose, Suzanne Wolk, and the entire production team at Penn State University Press, who helped turn an electronic manuscript into a true material text. Jessica Freeman at Potomac Indexing did superb indexing work.

As a special collections librarian, I must acknowledge the tremendous amount of unseen and all too often unacknowledged labor of librarians, library staff, and archivists—my colleagues in the professions—over many generations, in making the numerous manuscript collections and other printed sources examined in this book easy to locate, accessible, and well preserved in their respective repositories. Scholars locate and consult materials in archives and libraries only after many hands have spent long hours acquiring, identifying, arranging, describing, and preserving these materials and making them available to the public. I am most grateful for the invaluable assistance of librarians, curators, and archivists at the American Antiquarian Society; the American Bible Society; the Boston Public Library, Special Collections; the British Library; the Columbia University Rare Book and Manuscript Library; Duke University's David M. Rubenstein Rare Book and Manuscript Library; the Grolier Club Library; the Historical Society of Pennsylvania; Special Collections, Baker Library, Harvard Business School; Houghton Library, Harvard University; the Library Company of Philadelphia and its fellows seminar series; the Massachusetts Historical Society; the New York Public Library, Division of Rare Books and Special Collections; the Louis Round Wilson Library at the University of North

Carolina–Chapel Hill; the Herbert D. Katz Center for Advanced Judaic Studies, University of Pennsylvania; the Kislack Center for Special Collections, Rare Books, and Manuscripts at the University of Pennsylvania; the Presbyterian Historical Society in Philadelphia; Special Collections at the University of Reading, UK; the Rosenbach Museum and Library in Philadelphia; and the Rare Book School at the University of Virginia.

A William Reese Fellowship in American Bibliography from the Library Company of Philadelphia permitted extensive work at the Library Company and the Historical Society of Pennsylvania, and a stay at Reese House at the American Antiquarian Society was much appreciated.

An early version of chapter 2 was given as a paper at the Bibliographical Society of America's New Scholars Program panel at its annual meeting in 2015; an expanded version appeared in the *Papers of the Bibliographical Society of America* in December 2015. An early version of chapter 3 was given as a paper at the annual meeting of the Society for the History of Authorship, Reading and Publishing (SHARP) in Victoria, BC, in 2017, parts of which later appeared in *Printing History* in the winter of 2019. An early version of chapter 4 was given as a paper at the SHARP annual meeting in Montreal in 2015. I would like to thank the editors of *PBSA* and *Printing History* for allowing these articles to be reworked and expanded into chapters and included here.

My colleagues at Furman University, and especially in the Furman University Libraries, have been paragons of support, understanding, and encouragement during this process. Elaina Griffith and her staff tirelessly secured many obscure books for me via interlibrary loan over the course of many years. The Research and Professional Growth Committee of the Furman University faculty and the Furman Humanities Center provided much needed research, travel, and indexing support. Caroline Mills, Michele Speitz, and my colleagues on the board of the Furman Humanities Center have been incredibly supportive.

I am grateful to my parents for a lifetime of love and support. Karen and Rudy Edmundson are equally supportive and loved. Murray and Maggie provide companionship, love, insight, and much-needed perspective. Murray has been with me on this path from its beginning, and I owe him a debt of gratitude I cannot fully express. Kitsey, Remy, and Simone deserve recognition and thanks as excellent friends. The Warwick Road Cheese Club provided much-needed support and nourishment. Melissa Edmundson Makala has tirelessly supported and encouraged me in everything, and is a scholar whose work always leaves me amazed. This book, and the journey that led to it, could not have been completed without her.

Introduction

In the thirty-year period between 1810 and 1840, the printing trades and nascent publishing industry in the United States underwent a series of transformations that changed how books and other printed matter were created. These transformations changed notions of authorship and reading practices and began to break down an artisan-based model of printing and publishing that dated to the late medieval and early modern period. In a short time, the introduction of power presses, the adoption of stereotyping (printing from cast plates instead of standing type), the introduction of machine-made paper, and the growth and consolidation of local printers into regional and national publishers all presented challenges and opportunities to an existing trade, the localized artisan craft practices of which had not fundamentally changed since the earliest days of European printing in the fifteenth century. All of these innovations became market-ready, at least for some well-capitalized printers, in this thirty-year period. The most successful printers amassed capital (some of it in the form of stereotype plates) and secured wider distribution networks for their output, allowing them rightfully to be called publishers in the modern sense. Newly formed organizations such as the American Bible Society immediately grasped the ways in which these innovations in speed, size, and reach could allow them to dramatically increase the scale and impact of their mission to produce and distribute printed scriptures to the nation's citizens. The calculated growth and innovation of regional printing and publishing businesses during this time, together with their successes and failures, paved the way for the large-scale, nationally focused commercial publishing houses that would emerge in the United States by midcentury.

Publishing Plates investigates the development and significance of stereotyping and its companion process, electrotyping, in the United States, primarily through the lens of book history and literary studies. It argues that stereotyping was the most significant of these early nineteenth-century innovations that helped create the large-scale, nationally based publishing industry in the United States by 1850. If a publisher made the right choice of title and followed the right business model, investing in stereotype plates could secure a greater market share and provide years of cheap reprints. If they chose to publish the wrong text, it could tie up significant amounts of capital better used elsewhere. As some local printers grew into regional and national publishers, the decisions about when and how to invest in new technology became crucial to their growth and success. This book explores some of these decisions, including several unsuccessful ones. By mining the archives of nineteenth-century US printers and publishers, a detailed picture emerges of individual reactions to technological changes and disruptions in the printing trades, and of how American printing and publishing grew into the industry it is today.

In his 1816 inaugural address as the Rumford Professor and Lecturer on the Application of the Sciences to the Useful Arts at Harvard University, Jacob Bigelow celebrated what he considered the unique inventive achievements of the citizens of the United States. These accomplishments were not pursued with an eye to fame or fortune, he said, but with an inherently *American* spirit of improvement and interest in technological progress. Bigelow argued that the origins, government, and natural resources of the United States set it apart from other nations and created the unique conditions for its advancement: "The progress of our internal improvements, and the high state of the mechanic arts among us, as well as in our sister states, has entitled us to the character of a nation of inventors."[1] American invention, he argued, should serve a higher purpose than simply to make profits for a small group of owners, as in the Old World. Bigelow believed that labor without human progress and invention without improvement to society was a regressive model more suited to the older economies of Europe than to the unique character of the early US Republic. A new, representative democracy, unique in the world, naturally lent itself to new, democratic forms of innovation in the mechanical arts. In the United States, a spirit of quiet progress and steady innovation was the reason the new Republic had advanced so far in so little time, he thought, securing its freedom and becoming a progressive model for the rest of the world to emulate.

This early articulation of American mechanical exceptionalism closely linked democratic principles with technological improvement, and its object was to realize human potential and promote societal advancement. Bigelow's ideological position, here applied to technology, was not uncommon in the early national period, where the recognition and celebration of uniquely *American* ways of conduct, from political organization, to spelling reform, to medicine, architecture, and business, were commonplace in a new nation attempting to establish itself as an important, successful experiment on the world stage.

Bigelow himself expanded the meaning of the term "technology" to include its practical, applied aims when his expansive survey of American mechanical achievements, *Elements of Technology*, was published in 1829.[2] This work appeared, notably, in the same year as Thomas Carlyle's essay "Signs of the Times," with its negative portrayal of the machine. For many in the new Republic, mechanical innovation seemed to be a natural outgrowth of democratic values. Any early hesitation about the growth of applied industrial technology and its role in the new nation gradually dissipated as nineteenth-century innovations proved that technological progress and republicanism could reinforce each other for the betterment—if not of all, then at least of many. As John Kasson notes, throughout the early nineteenth century, public voices "hailed the union of technology and republicanism and celebrated their fulfillment in an ever more prosperous and progressive nation."[3] Thomas Jefferson, the champion of agrarianism, also had an Enlightenment-based sense of optimism about the progress of science in solving real problems and improving the lives of ordinary people. As the young nation's first secretary of state, he reviewed the first US patent applications in the 1790s. As president, he championed the newly formed Patent Office (1802) as a symbol of US ingenuity. In Jefferson's view, a republican government could help encourage and cultivate native talent in the mechanical arts in ways that other forms of government could not. He wrote to Robert Fulton, the inventor of the steamboat, in 1810, "I am not afraid of new inventions or improvements, nor bigoted to the practices of our forefathers."[4] Jefferson, with his ideal of the independent yeoman farmer, was wary of the new Republic's becoming a nation of manufacturers, but he felt that technological improvements could alter the quality of life for its citizens in significant and meaningful ways.

Aileen Fyfe has recently argued, and I agree, that technological changes in the printing trades during the nineteenth century are often alluded to in other works of history, but exactly how they occurred on the ground is still little studied.[5] The introduction and impact of stereotyping is mentioned, for example, in all the recently published national histories of the book in the United States, Britain, Canada, and Ireland, and also in bibliographical manuals and other works on printing history.[6] But the last full-length monograph on stereotyping in the printing trades, George Kubler's *New History of Stereotyping*, was published in 1941.[7] Other disciplines could add some contributions to a deeper study of stereotyping in the United States. Scholars in the field of American studies have observed that a culture of uncritical technological positivism pervades much of the American history of technology, and they have argued that we need increased interdisciplinary attention to "stories of technological stewardship" and critiques of technology "as both substance and ideology in American cultural life."[8] As this book is primarily concerned with the meanings generated by the introduction of a newly invented physical object—the stereotype plate—into a long-established profession, an object that contains both textual and symbolic meaning in addition to embodied capital, it is important to consider the increased critical attention to how material objects resonate and create new interpretive meanings as individuals interact with them. Anthropological and historical studies of objects have become commonplace in the past few decades (the latter often grouped, for better or worse, into "material culture" studies), but objects and their meanings are also the subject of increased attention by literary scholars and cultural theorists.[9]

This book, then, is necessarily informed by critical studies in the history of technology. Printing historian Jessica Despain recently discussed the work of film scholar Rick Altman on "the social interplay that occurs between the creation of new technologies and the human usage of them." Altman refers to this approach as "crisis historiography," which understands that the uses of technology are socially constructed and are both *ongoing* and *multiple*. That is, the technology is never socially constructed once and for all. During a crisis, a technology is understood in varying ways, resulting in modification not only of the technology itself but also of terminology, exhibition practices, and audience attitudes."[10] Because the introduction of stereotype plates offered printers new options for reprinting, investment, and the expansion of their trade, the crisis they faced, in the form of decisions on how to best employ plates and the texts they chose to have cast into plates, fits well into this model. The multiple ways in which printers and publishers understood the significance of this new technology, its potential, and its limitations, and how this understanding continued to evolve and change over time, drives this study. Also, the significance of owning a newly cast set of stereotype plates as a piece of intellectual property, and the ways in which this physical change in publishing was managed through storage, shipping, and physical movement through urban and rural spaces, is worthy of greater attention and is considered here.

Different business models for owning and using stereotype plates and other new technologies in the printing trades will emerge in the narrative that follows. Some individuals and organizations successfully managed this transition; others did not. By looking closely at the decision-making processes of the people who worked through these changing times in their respective professions, we can avoid the trap of falling into one standard description of how the introduction of stereotyping and electrotyping played only a singular role in the transformation of the nineteenth-century printing trades and publishing industry. This simplistic shorthand, which is still found in many of the standard printing and publishing histories, also tends to embrace varying degrees of technological determinism and positivism. Michael Warner reminds us to guard against granting technology "an ontological status prior to culture," observing that "practices of technology ... are always structural, and that their meaningful structure is the dimension of culture."[11] The technological changes examined in this book are fully embedded in the cultures of the early US Republic and the artisan-based apprentice models of labor found in the printing trades in the modern West, and in their attendant ideologies: the Enlightenment and post-Enlightenment enshrinement of reason and progress, the Protestant work ethic, and the seemingly unlimited potential for human advancement offered by the boundless new American continent, brimming over with resources of every kind. But the ways in which this technology was deployed, as this book shows, were not at all monolithic or straightforward, nor are these ideologies without inherent contradictions, problematic aspects, and disastrous consequences for those without political or economic influence, such as Native Americans and enslaved and free Black citizens.

These theoretical areas of concern underlie the conclusions that follow in *Publishing Plates*, which discusses the ways in which stereotype plates became embodied objects of capital, corporeal manifestations of authorship and investment, instances of intellectual property and artistic expression—portable and infused with the potential for reproduction and distribution in ways that had not been seen before. By looking at printing, publishing, and authorship through a materialist lens, focused on the plates that enabled these changes to occur and the people who used them, we can better understand the transformations that took place in the printing trades and nascent publishing industry in the United States in the first half of the nineteenth century.

❧

Chapter 1 traces the European origins of the process of casting plates from set type and its first successful realizations in the United States, drawing a parallel with its multiple origin stories to the multiple national origin stories of printing itself in the fifteenth century. It updates the last histories of stereotyping written by George Kubler in the 1930s and 1940s and traces its first instances in the United States to the successful English precedents of Charles Mahon, Third Earl of Stanhope, and his circle of printers in the first decades of the nineteenth century. This chapter brings together, for the first time, all the earliest mentions of stereotyping in the United States in printing trade manuals and popular literature. It describes the first successful uses of stereotype casting in New York City in the 1810s and 1820s, the interconnections among the earliest American typefounders, stereotypers, and printers, and stereotyping's first introduction into the printing trades.

With chapter 1 having established stereotyping in the United States in 1813, chapter 2 focuses on the business practices of the Philadelphia publisher Mathew Carey as he navigated a changing national marketplace in quarto Bibles between 1813 and 1824. Carey already owned one of the only complete Bibles in standing type, from which he could print as many copies as he needed, and so the introduction of stereotyped Bibles by several New York typefounders in the mid-1810s complicated his market dominance and investment. As the production of multiple sets of quarto Bible plates threatened to upend the market, Carey was forced to make decisions about acquiring some of these sets for his own use. He was also forced to react to increased competition for the same product produced by competitors using a newer technology. Carey's main regional competitor, the New York printer and stereotyper Collins & Company, produced exactly the same range of Bible variants from its newly cast set of stereotype plates that Carey did, but Collins undercut Carey on price every time. As multiple sets of plates for the same book entered the market, only well-capitalized publishers like Carey could afford to invest in them. In order to maintain his market share, Carey purchased a complete set of quarto Bible plates, only to store it untouched for several years in an unsuccessful attempt to embargo it and maintain a fleeting regional monopoly on the quarto Bible trade. Within a few years, as multiple sets were used for the production of the same work in cities throughout the country, Carey's advantages dissolved as the marketplace for quarto Bibles became diffuse and oversaturated.

Chapter 3 turns to the work and influence of the New York–based American Bible Society (ABS), whose businessmen-founders eagerly embraced new advances in the printing trades to enhance their mission to produce and distribute cheap Bibles throughout the young nation. The ABS was established because its founders knew that stereotype Bibles could spread the gospel quickly and efficiently. Evangelical organizations such as the ABS and the American Sunday School Union were the first nonprofit groups to adopt stereotyping to further their publishing goals, effectively creating the first mass media organizations in the United States. For the ABS managers, ownership of the means to reproduce the Word at will was as much a sign of God's Providence as it was a technological or scientific advance. This chapter explores the printing and business practices of the ABS as it commissioned and amassed stereotype plates and printed cheap Bibles and New Testaments, from its founding in 1816 through its attempts in the late 1820s to supply every household in the country with a Bible. By looking closely at the ABS's decisions to employ new technologies in its printing work, we can better understand the newly emergent marketplace in stereotype plates, the risks and rewards of being early adopters of new printing technologies, and the ways in which the ABS's calculated growth and innovation became models for the large-scale commercial publishers that would emerge by midcentury.

Chapter 4's focus extends further outward, to the afterlife of stereotype plates as they were sold, exchanged, auctioned, and used to create multiple published editions. It investigates advertisements in the printing trade and looks closely at used sets of plates offered for sale at the industry trade sales between 1824 and 1900. Sets of plates were sources of capital for publishers; they were also, for the first time, true material texts, the physical embodiment of an authorial work and a self-contained, portable source of reproductive value. Reference works and scripture mostly lacked copyright protection, but some new works that were cast in plates were often sold or auctioned with their copyrights intact, offering second-tier or regional publishers the opportunity to acquire a relatively recent work to reprint. Some texts had long afterlives as they were bought, sold, and printed many times over the years. This chapter traces the stereotype plates of Solomon Northup's *Twelve Years a Slave* (1853) through their appearances at trade sales and through multiple reprintings and looks at Herman Melville's experience navigating the stereotype marketplace for his own works.

Chapter 5 examines some of the cultural changes caused by the introduction of stereotyping and stereotype plates into literary circles, in the American lexicon, and in the broader cultural landscape of nineteenth-century America, including African American authorship and publishing. Edgar Allan Poe advocated the new process of "anastatic" printing as a way for authors to stereotype their own writings and reconnect directly with the reading public, excluding publishers entirely. Walt Whitman wrote of "making poems," both as a poet and also quite literally as the initiator and owner of the stereotype plates for *Leaves of Grass*. Henry David Thoreau, an author whose livelihood and family prosperity were deeply embedded in the supply chains of the stereotyping and electrotyping industries, also evolved his own literary uses of the term "stereotype." Common language quickly appropriated *stereotype* and *stereotyping* from terms specific to the printing industry to synonyms for copying, and finally to the pejorative definition that we use today. Finally, this chapter looks at the experiences of the authors Sojourner Truth and William Wells Brown and their intimate connections to the stereotype plates of their own narratives and identities, and considers the ways in which embodied forms of authorship in the form of plates could serve as vehicles for liberation, independence, and justice.

Together, these chapters explore a changing technological world in the printing and publishing industry in the nineteenth-century United States and the ways in which the introduction of stereotyping affected the broader cultural landscape. The digital humanities scholar Alan Liu writes aptly of "new media" encounters with older forms of media, "good narratives of new media encounter are in the end less stories than whole imaginative environments or, as I termed them, borderlands of surmise. Good accounts of new media encounter imagine affordances and configurations of potentiality.... We want a way of imagining our encounter with new media that surprises us out of the 'us' we thought we knew."[12] The same spirit informs *Publishing Plates* and its exploration of the changing media environment in US cultures of print during the nineteenth century, specifically the introduction and uses of stereotyping and electrotyping. The book examines how the printing and publishing worlds of the era reacted to change; how individuals, businesses, and organizations used these new technologies to further their aims; and how the cultures of plates that emerged had broader meanings that rippled out and influenced popular culture, everyday life, and language through their ultimate products: printed material texts. This new understanding of the role of material texts pervades nineteenth-century American culture, from the physicality and ubiquity of the plates themselves to the popular uses of the term "stereotyping" as a metaphor for the expansiveness and the limitations of rapid technological change. Carlyle was right: the early nineteenth century was most certainly a mechanical age, with all that the term implies, and nowhere more so than in the adaptive technological environment that grew up in the printing trades and publishing industry.

CHAPTER 1

 The Development and Spread of Stereotyping in Europe and North America

In 1832, the mathematician, economist, and computing pioneer Charles Babbage published a long treatise titled *On the Economy of Machinery and Manufactures*. At the end of an early chapter titled "Of Copying," Babbage invited his readers to consider the printed letterforms that made up the book they held in their hands. The page before them was the final product, he noted, of "six successful stages of copying": the initial carving of a punch, the creation of a matrix, the casting of type from the matrix, the forming of a plaster mold from the set type of the book's page, the casting of a stereotype plate from that mold, and, finally, the reverse impression of that plate, made in ink, on paper.[1] These six steps summarize the mechanical processes needed to print a book in 1832 using the new process of stereotyping.

Babbage chose this example of new developments in typefounding and printing technologies carefully. He wanted his readers to pause and consider the hidden nature of printing and print culture in everyday life. And he wanted to highlight a significant new technological advance in an old artisan and a new industrial practice, one that had always sought manufacturing consistency and uniformity of output as its two primary measures of pride and accomplishment. The complex set of skilled industrial processes required to print a book was not usually noticed by the consumer, who only judged the finished product against a world of similar printed matter. Machine parts and other objects of industrial manufacture—pieces of type and stereotype plates, for example—had to be precise copies of one another in order to maximize manufacturing productivity and uniformity in output. Likewise, the advances in the printing trades that incorporated these new stages of copying—in effect complicating the manufacturing process—show how, relatively soon after their adoption, something approaching perfection might be achieved, a perfection potentially applicable to all forms of industrial manufacturing. It is significant that creating a stereotype mold from standing type—the fourth of Babbage's six stages—is the stage in which he notes "the union of the intellectual and the mechanical takes place."[2]

Babbage's example helps frame the subject of this book, in both its scope and its aims. This chapter investigates the earliest days of stereotyping in the United States following its introduction from England in 1812. The invention and rapid adoption of stereotyping in the late eighteenth and early nineteenth centuries constitute the first significant change in European printing technology since printing with moveable type was perfected in the fifteenth century. Just as Babbage showed his readers how the products of technological advancement lay essentially hidden in everyday life, so too has the process of creating and using stereotype plates in printing received insufficient attention from bibliographers, historians of technology, textual critics, and literary historians. My aim here is to explore several aspects of a larger series of questions surrounding the early adoption, uses, and significance of the shift from printing exclusively from standing type to printing with stereotype plates in the United States.[3] Using methodologies and critical perspectives from analytical bibliography and new work in the history of the book (or book history, or critical bibliography), I also consider the greater cultural significance of stereotypes and other types of plates in this newly emergent "culture of plates" within the framework of American studies and material culture studies.

The widespread adoption of stereotyping fundamentally changed the way in which books (and, later, periodicals and newspapers) were printed. The book historian John Carter calls it the "one really radical invention" in printing to take place between the pioneering work of Johannes Gutenberg in the mid-fifteenth century and the shift to photo and then digital composition in the mid- and late twentieth century.[4] The commissioning of plates by printers and publishers altered local shop practices, distribution methods, the relationship between authors and publishers, and labor and management issues in the printing trades. A new, secondhand market in stereotype plates developed that would further complicate the production, reprinting, and distribution of books and material texts throughout the nineteenth century.

The first American stereotype plates were cast in New York in 1813. Within only a few years, typefounders in New York, Boston, and Philadelphia were producing thousands of plates that they sold to printers and publishers along the East Coast and even into the West. High-demand items such as schoolbooks, New Testaments, and complete Bibles were the primary texts cast into plates, and new organizations like the American Bible Society were early adopters of the new technology.[5] Mathew Carey, the largest publisher and the highest-volume seller of Bibles in America before the advent of stereotyping, commissioned a set of New Testament plates early on. Carey quickly realized that the production of multiple copies of plates for the same text would fundamentally alter the dynamics by which publishers brought certain works to market. By 1840, stereotyping was firmly established as a cost-effective model for many genres of printed matter, and a more diverse array of steady sellers, including novels and some periodicals, were beginning to be stereotyped. Later in the century, with the advent of high-volume power presses, newspapers would use stereotyping to print copies of the same edition of a newspaper, employing multiple sets of plates on multiple presses running at the same time, which sped up the printing process dramatically. The growth and development of printing with plates also has implications for our understanding of some broader topics in the study of nineteenth-century print culture, such as the practices of reprinting, the significance and growth of religious publishing, the role of serials, and our understanding of a transatlantic literary culture relating to the transmission and distribution of texts that moves from the United States to Europe as much as in the opposite direction.

In the handpress period in the West, which lasted from 1450 until roughly 1820 (or later, depending upon where one looks), books, pamphlets, periodicals, and broadsides were all produced in the same way. Individual letterforms made of type metal, an alloy of lead, tin, and antimony, were picked from a type cabinet by a compositor and arranged, letter by letter, to form words and sentences. These lines of type were placed on a composing table or on the press bed itself, with added spacing between words and lines, and the whole unit of individual pieces of type and spacing then became a form, which could comprise one page or many pages arranged together, depending on the text and its use. The form was locked tightly into place on the bed of a press made of wood or iron, inked, and pressed under the weight of a platen to make a reverse impression of the type onto a sheet of paper or parchment.

Two or three men worked the press as a production team, adding and removing sheets, re-inking the type, and pulling the large platen lever to make the impression. After the press run was complete, the form was cleaned and unlocked, and the individual pieces of type were put back into their cabinets for reuse while the completed print job hung or was stacked to dry. With careful use, type fonts could be used and reused for different printing jobs for many years, sometimes decades. Small changes in the size and shape of presses notwithstanding, this artisanal practice of printing books, newspapers, pamphlets, and smaller jobs such as indulgences or business forms persisted essentially unchanged for nearly four centuries. Gutenberg could have walked into a printshop in lower Manhattan in 1820 and recognized every piece of equipment, type, ink, paper, and furnishing around him.

Stereotyping involved making a copy of the composed type, which could be used to print the text, replacing the type itself. A plaster of Paris mixture was spread on top of the form of set type, with graphite or some solution added first to aid in the removal of the hardened plaster. When ready, the hard plaster mold was removed and its reverse impression was used as a mold to which hot metal was added to form one sold piece of type—a stereotype plate—which was then broken off from the plaster, cleaned, beveled, and shaved to a uniform size and thickness. The new plate was thus a perfect copy of the set type in the form, which could then be redistributed for another job, never having been printed from. Because the plates were thin, metal or wooden blocks were needed to raise them to type height; they could then be added to the press bed and locked up like any other form of type (fig. 1). In addition to type, woodcut illustrations could be stereotyped in this way, individually or as part of a locked-up form along with type. Later in the century, papier-mâché was successfully used instead of plaster to make an accurate—and less messy—copying medium.

Stereotyping brought about a new level of uniformity in printing output. The stereotyped plates of a book, once cast and initially printed from, could be stored and printed from at will, over many years and through many smaller press runs. For multiple successive impressions, stereotyping offered a clear advantage over having to compose new settings of type for each reprint. The

FIG. 1   Two electrotyped book plates, ca. 1890. Photograph © Richard Jones. Used with permission. Author's collection.

initially higher cost of a set of plates for the right sort of steady-selling item would pay for itself over time and multiple press runs. Bibliographers and textual critics have shown conclusively how books printed during the handpress period were anything but textually consistent, even from copy to copy.[6] At the very end of the handpress period, the adoption of stereotype plates, which themselves were occasionally created in multiple copies, allowed for some greater degree of textual authority. At least this was what publishers of stereotyped titles claimed, though the ways in which this authority was asserted, accepted, and challenged have yet to be fully studied.

As Babbage noted, in making a stereotype plate for printing, a full-page positive impression of a form of standing type was created. Liquid metal was then used to fill in the plaster mold and create a negative impression of the form as a plate with the impression of the full page of type. For a large and busy printshop handling multiple jobs at once, the advantages were clear: the type for one commission or job was used only once—to make the plate—and it could then be distributed immediately for use in other projects instead of being left in place for printing at a later date. Because the type used to create the plate was never printed from directly, it lasted considerably longer than if it were used for making multiple printed impressions.

Other advantages emerged later. As printing with plates was adopted more widely, publishers could print only as many copies of a book as were needed to satisfy the immediate demand. In the handpress period, a printed edition could take several years to sell out before another was needed. Now, if a new impression were needed, an additional press run could be made from the same plates with minimal setup time and effort. Warehousing sets of plates instead of the more fragile (and flammable) unbound sheets of printed books became especially attractive. Larger publishers were creating fireproof vaults by midcentury for their boxed collections of plates.[7] These sets of plates became objects of capital investment, true material texts, as works of intellectual property and skill in composition and casting became permanently embodied in a physical form for the first time in history. Plates became commodities that were commissioned and then bought and sold in the marketplace in ways that the loose type in the cabinets of a printshop's composing room were not.

For steady-selling items like Bibles, prayer books, schoolbooks, and dictionaries, the advantages for publishers were clear, provided the initial investment to purchase or cast a set of plates could be made. Early on, the cost of commissioning a set of stereotypes for a book was at least twice that of traditional textual composition. This limited the adoption of stereotyping, at first, to only the largest publishers and to evangelical concerns such as the American Bible Society, which could bear the up-front costs. Printed works of a limited temporal nature—almanacs, sermons, and other short ephemeral works—did not lend themselves naturally to reprinting, and so were mostly still printed from standing type throughout the century. The use of stereotyping coincided with a series of other technological changes that were beginning to transform the printing trade and publishing industry in the mid-nineteenth century, and thus stereotyping both solidified and hastened a transformation in print culture in other parts of the trades as well.

By the 1830s, as the commissioning of stereotype plates became common, the plates themselves became objects of capital investment. A publisher could hire out a set of plates to another publisher for an edition they did not want to reprint themselves. Publishers could also cooperate with one another on a joint edition using a shared set of plates. Upon death or bankruptcy, the stereotype plates—and any copyrights associated with them—represented substantial quantities of embodied capital that could be liquidated, thus inaugurating a secondhand trade in stereotype plates that took place at biannual printers' trade sales and also through direct sale and advertisement in printing trade journals (discussed in detail in chapter 4). In part because of the investment in creating plates and their selective use, the introduction of stereotyping was a primary influence on the maturation of the American printing trades from a loose affiliation of almost entirely local printers, at the end of the eighteenth century, to a true national publishing industry by the middle of the nineteenth.

EARLY STEREOTYPING EXPERIMENTS

The earliest claims about the invention of modern stereotyping are as unsettled—and almost as mythical—as the origins of printing itself. New research continues to shed light on our understanding of how the first European books were printed. In recent years, the early products of Gutenberg's press have been examined more closely than ever before, with the aid of bibliographical analysis and digital technologies that allow scholars to locate and compare evidence of repeated words or uniform letter combinations that are longer than individual pieces of set type, suggesting that some form of sand casting or other mold-made impressions of words or letter combinations were made during the earliest days of printing in Europe.[8] Several more or less successful later attempts to cast printing plates from set type were made from the sixteenth through the eighteenth centuries, each with its own nationalistic tradition, whether Dutch, Scottish, or English. Typefounders also experimented with creating larger blocks of cast letterforms for printing, though none of these experiments was ever successfully adopted for large-scale production. Many histories of Western printing refer to experiments in the Low Countries in the seventeenth century, in which set type was soldered together on its back to create a heavy, solid block that was printed from and, presumably, saved for later use.[9] Other scholars have examined early attempts by Dutch printers, especially by the Reverend Johann Müller in Leiden, to make impressions of type forms.[10] Nineteenth-century English and American printing histories and shop manuals often allude to these Dutch experiments. George Kubler, in his *New History of Stereotyping* (1941), credits Müller and a partner, a man named Van der Mey, with perfecting a process in which forms of set type were immersed in vats of liquid solder, fusing them together into a block. Kubler also mentions parallel efforts by Joseph Athias, an Amsterdam printer, around the same time.[11] J. Leander

Bishop, in his *History of American Manufactures*, states that stereotyping was invented by "John Mueller at Leyden in 1690."[12] Articles on printing and typefounding in young people's magazines, often following the lead of many of these sources and of popular encyclopedias, also point to the Dutch experiments as the forerunners of current practice, though an article in the Cincinnati-based *Family Magazine* also took pains to mention some eighteenth-century American experiments, fueling the nationalist fire for claiming precedents in innovation.[13]

William Ged, an Edinburgh goldsmith, succeeded in creating plates of text suitable for printing by the late 1720s. He secured backing from several London investors in the early 1730s, though he was not able to license or sell his invention, despite strong interest and trials at the university press at Cambridge.[14] Ged printed an edition of the two main works of the ancient Roman historian Sallust in 1739 that announced on its title page that it was printed entirely from plates ("non typis mobilius"), and he produced two impressions of a second book from plates in 1742.[15] Ged died in 1749 having failed to establish his plate-making business.

The prolific Scottish printer Andrew Foulis partnered with Alexander Tilloch to take out a patent for plate printing from molds in 1784 and printed several books using the process before abandoning it.[16] There is some evidence that Tilloch had seen one of Ged's old plates being used as a paperweight in the London offices of the publisher John Murray, who had received it as a gift.[17]

In the modern era, the French firm of Didot "coined the name 'stereotype' [in French, *cliché*] for printing from solid lead plates" in 1795, from which they printed several works in the 1790s.[18] Didot used type made from an alloy different from type metal for its stereotyping process, a harder alloy than traditional type that stood up better to the molding process. The set form of type was then used as a large punch to impress its letterforms into another, softer lead plate, which formed the matrix. The matrix was then used to cast a metal plate, which was pried from it by means of a knife. Armand Camus, writing about Didot's work in the 1790s, described another method used by the firm in 1798 in which copper forms were made from a new plate, with the mold made from hardened earth or clay, but this method produced a lesser result than the metal-stamping process.[19] Didot's stereotyped works were continually published thereafter using these methods.

Most Anglophone histories of printing point to the Englishman Charles Mahon, Third Earl of Stanhope, rather than to Didot, as the modern originator of stereotyping, though Didot brought stereotyped books to market using their own process a decade earlier. While Didot's method was known in England, Lord Stanhope, in addition to inventing the modern iron printing press, succeeded in perfecting his own stereotyping process using plaster casts of type instead of lead plates (fig. 2). At one point in his experiments, he made the acquaintance of Alexander Tilloch and was able to carry Tilloch and Foulis's experiments further, producing plaster molds of set type from which he was able to cast usable plates. By 1802, Stanhope had worked out the difficulties of plaster casting and claimed that his method of English stereotyping could be adopted by the industry in volume. Preferring it to Didot's version, Partington's *Printer's Complete Guide* (1825) stated that Stanhope's stereotype plate was "a fac-simile of the page from which it was taken."[20] At the beginning of the nineteenth century, these two parallel processes of stereotype casting were widely known and reported on in newspaper accounts throughout Europe and the Americas. The Napoleonic Wars likewise helped polarize these two origin stories, making them part of nationalist mythologies. In both England and France, however, stereotyping remained a small niche process within the

FIG. 2   Stereotype foundry, showing plaster being broken off a newly cast plate. From "The Commercial History of a Penny Magazine—No. III: Compositors' Work and Stereotyping," *Monthly Supplement of the Penny Magazine of the Society for the Diffusion of Useful Knowledge* 107 (31 October–30 November 1833): 472. Author's collection.

printing trades that was not quickly or universally adopted owing to its high cost and complex set of steps. Once introduced into the United States, though, stereotyping was adopted more widely and at a more rapid rate.

Stanhope's stereotype process was used to print books in London in the first decade of the nineteenth century, though today Stanhope is better remembered for his improvements to the mechanics of the iron printing press. There is some evidence that he attempted to license his inventions to Americans during this time, meeting and corresponding extensively with US papermaker Joshua Gilpin, though by 1806 Gilpin's business interests were directed elsewhere.[21] In perfecting his process, Stanhope partnered for several years with a master printer, Andrew Wilson, to bring his experiments to fruition. Wilson later went on to run his own printing business, which used stereotyping.[22]

Some experiments also took place in colonial America and the early Republic to "fix" the text of printed works by making impressions of set type. Almost inevitably, when looking at innovations in colonial American printing, one documented attempt involves the experiments of Benjamin Franklin. Franklin corresponded extensively in the 1740s with the later governor of New York Cadwallader Colden about methods for fixing set type into blocks, concluding that it could be done, though he never attempted it himself.[23] Later experiments by Franklin's nephew Benjamin Mecom suggest that, while working in Philadelphia in 1775, Mecom succeeded in casting plates for several pages of a New Testament but did not finish casting the complete book.[24]

Isaiah Thomas mentions stereotyping in his *History of Printing in America*, which he published in 1810 after a decade of research and compilation, and before the process was commercially used in the United States. Thomas's book is an extensive, evidence-based chronology for which he made considerable efforts to gather and verify source material. Though no one was casting stereotype plates in the United States in 1810, Thomas and others in the young nation were aware of British and French books printed using the new process through their appearances in American booksellers' shops. Perhaps to undercut the French influence, Thomas cited evidence that the Dutch printer in Leiden, Van der Mey, had been successfully experimenting with creating plates in the late seventeenth century, long before Didot brought out editions in the 1790s, and he quoted extensively from an article that summarized the work of the Dutch printers.[25]

In the 1820s and 1830s, Thomas revised his history with the aim of bringing out an updated edition, but he did not live to see it in print. The second, revised edition of *The History of Printing in America* was published from his notes and emendations only in 1874. In it, Thomas shortened his description of the process of casting stereotype plates, eliminating its European origins altogether (fig. 3). And while it was a common practice in the United States among larger publishers in the years in which he made his revisions, the text instead shifted its focus to American antecedents. Thomas mentioned his contemporary Benjamin Mecom's attempts to create stereotypes in 1775 and summarized his post-1810 revisions to the original text succinctly: "Stereotyping is now very common in the United States, and is well executed."[26] Thomas also cited the evidence that Cadwallader Colden had corresponded with Benjamin Franklin in the 1740s on how to fix a form of moveable type in order to make impressions from it.[27] Thomas further mentioned the work of Jacob Perkins of Newburyport, Massachusetts, who created a new method for copying engraved bank note plates to prevent counterfeiting or forgery. Perkins's experiments, which employed a slightly different form for making casts of plates, took place in the first decade of the nineteenth century. Perkins also wrote and published an eight-page students' writing manual printed entirely from copies of cast-steel engraved plates.[28]

DOCUMENTING THE NEW TECHNOLOGY

While Didot's stereotype process used lead plates together with type to form a matrix, the English method of plaster casting was learned by more Americans and was the method ultimately adopted in the United States. Each step of the Anglo-American stereotype process, while initially proprietary, had been well documented since the 1810s and could be found in many printer's manuals and descriptions of typefounding.[29]

Anglophone printers' manuals on both sides of the Atlantic privileged the Stanhope plaster of Paris (or wet plate) method. The first to appear, a short work of sixty pages titled *The Method of Founding Stereotype, as Practiced by Charles Brightly*, was printed for Brightly in the small market town of Bungay, Suffolk, outside London, in the summer of 1809. In this work, Brightly described his own process, a slight variation on Stanhope's plaster of Paris method, in sufficient detail that it could be replicated by a competent typefounder. As a working printer, Brightly also commented on the nature of the initial kinds of type used for composition and casting, their height and hardness in particular, from which a suitable impression could best be taken. Illustrations complemented the text, making Brightly's pamphlet an extremely useful

STEREOTYPE FOUNDRY.

FIG. 3   Stereotype foundry, showing casting and cleaning newly cast plates. From "Stereotyping and Electrotyping," in *The Great Industries of the United States, Being an Historical Summary of the Origin, Growth, and Perfection of the Chief Industrial Arts of This Country* (Hartford: J. B. Burr & Hyde; Chicago: J. B. Burr, Hyde & Co., 1874), 177. Image courtesy of Special Collections and Archives, Furman University Library.

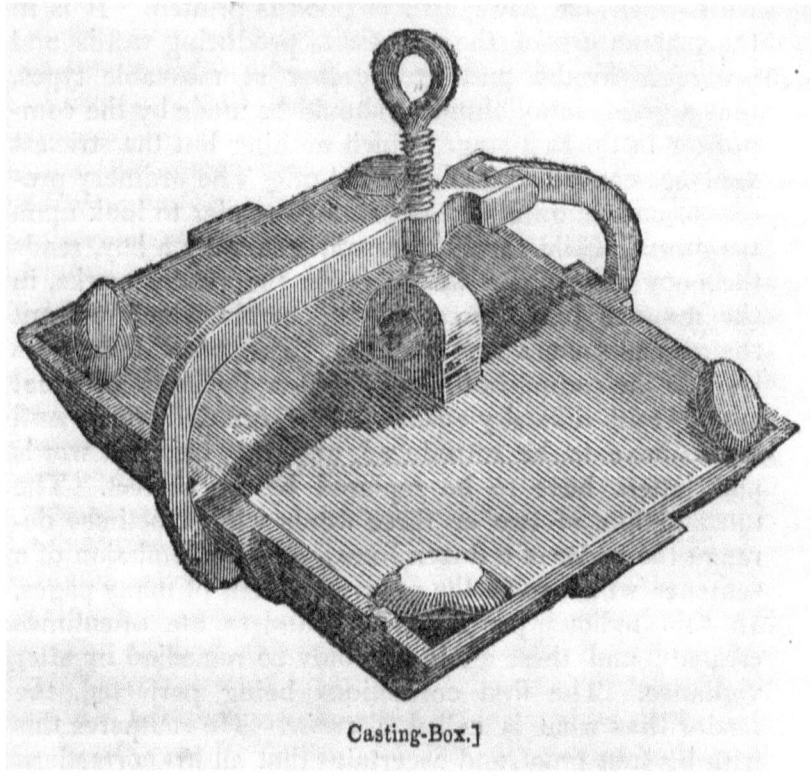

FIG. 4   Casting box for making a plate. From "The Commercial History of a Penny Magazine—No. III: Compositors' Work and Stereotyping," *Monthly Supplement of the Penny Magazine of the Society for the Diffusion of Useful Knowledge* 107 (31 October–30 November 1833): 470. Author's collection.

description of a hitherto proprietary technology (fig. 4). In its final pages, Brightly answered and corrected a defense of stereotyping made by Andrew Wilson, Lord Stanhope's printer, in a May 1807 article in the *Monthly Magazine*, in particular Wilson's assertion that stereotyping would save the reading public between 25 to 40 percent of the price of a common book when stereotype plates were used to print it.[30] Brightly pointed out that such savings could be achieved only if the right works were chosen, and then only for the printer or publisher, not the consumer. Nor would these savings be realized, he noted, until multiple editions or reprintings were made, which in most cases would take years, assuming a standard edition that went through four or more reprintings from the same set of plates. Brightly was not trying to dissuade other publishers from using the new technology, he said, but merely to counter Wilson's overly optimistic assertion.[31]

Brightly predicted innovations that would improve consistency in creating plates so that production costs would become as low as printing from set type. Wasted paper stock from multiple sets of page proofs would be minimized with corrected, consistent sets of plates. Brightly himself had no direct connection to Wilson or Stanhope, so how he learned the process well enough to practice it at this level is still unknown. Other printers in his circle had some connections to the university press in Cambridge, not far away, so Brightly may have had some exposure to the process there, as Wilson and Stanhope had attempted to interest the university press in their experiments earlier in the decade.[32] As the first true exposition of how the new process worked, this pamphlet would have been known and in demand among publishers and typefounders on both sides of the Atlantic.

Thomas Hodgson's *Essay on the Origin and Progress of Stereotype Printing* was printed in Newcastle in 1820 in a modest edition of 306 copies under the patronage of the Newcastle Typographical Society.[33] Hodgson and his brother worked in the family's printing firm. Hodgson acknowledged the work of Armand Gaston Camus, whose 1801 *Histoire et procédés du polytypage et de la stéréotypie* was first published in the *Mémoires de l'Institut*. Hodgson noted that there were twelve establishments in London making stereotype plates and a few known foundries elsewhere in the United Kingdom. It is thus not surprising to learn that when a fire destroyed the Caxton printing office in Liverpool in 1821, the firm already held some "ten thousand pages of stereotype plates."[34]

Hodgson dedicated his *Essay* to the Literary and Philosophical Society of Newcastle, of which he was a member. Less a technical manual than a compiler's history, the work is notable for its acknowledgment of the assistance of Alexander Tilloch and Andrew Wilson, two of the men who were responsible for making the first successful English experiments along with Lord Stanhope. Also of interest is Hodgson's acknowledgment and account of a US innovation in stereotyping that made its way to Britain in 1819, the process of "polytyping" engraved plates, known as siderography, which was developed in Massachusetts by Jacob Perkins.[35]

The first printer's manual published in the United States was *The Printer's Guide* (1818), written and printed by Cornelius van Winkle in New York City. As the printing historian Rollo Silver has written, "For the first time American printers had their own manual with descriptions of American presses, specimens of American typefounders, price lists for printing, and information on supplies." Some parts were taken almost verbatim from English manuals, but "it was prepared by an American printer for the use of American printers."[36] *The Printer's Guide* included a type specimen list from the firm of E. White in New York and another from the firm of D. & G. Bruce that also noted "stereotype blocks to order" in its list of printing supplies that could be ordered by other shops.[37] E. White's specimen list included a five-page series of illustrations titled "Stereotype from Wood-cuts," all stock images that originated in wood and were transferred uniformly to metal by stereotyping. This shift was new: all sorts of uniform cuts, illustrations, and decorations could now be copied and cast as multiples. Cast type illustrations and decorations were generally small, with woodcuts used for larger illustrations. Now, for the first time, a large woodcut could be copied uniformly in cast metal in as many copies as were needed, to order.

Van Winkle's *Guide* went through several editions, but the first description of the stereotyping process appears only in the third edition, published in 1835. Following a summary of the history of printing, Van Winkle mentions stereotyping in a historical note before describing the minutiae of composition, imposition, and presswork. He refers to a *London Magazine* article on Dutch perfections of a new printing process similar to stereotyping and mentions Ged, Didot, and Stanhope. In his discussion of Stanhope's work, Van Winkle quotes the printer Andrew Wilson as saying, "the various processes of the stereotype art had been so admirably contrived, as to combine the most beautiful simplicity, with the most desirable economy—the *ne plus ultra* of perfection, with that of neatness."[38]

While many of its early practitioners were quick to note the advantages of stereotyping as a technological advance, not all printers were as favorably disposed to the new process and its potential. In addition to a quick dismissal in the April 1807 edition of the *Monthly Magazine*, publisher and printing historian T. C. Hansard wrote that "no printer should stereotype who wishes his type to be a credit to his house: the wear of the material in casting is miserable, the gypsum is at best a fine powder, and grinds away the edge and face of the letter when rubbed in with a brush, in a frightful manner. The letter can never be entirely freed from the plaster and will present a very dirty appearance ever after" (fig. 5).[39] In *Typographia*'s extensive discussion of stereotyping, Hansard quoted at length from Andrew Wilson's May 1807 article in the *Monthly Magazine*, in which Wilson systematically described the advantages of stereotyping in terms of cost-effectiveness, efficiency, and uniformity of

[Moulding-Frame.]

FIG. 5   Molding frame for making a plaster impression of type. From "The Commercial History of a Penny Magazine—No. III: Compositors' Work and Stereotyping," *Monthly Supplement of the Penny Magazine of the Society for the Diffusion of Useful Knowledge* 107 (31 October–30 November 1833): 470. Author's collection.

output. Hansard dismantled Wilson's arguments point by point from the perspective of a publisher who had stereotyped many works and could accurately report on how they worked in practice. Hansard argued that Wilson's alleged advantages were either complete fictions or grossly exaggerated. He objected to Wilson's claims that stereotyped works would always be cost-effective in the long term, and, mechanically speaking, that the final impressions were always excellent and the wear on the type in making plates insubstantial. The expensive plates, Hansard argued, would be printed from so many times that they would wear down considerably, each impression looking worse than the previous one, especially with old plates. A printer working from type would therefore necessarily produce better-looking reprints, for his type would be systematically replaced over the years as it gradually wore out. For Hansard, the process of stereotyping cheapened the quality and appearance of certain types of reprinted works to an unacceptable level.

Despite these objections, Hansard conceded that "stereotyping is much used, and very advantageously, for Primers, Spelling-books, Religious Tracts, and other works requiring no variation of editions, or great excellence of execution."[40] Correcting an error on a plate was more involved than simply replacing a piece of moveable type in a set form, but corrections to plates necessarily became a part of the workflow of the stereotype foundry. To correct a plate that was found defective, a piece of moveable type was cut down to size and inserted into the plate at the correct thickness (fig. 6; see also appendix B). Other early printing guides noted the quality and efficiency of stereotyping in copying relief woodcuts and wood engravings for printing. "Such is its accuracy," claimed Charles Frederick Partington, "that plates may be cast from copper-plates as perfect as the engraving itself. Woodcuts and ornaments of every kind may be cast in the same manner."[41]

Fears that the widespread adoption of stereotyping would cost many compositors their jobs figured heavily in these debates. Given that the authors

FIG. 6   Stereotype block for raising a plate to type height. New York: F. Wesel Manufacturing Co., ca. 1895. Author's collection.

of most of the first printing manuals were printers themselves, trained under the apprentice system, the introduction of stereotyping was a potential threat to an entire artisan- and apprentice-based profession. John Johnson, a printer and printing historian, in his *Typographia, or The Printer's Instructor* (1824), was equally skeptical and dismissive of the benefits of this new technology:

> When we reflect, that so many of our brethren who well deserve (from their ability) a comfortable subsistence, and who ought to be enabled (from their profession), to move in a respectable sphere of life, are now, through this process, reduced to a very humble pittance, thereby bringing the first Art in the world down to a level with the lowest; and, at one season of the year, nearly one half of the valuable body of men alluded to may be considered as totally destitute of employ, on account of the standard works, which was the summer's stock work, having been Stereotyped.[42]

An examination of publications actively debating the nuances of stereotyping shows that by the 1820s some changes in workplace practices were beginning to occur. The "black art" passed down to apprentices in the old artisanal tradition was beginning to break down, as several new technologies and labor practices began to affect the makeup of the trades. What had been a set of trade secrets passed down from masters to apprentices was now openly debated in print down to the smallest level of detail and nuance, in published discussions of the value of stereotyping and other potentially transformative new technologies and innovations.

In the United States, commentators on the rapidly spreading technology of stereotyping were more uniformly positive. In his 1829 *Elements of Technology*, Harvard professor Jacob Bigelow described the process in detail, concluding that "stereotype printing is chiefly useful for standard and classical works, for which there is a regular demand, and of which the successive editions require no alteration. It is now executed with such increased economy, as to be applicable to works of even less durability."[43] An 1837 children's book about various trades devotes one page to the stereotyper; it describes the process of making a plate from set type and provides a brief history of the practice. It concludes with a note on Stanhope and Wilson's final innovations in 1804 and printers' strenuous opposition to this new technology, "the printers supposing, perhaps with some reason, that it would prove injurious to their business."[44]

By the 1840s, the early trade secrets and techniques of stereotyping were uniformly known and commonly practiced throughout the printing trades.

Printers' manuals and trade surveys accurately described the rudiments of the process, and stereotyping became part of the business model for larger-scale printers and book publishers. By midcentury, attention also turned toward electrotyping, stereotyping's refined successor process, which allowed for the detailed copying of images and larger engravings. Large newspaper publishers, who now operated power presses and were concerned with issues of volume and speed in production, began to experiment with casting curved plates to fit onto large cylinder presses. Multiple plates of the same newspaper page could be created and printed from simultaneously on multiple presses, doubling or tripling output, which allowed more rapid dissemination of the news. As one survey of American industrial progress noted, "Plates for use upon the cylinders of printing machines are made with the curve of the cylinders, the forms themselves in which the type are paged having a convex surface, which gives them the name of 'turtles.'"[45] Electrotyping began to be used commercially as early as 1850, and by 1860 most stereotype establishments had added an electrotype plant for certain types of output.[46] Book production remained an important part of the stereotyping business throughout the nineteenth century, but the massive growth of daily newspapers and weekly news magazines by midcentury allowed stereotyping to flourish as the best solution for high-volume, high-speed applications.

THE DEVELOPMENT AND SPREAD OF STEREOTYPING IN THE UNITED STATES

An 1811 advertisement in the *Long-Island Star* announced that a press maker named Francis Shield, recently arrived from London and living in New York, "is also in possession of the art of making *Stereotype plates*, and has specimens in his possession."[47] Shield had built Stanhope presses in London before emigrating to North America and presumably had some knowledge of the Stanhope stereotyping process, which had not yet been introduced in the United States. John Bidwell speculates that Shield worked with John Watts, who would later cast the first set of stereotype plates in the United States in 1813. Both men had earlier associations with Stanhope, from whom they learned at least part of his secret process.[48] No books bearing Shield's name as stereotype founder have come to light, and it is unlikely that his advertisement brought him any stereotyping work from New York printers or publishers.

Printing historian Rollo Silver has argued that by 1811 at least three other people in the United States were interested in stereotyping and beginning to experiment with it: David Bruce, a New York typefounder who traveled to England hoping to learn the process; John Watts, whose brother was one of Lord Stanhope's first pupils and who had come to New York in 1809 and would later succeed in casting plates; and S. W. Johnson, a Baltimore founder who advertised lessons in stereotype founding.[49] Johnson does not appear in any printers' listings or Baltimore city directories. His biography and training, and the outcome of his advertisement in the *Baltimore American*, are not known. The first known book printed with plates in Baltimore appeared only in 1816. In addition to Bruce, Watts, and Johnson, Mathew Carey in Philadelphia (as we shall see in chapter 2) received a firsthand account of the stereotyping process several years before it was actively practiced in the United States. Isaiah Thomas in Worcester, Massachusetts, was also keeping abreast of the latest English and continental innovations in the printing trades at this time.

The first American book printed with stereotype plates was a complete octavo Bible published in 1812 by the Philadelphia Bible Society. The Society commissioned and received a set of plates, at significant expense, from a London typefounder in October of that year, just after the outbreak of war with Britain. The Philadelphia Bible Society also purchased additional sets of stereotype plates from the same foundry in 1816, even though domestic manufacturers existed by then.

Kubler says that John Watts, the first successful stereotyper in America, trained in London and spoke French, and that his stereotyping method was a combination of the Stanhope and Didot processes. As noted above, Watts came to the United States in 1809 and produced his first commissioned set of plates in 1813. They were to the Westminster *Larger Catechism*, which was published in June of that year by the firm of Whiting & Watson for the New-York Religious Tract Society. Watts next surfaced in 1815, when he cast several sets of plates to Lindley Murray's *English Grammar* for the typefounding and printing firm of Collins & Co., one of which it subsequently sold to Mathew Carey. Collins & Co. kept one set for itself and published an edition from it, and sold an additional set to a Poughkeepsie publisher, Stockholm & Brownejohn. Watts then apparently sold his business and process to the Collins brothers, Quaker printers originally from New Jersey who had set up their business in New York. Watts then moved to Austria, where he next appears in the record in 1820.[50]

After the War of 1812, as printing business began to increase again, a number of US firms began to develop their own stereotype foundries. "The bookseller had more customers, and he was not obliged to pay for setting the type anew for each edition," Leander Bishop explains. "So books were cheapened, and purchasers increased, making the publishing business more steady as well as more profitable, and enabling some publishers to realize competencies and fortunes."[51]

David and George Bruce were the foremost typefounders in New York at this time and also had a printing business. Their chief competitor, Collins & Co., had a much wider reach, selling its own sets of stereotype plates up and down the East Coast, from Boston to Philadelphia, Baltimore, and Georgetown, South Carolina. The Bruces and Collins & Co. shared in lucrative Bible society commissions, producing both plates and printed editions for several Bible societies, though the Bruces' markets were primarily limited to Boston and Philadelphia.

In the early years of the nineteenth century, New York had not yet taken over from Boston and Philadelphia as the center of the printing and publishing industry in the United States. While the vast majority of stereotype foundries were in New York, one early adopter, J. F. and C. Starr, were making plates in Hartford as early as 1815 and supplying printers in New York State and New England. Later, Charles Starr moved his operations to New York City, where he and several of his brothers owned printing, typefounding, and stereotype businesses.

Rollo Silver argues that the introduction of stereotyping in America started "a touch of speculative fever" for innovation in the trades. Only a few years after the first plates were printed from in 1812, this proved to be true. In Connecticut in 1813, a group that included Eli Whitney, the printers Hudson & Goodwin, and the Yale chemist Benjamin Silliman incorporated the Stereotype Company for "the purpose of manufacturing stereotype plates and other plates and types, and of printing and vending literary works maps and charts."[52] Their operation needed to raise $100,000 before they could begin their work. William Charvat notes that a similar venture was incorporated in Connecticut two years later with starting capital of $150,000, an incredible sum, though neither operation ever advanced to the manufacturing stage.[53] Clearly, there was widespread interest in the new technology, along with substantial investment capital. Hudson & Goodwin, a large firm in Hartford, kept up its interest in the new technology as well and was printing from plates made by other founders later in the 1810s.

Boston and Philadelphia, the older, more established centers of printing in the United States, were at first resistant to using stereotype plates. Only a few titles printed with plates were published in those cities before 1820. More stereotyped editions came from publishers in smaller cities experimenting with the new technology, places like Hartford, Albany, Baltimore, and Brattleboro, Vermont, where the plates were nearly all cast by New York typefounders. Elihu and Henry Phinney inherited their father's printshop in Cooperstown, New York, in 1813, and by 1820 had added a stereotype foundry and a paper mill. They printed more than 150,000 copies of their stereotyped family Bible in subsequent years.[54] The Boston publisher Crocker & Brewster commissioned a six-volume Bible cast in stereotype plates in 1820, publishing each volume separately as the plates were cast over a two-year span. In his memoir, Uriel Crocker noted that the firm printed some twenty or thirty thousand copies of the Bible from those plates, about five hundred per run, as needed, for as long as it was in business, and he then sold the usable plates of it to H. O. Houghton & Co. in 1876 when he retired.[55] Silver writes of these regional biases, "Conservatives in the trade shied away from the new technique until their more hardheaded colleagues demonstrated that it was no longer experimental, but practical to use."[56]

Among the titles made into plates, most took the form of steady sellers that would justify the substantial initial cost of commissioning them: Bibles and New Testaments, Books of Common Prayer, dictionaries, and schoolbooks such as Lindley Murray's best-selling *English Grammar*. But there were also some idiosyncratic choices. The Starrs in New York stereotyped several small children's books for the Hartford printers Sheldon & Goodrich in 1815. Sheldon & Goodrich published new impressions of these works from the same plates, but with new title pages, every few years, well into the 1820s. More surprising was a guide to hairdressing in English and French titled *The Complete Coiffeur*, by John LaFoy, with added poems and songs, that was stereotyped and published in 1817, and apparently reissued under different publishers as the plates later changed hands. The work was advertised as having been published by Van Winkle & Wiley in the *New-York Columbian*, though New York printer Cornelius van Winkle did not commission another stereotyped title in the 1810s.[57]

The earliest stereotypers and typefounders in the United States had many close interconnections. George B. Lothian was the son of a Scottish typefounder who moved to the United States to set up a typefounding business, which failed in 1810. The younger Lothian then worked for John Watts for several years in New York, where he presumably learned about stereotyping, and then moved on to the New York stereotyping firm of Collins & Hannay (a branch of Collins & Co.) for two years before striking out for Pittsburgh to establish his own type foundry. It was not successful, so Lothian returned to New York and worked for D. & G. Bruce. All of this occurred during several years in the 1810s.[58]

Lawrence Johnson, a Philadelphia typefounder, was born in England in 1801 and began his career with the firm of John Childs & Son in Bungay, the same market town where Charles Brightly was experimenting with stereotyping. He emigrated to the United States in 1819 after completing his apprenticeship and found work in New York with B. & J. Collins, one of the two principal stereotyping firms in New York at the time. In 1833, he and his partner, George Smith, bought the long-established Philadelphia type foundry of Binney & Ronaldson, the primary American foundry in the early Republic.[59]

The quick adoption of stereotyping by United States typefounders and printers, in contrast to their counterparts in Great Britain, was the subject of notice. As one English traveler to New York noted in 1817, "Stereotyping is practiced: Messrs. —— are now engaged upon a work larger than any which has ever been stereotyped in England."[60] Up-front costs remained substantial, often reaching twice the price of standard type composition, though as the industry expanded, prices fell considerably. By 1894, creating a stereotype or electrotype plate cost on average only 30 percent more up front.[61] For larger works with considerable reprinting potential, stereotyping was an immediately popular option. "By 1825 the stereotypers of New York, Philadelphia, and Boston were supplying printers with popular texts which could be published in each city simultaneously without the labor of composition or the expense of standing type," writes Silver. "Thus, as the first quarter of the nineteenth century ended, the American printer was becoming familiar with iron presses, stereotyping, lithography, and the use of power. These were ingredients of the industrial revolution in printing."[62] The practice grew steadily, with foundries appearing primarily in the major cities and being centered there for much of the nineteenth century. Silver writes, "The promising new process immediately attracted the attention of all typefounders, some of whom added stereotyping to their techniques."[63] Of all the members of the printing trades, typefounders had the most direct experience to add a stereotyping foundry as a side business, and many did. At the end of the century, the *American Dictionary of Printing and Bookmaking* could report, "By 1820 the number of stereotypers in New York had increased to five, and by 1830 to eight or nine.... Plates were made for books and for advertisements freely in the year 1840, but even in 1855 little was done in stereotyping in small towns. There were no foundries, for instance, in Syracuse, Troy or Utica before the war, and only one in Rochester."[64]

In part because of its natural deep water harbor, New York City surpassed Philadelphia in population for the first time in the 1820 census. Commerce and manufacturing were centering in and around New York, and the opening of the Erie Canal in 1825 connected New York and Albany with Buffalo and the Great Lakes, further securing New York's position as the engine and center of US manufacture and commerce. The combined printing trades in New York in the 1820s and '30s were larger than the trades in Boston and slightly larger than those in Philadelphia, but by 1840 New York was the center of American printing and publishing.

Because of the cotton trade, New York also became the center of European commerce in the United States and of the shipping trade to the South. New York (and European) goods in turn supplied the southern states in greater quantities than any other northern port city, and books printed in New York likewise found a ready home in southern bookstores. The printing trades consolidated in New York City in part because of such distribution networks. Because of the nature of commercial, or job, printing, customers needed close contact with their printers. The periodical and newspaper press that jobbed its work out likewise needed printshops close to the centers of commerce and activity, so urban printshops in New York flourished. Thanks to the mostly compact footprint of printshops, the organization and layout of which had not changed significantly since the fifteenth century, presses could be located in cities, and type and stereotype foundries were similarly constructed in urban centers. Where clothing mills and other large-scale manufacturers needed huge spaces and ample water power, new innovations like steam-powered printing could take place within a relatively modest urban footprint. Boilers were located in New York basements and subbasements to power the new, larger steam presses required for large-scale book and newspaper production in the 1840s.

Single-page plates made from set type for book printing were only one part of a typefounder's potential output from the new stereotyping trade. Adoniram Chandler, listed as a typefounder in the 1820 New York City directory, appeared in subsequent years as a stereotype founder. His first specimen book, also from 1820, contained more ornaments and decorated rules than it did type.[65] His second specimen book, *Specimen of Ornamental Type and Printing Ornaments* (1822), includes a note that reads, "The ornamental types exhibited in this specimen are cast in stereotype plates, and the letters separately fixed to wooden bottoms. A great quantity of this kind of job type has been in use for three years past, and those who have tried it, speak decidedly in its favour."⁶⁶ This display type, where each letter was fixed to wood, sold at eighteen cents per letter, which was much cheaper, according to Chandler, than purchasing full lead type metal at forty-two cents per pound, and would last just as long.

Chandler's 1822 specimen book also offered this argument for stereotyping:

> The principal objections which have been urged against stereotype plates are the inequality of their thickness, unevenness of their surface, &c. and the consequent difficulty of obtaining a fair impression from them. The subscriber, having spared no pains in obtaining a knowledge of, and adopting the best practical operations in this business, together with essential improvements, which some years' experience has suggested, feels justified in assuring those whom it may concern, that the plates cast at his foundry are not surpassed by those from any other foundry either in Europe or America. Works of several hundred pages, on small type, have been put to press with as little difficulty, as respects *overlaying* and register, as the same work would require if done on separate type.⁶⁷

As urban printers and publishers amassed multiple sets of stereotype plates, proper warehousing to protect these new investments became necessary. Housing stereotype plates became a serious business that had implications for a publisher's survival if disaster struck. Reporting on the Harper & Brothers fire of December 1853, which destroyed the publisher's entire printshop, *Norton's Literary Gazette* noted, "Their stereotype plates were nearly all preserved, and a week had hardly elapsed before the best presses from Boston to Cincinnati were in motion to renew their vast stock of books."⁶⁸ Immediately after the fire, plates for commissioned works were taken from Harper's New York vaults to several job printers so that printing from them could be resumed without interruption. The January 1854 issue of *Harper's Magazine* was rewritten and published without any delay. In all, Harper estimated that it lost $1.15 million in the fire ($800,000 of which was from printed stock), but its single largest surviving asset was its collection of stereotype plates, which it valued at $400,000. To raise some ready cash, Harper sold Hartford poet Lydia Sigourney the plates to four of her works for $1,000.⁶⁹ The firm survived, in large part, because it chose to cast plates for all its works without question and protected them from damage. Other publishers who printed and warehoused their entire output as printed sheets would have lost everything to the flames and been driven out of business.

Within a generation of its first successful castings in the United States, stereotype plate output increased substantially. By 1845, one of the two largest stereotyping operations in Boston claimed to produce more than seven thousand stereotype plates per year and used steam power to trim and shave them to type height.[70] Harper & Brothers claimed that by the mid-1850s it was warehousing nearly ten thousand plates for *Harper's Magazine* alone, not counting each of the published books the firm had stereotyped during the previous twenty years, also in storage. Harper's plates were stored in subterranean vaults beneath the company's new building, constructed as a state-of-the-art fireproof stereotyping, printing, and publishing headquarters in 1855, two years after the fire.[71]

STEREOTYPING AND LABOR IN THE PRINTING TRADES

American printing and publishing underwent a tremendous period of growth and change in the first half of the nineteenth century. Urbanization, the growth and proliferation of educational institutions, and national trade and communications networks all contributed to creating a larger reading public with an increased need and desire for printed matter.[72]

Industrial capitalism introduced several new forms of technology into the printing trades and altered labor practices in larger shops. The traditional master-apprentice model began to break down as dedicated unskilled tasks for workers replaced the holistic training earlier printer's apprentices received in smaller shops over the many years of their apprenticeships. As larger printers and publishers consolidated, they fundamentally transformed what had been an artisan craft, with skills and traditions that were passed down from master to apprentice, into an industry that depended instead upon the deskilled division of labor and shop practices. As the labor historian George Barnett put it:

> At the beginning of the nineteenth century a journeyman printer was ordinarily able to do all the parts of the work necessary for the production of printed matter, although in the larger offices even at that time some workmen were employed exclusively as compositors and others as pressmen. As the volume of production and the size of the offices has increased, and

> as new machinery and new processes have been introduced, the work of the large printing office has come to be divided among many different classes of workmen.... Despite a certain amount of overlapping, it has been readily conceded that the pressmen, stereotypers, and electrotypers, photo-engravers, and mailers are engaged at work for which the printers are not trained.[73]

As steam-powered presses were introduced into firms, printshop tasks became increasingly segmented and stratified. No longer were apprentices required to learn every aspect of the job, from composition to handpress work. With power presses, the dedicated job of press feeder required a far less skilled worker to feed paper into the machine. Larger publishers capitalized on this change and increasingly hired women as press feeders, paying them considerably less than their unskilled male equivalents. This not only cheapened skills, as Bruce Laurie notes, but fragmented trade knowledge, further alienating the remaining journeymen compositors who trained under the apprentice system.[74]

By the mid-1830s, the printing trades in the United States had grown to such extent that there was an oversupply of skilled workers seeking regular employment. Because of the resulting lowering of wages by printshop owners, journeymen compositors attempted to organize themselves into citywide typographical associations in order to keep wages standardized in their respective cities. The master-apprentice model produced a large number of trained journeymen who lacked the capital to purchase their own printing establishments and who would not inherit a shop or be taken on as a partner by their former masters. The high costs of the new powered cylinder presses made it nearly impossible for a journeyman to become a master printer and owner of his own establishment. Instead, journeymen frequently worked as itinerant printers, being paid by the piece, as much or as little as they chose to do, and moving from shop to shop and city to city, earning them the name "tramp printers." Skilled journeyman printers were among the most mobile artisans in early America. Many eventually moved from large eastern cities to smaller towns in the West in search of better opportunities than could be found in the urban East, running newly founded newspapers and printshops for owners in small towns that formerly had none. There is a rich literature of anecdote and memoir by tramp printers in the nineteenth-century United States.[75]

By 1833, New York's journeymen printers were complaining that the growth of stereotyping had rendered it steadily more difficult for compositors to support their families; a few years later, their complaints were focused on denouncing the introduction of steam-powered presses and the displacement of pressmen in the city's largest periodical and book-printing firms. William S. Pretzer writes, "As the ranks of compositors swelled with semiskilled hands, their status and security declined. Taken together, the machine presses, stereotyping, and expanded reliance on semiskilled workers drove down wages for both presswork and composition. Starting in the 1820s and cascading in the 1830s, the result was a full-scale labor crisis."[76] The Panic of 1837 seriously affected the printing trades just when urban typographical associations were having modest success in creating uniform wage scales. Some early effects were felt by 1834, and the resulting depression did not ease until 1843. "Throughout the panic," writes George Stevens, "the union refused to officially sanction a suspension of its wage scale."[77] By 1845, with New York established as the center of publishing in the United States, automated presses had become the norm for large shops, and former pressmen were relegated to the role of feeder on these steam-powered presses. The deskilling of printshop labor caused by the introduction of power presses was a classic form of labor displacement in an industrial revolution.[78]

Journeymen's wages were also threatened by increasing forms of competition for their skilled labor. The arrival of country printers seeking higher urban wages steadily increased throughout the nineteenth century. Many shop masters were increasingly willing to give jobs to recent immigrants, who may not have had years of printing experience, and to use boys known as "half-way" boys or "two-thirders," apprentice compositors who had not completed their full apprenticeships before striking out as unverified journeymen.

Stereotyping was the first but clearly not the only threat to the established order of printing trade labor during this period. Because of these pressures, journeymen began to have an oppositional relationship with owners of printing establishments. Many attempted to organize themselves into citywide typographical societies in an attempt to stabilize the prices for hired composition within a metropolitan area. Another function of the typographical societies, which evolved into modern trade unions, was to police their own members, making sure they stuck to the agreed-upon price structure for composition work. Certificates of membership were given out by the typographical associations so that one member could take a job in another city and be vetted as association-approved.

The rising number of European immigrants who claimed to have some printing experience was also attractive to shop owners as cheap labor. With the increased movement of printers around the country, many former apprentices who had not completed their terms of apprenticeship attempted to move to other cities and falsely claim journeyman status. Identifying and excluding these "two-thirders" from work was a significant topic of discussion at the first national printers' meetings. Occasional attempts by shop owners to train women and nonapprentices as compositors continued this process of deskilling in the trades.[79] This trend accelerated when the Adams power press was introduced in 1830, its use becoming widespread within a few years; the Adams press was a large-scale book-printing press that required dedicated sheet feeders and sheet receivers instead of trained pressmen. By 1855, the new state-of-the-art Harper & Brothers headquarters boasted a workforce that was equally divided by gender and by task, women making up the bulk of press feeders, binders, stampers, and packers. Men filled the roles of compositor, stereotyper, steam and press engineer, and warehouse staff.[80] The older apprentice and journeyman system of thirty years before was completely displaced in the book trade. In newspaper offices, the deskilling of labor was felt even more acutely. "Printers"—that is, apprentice-trained journeymen—were replaced by "typesetters" whose skills could be learned in months. The *New York Tribune* stated that the new demand for labor was for "mere type-setters, and not printers . . . in the strict sense of the word." The *Tribune* itself listed no printers among its employees in 1853, only "compositors" and "feeders."[81]

By the 1840s, journeymen printers were feeling threatened from all sides. Bruce Laurie writes of Philadelphia journeymen:

> Preoccupied with the immigrant menace, they stood idly by as their trade underwent a boom marked by expansion and modernization, as well as by mushrooming small book and job shops. Printers who had once worked their trade in the casual setting of the small shop now faced the choice of doing increasingly specialized tasks in large factories or sweatshops. They saw their work traditions assaulted as employers divided up skills and hired "half-trained" men and women, many of whom had their hours extended to eleven and twelve a day. On top of this, wages hardly improved in the course of the decade, and journeymen printers, still the best paid of all artisans, were beginning to grow restless.[82]

The Typographical Association of New York, a militant trade union, was formed in 1831. Earlier associations of printers in New York dated back to the 1809 establishment of the New York Typographical Society, founded to standardize composition prices in the city. The Typographical Society arose from the need to organize around a number of threats to the profession, among them stereotyping and youth labor, both of which were taking work away from compositors.[83] The several extant citywide typographical associations in the United States came together in 1852 to form the National Typographical Union, the first national trade union in the United States. It became the International Typographical Union in 1869 after it began organizing members in Canada.

At the second national convention of journeyman printers in 1851, members petitioned Congress to add duties to imported stereotype plates, thus encouraging more domestic production; the duty would raise the cost of imported plates "up to the rates paid in the United States for their composition and casting."[84] The motion went to committee but did not make it to a floor vote. This petition by organized journeymen echoed the argument made by publishers to Congress fifty years earlier about the dangers posed by Bible societies that imported foreign sets of plates at the expense of domestic production.[85]

Despite this opposition from journeymen, the creation of independent stereotype foundries in major cities, and the increasing adoption of plates by printers and publishers, had only a minor effect on labor issues in the printing trades in the United States. Journeymen compositors, skilled workers who were among the highest-paid artisans in the nineteenth century, increased so much in number by midcentury that the relatively small number of stereotypers producing plates never presented a significant threat. Compositors still had to create stereotype plates from set type in a printshop, so the threat to their livelihood due to an increase in platemaking was indirect at most. As the industry consolidated, journeymen printers had to contend with more immediate and multiple threats in the form of two-thirders, foreign and youth labor, and the rise of power presses.

The 1830s and '40s brought "swift mechanization" to the printing trades in a way that was unlike any other urban craft or industry in the United States.[86] Other light industrial and manufacturing trades in urban environments did not undergo a similarly swift change in operations as they became mechanized and altered their labor practices. The transformations caused by the introduction of stereotyping were likewise changes in degree rather than revolutionary. Stereotyping added one additional step to the typefounding and printing process by its own unique skilled labor practice. It furthered the transition from small printshops to larger publishers, and it helped capitalize the printing trades in new ways while also offering greater efficiency for printers and nascent publishers wealthy enough to invest in and exploit it.

By the later 1840s, stereotyping was an established option for larger publishers in printing books and periodicals. The commissioning of a set of plates for certain types of new works became the mark of a well-capitalized firm, even in smaller towns, though foundries themselves remained located primarily in major metropolitan areas. Typefounders also used stereotyping and electrotyping to reproduce stock images ("cuts") from an initial woodcut or wood engraving quickly and in large quantities. These copied images could then be listed in type specimen books and sold in quantity to every smaller printer or newspaper around the country, standardizing the visual vocabulary found in antebellum newspaper advertisements.[87] The word *stereotype* entered the lexicon as a term for a mirror image, and even for copying itself.

CHAPTER 2

൪ Mathew Carey and the Family Bible Marketplace

In 1813, Mathew Carey owned the largest and best-capitalized publishing firm in the United States. As a young man in Dublin in 1779, he had gotten into trouble with the authorities for writing a pamphlet on Catholic rights and fled to France for a year. There, he found work as a printer outside Paris in Passy, where Benjamin Franklin had set up a modest press for publishing political pamphlets during his time as agent for the Continental Congress. While in France, Carey met the Marquis de Lafayette, a member of Franklin's circle of friends and acquaintances. Returning to Dublin in 1783, Carey followed his interests in politics, editing, and printing, founding a newspaper, the *Volunteer's Journal*, which also landed him in trouble with the state for its progressive politics. He was again forced to leave Ireland, and this time he emigrated to the United States in 1784. Lafayette was staying with George Washington at Mount Vernon at the time, and when he learned of the young Irish publisher's arrival, he sent him a check for £200 to restart his business in the new Republic. And so it was, with this near-mythic start, that Carey's long and successful career in the United States began.

Carey moved to Philadelphia, where he set up a press and published a magazine, the *American Museum*, and fell into the rough-and-tumble world of partisan politics in the nation's capital and center of publishing. Carey, a Catholic and an ardent republican, took pains to disabuse critics of the notion that the new Irish immigrants to the United States had any loyalties to foreign or religious authorities other than their new government. He famously scrapped with the British loyalist William Cobbett, who, writing as Peter Porcupine, skewered many aspects of the new Republic's government and actions. After Cobbett returned to Britain and began a second career as a reformer and parliamentary reporter, they would keep up a regular correspondence with each other into old age.

Carey's business grew and prospered in Philadelphia. In addition to his magazine and job printing, he brought out books under his own imprint in the 1790s, and in 1794–95 entered into agreements with other publishers for ten jointly published books, including an edition of Jedidiah Morse's *American Universal Geography*, on which he partnered with the prominent Massachusetts publisher Isaiah Thomas. Carey had also, significantly, earned enough to invest in publishing an edition of William Guthrie's *New System of Modern Geography* in two large quarto volumes with an added atlas volume of plates. The Guthrie was his largest project to that point. After it was published, Carey let his eight printers go and focused entirely on bookselling and publishing, hiring local printers to complete new titles under his imprint. As James Green has remarked, "from 1794 on he was more nearly a publisher in the modern sense than any other American."[1]

From Philadelphia, Carey maintained an unrivaled network of book sales agents and distribution connections across the South and West. He actively traded his books with other publishers and booksellers across the country, from South Carolina to northern New England and abroad.[2] Carey was well known in his own time as one of the few publishers to maintain complete works set up in standing type, an extraordinary investment in materials and warehousing. In the handpress period, printing jobs were composed from loose type, set up into forms, corrected, proofed, and then printed from, all in a relatively short period of time. Once the work was complete, the type was cleaned and put back into its cases, ready for the next job. This workflow, producing many different books from the same fonts of type, was the most efficient for printing shops, as type was a major investment and could not be added to easily or without significant expense. Publishers also needed to estimate the demand, and hence the size of an edition, for a work in press, and then be prepared to hold on to printed copies of it to sell and exchange for some time as the edition gradually sold out, or until sufficient demand required a reprint. Editions of schoolbooks, geographies, and other works printed in the United States at this time would often not be reprinted for several years, when the edition sold out of its initial print run.

Rollo Silver notes that the Worcester publisher Thomas & Andrews probably printed Noah Webster's *American Spelling Book* from standing type in the 1790s. When Joseph Charless of Lexington, Kentucky, purchased the western rights to the book in 1806, he had forms of standing type to it shipped to him from Philadelphia. Isaiah Thomas in Worcester advertised in 1797 that he had four Bibles (folio, royal quarto, large demy octavo, and demi-duodecimo) set up in standing type, "in the same manner as they are at the Royal Printing Offices in London and Edinburgh, and the University Printing Houses of Oxford and Cambridge." Thomas imported at least one of these Bibles from England.[3]

By 1803, Carey owned two complete Bibles set up in standing type: a quarto family Bible (a large, lectern-sized book in which families recorded births, deaths, and marriages) and a duodecimo school Bible (pocket-sized, for personal use or in schools), the latter having been commissioned by the New York printer Hugh Gaine from England in the 1790s and later purchased from him. He also maintained a separate New Testament in standing type.[4] Carey innovated by selling Bibles by subscription in rural America through networks of traveling agents. He also sold his family Bibles in a variety of different options and prices—on different papers, in several choices of binding, and with or without maps, illustrations, commentary, and supplementary materials—initially some twenty different varieties, ranging from a modest $3.75 copy up to $18.00, an extraordinary sum for a single volume.[5] By 1810, Carey had essentially cornered the American market in quarto family Bibles and would go on to be "the foremost printer and publisher of the Bible in America during the first quarter of the nineteenth century."[6] By 1813, he was offering about fifty Bible variants to the trade and for retail sale and subscription.

Carey and his fellow booksellers and publishers understood the need for steady sellers, works that were in constant demand and provided some measure of stability. Holding an entire work in standing type allowed a publisher to warehouse the type instead of printed stock (on paper that had to be purchased in advance), and to print additional copies whenever there was sufficient demand. This involved a significant initial expense, but over time the investment paid off. The publisher did not have to pay compositors to reset the work, and new impressions could be brought out to satisfy demand considerably faster. For works like family and school Bibles, this also meant that minor errors, once discovered, could be corrected in the standing type, which allowed Carey to claim that his Bibles were the most textually correct editions of scripture available in America. Carey's use of standing type was a landmark of sorts within the printing trades and was widely known. Philadelphia city guides of the early nineteenth century frequently mention his innovation as a mark of the progress of industry in that city.[7] The practice of well-capitalized publishers' owning works in standing type offered a precedent for their decisions later on whether to invest in casting a set of stereotype plates to a new work, which offered the same advantages but with even less risk.

Mathew Carey knew about European advances in creating stereotype plates well before the technology came to the United States. Accounts of stereotyping and advertisements for stereotyped works published in England and France began to appear in American newspapers as early as the mid-1790s. In 1807, Carey copied into his personal memo book a letter from the English stereotyper Andrew Wilson to the New York printer John Watts outlining the up-front costs of casting stereotype plates to books. Watts presumably showed the letter to Carey on one of his frequent business trips to New York around this time. As this is the earliest known enumeration of the costs of stereotyping, it is worth transcribing here in full:

April 19, 1807

Statement of the Expense of Johnson's dictionary, from A. Wilson's letter to John Watts, dated Dec. 11, 1806.

Casework, 176,000 letters @ 77—£8	5.10:0
Reading 4d in the Shilling for English Dictionaries	1.17
To be doubled—7.7	14.14
Plates, weighing average of 32 lbs. per sheet 6/6	10.8
Editor, who inserts every useful & new word,	
not to be found in Johnson's, by agreement	3.3
	28.5
Number of sheets	40
	£1130.
Condition of my refusing to stereotype	
the same work for any other person	282.10
Total expense retaining the press work	
(This is the American price)	1412.10
Condition of giving up the plates when finished	565
Total expense retaining the press work	1997.10
A second set of plates & of the first	706.5
Total expense of 2 sets of plates	2683.15
=	11912.52

My terms of payment are, one half when a work is print in hand, & and the other half when the plates are finished; because, in stead of printing 10,000 copies in one Edition of such a Book as the above, the market may be equally well supplied by Editions of 1,000 copies; which leaves nine tenths of the capital hitherto employed in paper & press work. Were two editions of the above work compared from beginning to End, with moveable types, the expense w^d exceed £6000.[8]

Carey's response to this letter is not in the archives, nor is there any extant correspondence between him and either Watts or Wilson. This detailed cost breakdown came to him only four years after his first Bible in standing type was published, and it must have made a strong impression. If successful in the United States, a stereotyped work could be either a more efficient way of publishing a book or a direct challenge to Carey's innovative business model. Carey kept up a steady network of correspondence with foreign publishers, especially those in England and his native Ireland. They supplied him with books and with information about the printing trades and political developments in Europe, allowing him to keep abreast of the growth and impact of stereotyping, especially in England, and its effects on English publishers and the book trade.[9]

Carey would also have recognized that this new technology provided one way to circumvent the problem of keeping large quantities of valuable type tied up exclusively for one book and not put to more efficient use, especially for smaller publishers. In the letter, Wilson's condition of requiring payment for *not* stereotyping another copy of Johnson's dictionary for someone else—an effective copyright—raised an entirely new series of questions and challenges for publishers and typefounders alike. Wilson demanded a significant sum (£282.10) to effectively grant one publisher sole access to a work that he had stereotyped. Once other English typefounders began offering stereotyping services in their own shops, as they would soon do, Wilson's monopoly would end and he would have to compete in a marketplace of stereotypers for a publisher's business. The printer John Johnson, in his *Typographia* (1824), argued against stereotyping, as it might enable unscrupulous founders to surreptitiously cast multiple copies of a work for sale despite agreements to the contrary, thus eliminating a publisher's advantage in keeping a newly stereotyped work solely his own property.[10] When John Watts first began creating stereotype plates in New York in 1813, and firms such as D. & G. Bruce and Collins & Co. followed suit the following year, American publishing and typefounding underwent the same changes that their English counterparts had a decade earlier.

A GROWING MARKET FOR STEREOTYPE PLATES

Beginning in 1813, several typefounders in New York began experimenting with casting stereotype plates from set type. They soon contacted the nation's prominent booksellers and publishers, including Mathew Carey, with offers for plates to Bibles and other popular works. Carey was also offered copies of the first stereotyped work in America, the Westminster *Larger Catechism*, of which he purchased a large quantity after first examining a sample (fig. 7). In a letter of 19 August 1813, the New York bookselling and publishing firm Whiting & Watson wrote to Carey about its preexisting arrangement to receive copies of his Bible on exchange. Whiting & Watson specialized in theological works and sold Carey's family Bible in its New York bookstore. In the past, the firm had sent smaller, cheaper editions of the Bible to Carey and received in exchange copies of his larger family Bible. In addition to agreeing to receive some copies of Carey's latest works, Whiting & Watson offered Carey thirty copies each of the firm's latest publications, including the "Westminster Larger Catechism, stereotype, with proofs, selected by Dr. McLeod, reducing the size of the book. 142 pp. 12mo. Fine (our $6 paper) neatly bound at 0/37 C."[11] Whiting & Watson had commissioned John Watts, an English printer living in New York and trained in stereotyping, to create the first set of domestically produced stereotype plates for the *Westminster Catechism*. Watts had set up his printing business in New York by 1809. After a few years, he returned to England, having been unable to make a living exclusively as a stereotyper.[12] Carey agreed to purchase the thirty copies of the *Catechism* on exchange, and Whiting & Watson sent him the first eight copies of his order, which reached Philadelphia on 30 September 1813. He now had copies of the first domestically produced stereotyped book in hand to examine and sell.

The remainder of this chapter relies on a close examination of the records of the firms of Mathew Carey and Carey & Son held by the Historical Society of Pennsylvania in its Lea & Febiger Records collection. By reconstructing and interpreting Carey's subsequent decisions navigating the new marketplace for plates and printed stock, we can see how stereotyping gained a foothold in the United States as a new publishing option. And we can document how it began to shift certain dynamics of power and control in the printing trades and publishing industry as the Bible marketplace changed. Carey's principal steady seller, the quarto family Bible, was about to be challenged by several newly cast stereotype editions.

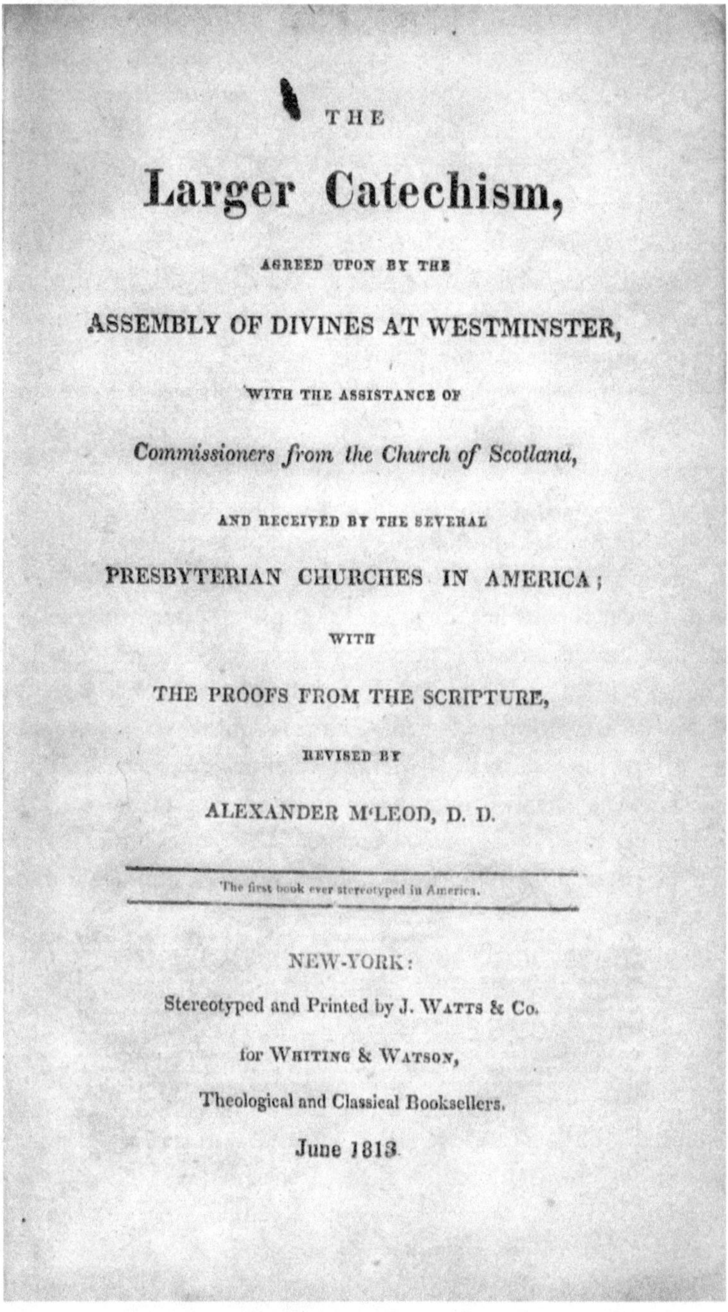

THE

Larger Catechism,

AGREED UPON BY THE

ASSEMBLY OF DIVINES AT WESTMINSTER,

WITH THE ASSISTANCE OF

Commissioners from the Church of Scotland,

AND RECEIVED BY THE SEVERAL

PRESBYTERIAN CHURCHES IN AMERICA;

WITH

THE PROOFS FROM THE SCRIPTURE,

REVISED BY

ALEXANDER M'LEOD, D. D.

The first book ever stereotyped in America.

NEW-YORK:

Stereotyped and Printed by J. WATTS & Co.

for WHITING & WATSON,

Theological and Classical Booksellers.

June 1813.

FIG. 7 The first book stereotyped in the United States. Title page of Alexander M'Leod, *The Larger Catechism* [. . .] (New York: Stereotyped and Printed by J. Watts & Co. for Whiting & Watson, 1813). Author's collection.

The New York typefounding firm of D. & G. Bruce wrote to Carey in the spring of 1814 to inform him, "We are now Stereotyping the octavo Bible as per specimen page, and expect to complete it in the course of the year. We wish to sell a set of the plates in Philadelphia, and offer it to you in the first instances. The Old and New Testament and Apocrypha will be completed in 1128 pages. The plates of which will sell at $3.50 each, making a total of $3948." The letter continued, exaggerating more than a little, "The cost of these plates is only about one third of what it would cost to get the same work up with common types, and they will last much longer."[13] While the plates would last longer, the cost of creating plates in these early days was at least one-third *higher* than paying for composition alone. David and George Bruce were clear in their intent: to give the first right of refusal to the largest publisher in America, someone who controlled Bible distribution to all the southern states and out west as far as Ohio. The price, while high, was fair. Carey claimed to have paid $7,000 for his duodecimo Bible in standing type several years prior to this offer.[14] An octavo Bible, smaller than his quarto family Bible, could be sold as a personal Bible to a wide audience at lower prices. The Philadelphia Bible Society had imported a set of plates to one from England in 1812. Since that time, no other British-made stereotype plates had come to America. The Bruce brothers, natives of Edinburgh, had been in the United States since the mid-1790s working in the printing trades. David Bruce spent a year in England around 1812, where he was said to have purchased the trade secrets of stereotyping in order to bring the practice back to his New York business. The firm of D. & G. Bruce prospered as stereotypers and typefounders in the early nineteenth century.[15]

The octavo Bible the Bruces offered Carey was set up as a more modest production than Carey's flagship quarto family Bible. In the Bruces' edition, there were no footnotes or annotations. If Carey purchased this set of plates, he would have the advantage of being able to print Bibles in quarto, octavo, and duodecimo whenever the need arose. The Bruces made clear, however, that they were in the business of copying the Bible and stereotype plates in multiple sets, and thus Carey would not be the exclusive holder of that set of octavo Bible plates. Unlike Andrew Wilson's letter, quoted above, they did not propose a fee for the exclusive right of casting only one set of plates. As they said, Carey would be the owner of the "Philadelphia set," with other sets presumably already being offered to publishers in the New York and Boston markets. If the Bruce brothers could produce and sell one set of plates, as they claimed, for a third of what it would cost to compose them independently, then they had to have produced multiple sets of plates from their initial setting of type simply to make up their own composition and production costs.

Carey eventually declined to purchase this set of stereotype plates, but he countered with an inquiry about the cost of a New Testament instead. The Bruces replied in April 1814, "We have the Testament in hand, and would sell a set of the plates at $2.25 per page, amounting to $756. We would allow 25 per cent for your Old Testament on account, if you would deliver it immediately, as the value of metal must fall soon. Our Testament will be completed in July. We have no scale of prices for stereotyping and do not intend to make a general business of it."[16] Carey agreed to purchase this set of plates and to supply the Bruces with his New Testament in standing type as part of the purchase. In the fall, the Bruces wrote that the plates were all cast and being corrected. They also apologized in November for the delay, explaining that their "men are much out on military duty."[17] The complete New Testament, 336 plates in all, shipped from New York to Philadelphia on 17 November 1814. Carey was charged $2.25 per plate, for a total of $756. He sent the Bruces a substantial quantity of old type over the course of the summer, valued at $421.88, leaving his out-of-pocket cost at $334.12. Carey did quite well on this transaction, selling his old type to New York for the Bruces' use during wartime and bringing his own actual cost for the New Testament down to almost exactly one dollar per plate.

Carey wisely printed one final impression of his standing-type New Testament before he sent the type to the Bruces. Once he received his New Testament plates in the fall, he had no immediate need to print from them. Instead, they were warehoused while he continued to sell copies of his final 1814 impression. (Carey unsuccessfully attempted to sell these New Testament plates to a New York printer two years later, an attempt discussed below.) Also in 1814, Carey purchased a second set of stereotype plates, to Lindley Murray's *English Grammar*, another guaranteed steady seller, this time from the New York typefounding and printing firm of Collins & Co. Isaac Collins (1746–1817) and his son Benjamin were Quaker printers, originally from New Jersey, who had been printing and selling Bibles since the early 1790s. Carey again did not pay full price but instead exchanged copies of his "Coarse Bible," his family Bible printed on cheaper, coarser paper, for the new set of plates. Collins's offer was to receive as many coarse Bibles, at a one-third discount, to make up the equivalent of the $900 asking price for the set of plates to the *English Grammar*. On 19 October, Collins & Co. sent Carey three hundred copies of the *Grammar* in sheets, newly printed from their set of plates. They also mentioned sending along "thy" set of plates to it once it was finished, clearly noting that there were multiple sets and that the Collinses would be keeping one for their own use. These plates were also stereotyped by John Watts.[18] Collins & Co., like D. & G. Bruce, was trading in multiple sets of plates to the same work, and it attempted to place a set with a publisher in each regional market. Carey's edition of Murray's *English Grammar* was published in 1815, with a title page noting that it was "Carey's Stereotype Edition." He would later write to Collins saying that he had an edition of two thousand copies in press. Carey again had made a shrewd business decision, acquiring a set of plates without investing any cash, and exchanging a large stock of printed Bibles for his copy of the *Grammar* in plates.

The mechanics of printing with plates on a handpress necessitated some way to raise the relatively thin plates up to type height on the press bed. The Bruces and Collinses both proposed solutions. D. & G. Bruce wrote to Carey while his New Testament was being prepared, "We shall use mahogany blocks, worth two dollars a piece, as is now the general practice in London. They may be surrounded by four pieces of wood, and ground up at the corner-irons of the press, the same as in a chase, and need not be unlocked until the edition of the work is completed."[19]

Alternately, Collins & Co. presented two options to Carey for the *English Grammar*: "We can get them of mahogany at about 30 dollars and of brass at 54 dollars—for our own set we have a set of brass blocks as we found them made of wood were troublesome & often out of order. . . . P.S. The brass blocks are double that is they take 2 pages on a block while the others are calculated for one page each only."[20] Carey was corresponding with both typefounders simultaneously at this point about the utility of using wood or brass blocks for his New Testament plates, attempting to learn which option would work best and be most cost-effective. On 24 February 1815 he wrote to Collins & Co., asking, "At what rate can these brass blocks be made in New Yorke?"[21] On 3 March, he requested a set from Collins. The invoice, dated 6 March, lists "6 Brass Blocks for 12 Pages of 12mo @ 9 dolls . . . $54."[22] On 18 April he wrote, "The Grammar I expect to ship and will have an edition of 2000 copies under way. The blocks you sent me for the Test. being too small I shall therefore have to procure and if contrary to your declaration can you agree to have them returned."[23]

The Bruces wrote to Carey on 26 April to say, "We have 24 blocks on which we have struck off an edition of our Testament. They will answer you equally well, and as we shall not want to print more for some time, you can have the whole or 12 of them at two dollars a piece."[24] Carey wrote back on 29 April stating that he wanted brass, as the mahogany blocks were liable to warp and become useless. The Bruces had sent him sample mahogany blocks to examine, but he returned them, writing, "I have but two stereotype works The Grammar & Testament. I have brass blocks for the former."[25]

The following year, Collins & Co. began to stereotype a complete quarto Bible. The firm was quick to announce this to the trade, both to claim the American precedent for a stereotype family Bible and to identify potential purchasers for its plates. The Collinses wrote to Carey in February 1815 about this new venture, "We do not expect to have any Bibles finished from our Stereotype Plates under 5 or 6 months. . . . We sincerely hope that we shall carry on the Bible Business with a mutual good understanding believing it necessary to insure a mutual advantage."[26] The "mutual advantage" was the understanding that both Collins & Co. and Carey & Son would now be competing for customers for their respective family Bibles. Collins & Co. could at least make the claim that its stereotype Bible was a newer, more attractive, and more authoritative innovation than the Carey standing-type family Bible.

In June, Collins & Co. wrote a long letter to Carey, stating, in part, "We have 2 sets of our Stereotype Quarto Bible cast, & should be glad to sell thee one of them in preference to any other person in Phila. and Baltimore as it would not then increase the Printers of Quarto Bibles in the U. States. Would it suit thee to purchase and send one set to Pittsburgh or Baltimore We shall probably sell to some Bookseller South of thy city in the course of this year. Suppose thou reflects a little on this subject & please drop us a line of mail. Thy friends, Collins & Co."[27]

With this courteous threat to sell a set to a potential competitor of Carey's, Collins & Co. clearly hoped to push Carey to agree quickly to purchase a set of plates. The Collinses also agreed to Carey's proposal to print two thousand coarse and one thousand fine concordances to accompany their quarto Bible, stating that they had thought of stereotyping it but that if Carey gave them favorable terms they would take his printed copies instead. Collins wanted to do business with Carey, but also to tell him how many Bibles the firm planned to publish for the New York and New England markets. Two months later, Carey declined to purchase the quarto Bible plates, as his own standing-type family Bible was in reasonably good shape. But a setback came shortly afterward, when Collins & Co. informed him that it was going to stereotype two sets of Brown's Bible *Concordance* and print from it after all, as "they will cost us printing from the Plates less than thy offer."[28] Carey had just been undercut on price for a printing job as a result of stereotyping. For the properly capitalized publisher, the value of investing in a set of plates to produce cheaper editions over time was becoming much more evident and attractive.

The proposed Collins & Co. quarto family Bible was not Carey's only competition. Isaiah Thomas already had a family Bible set up in standing type for the New England markets, and the Brattleboro, Vermont, booksellers and publishers Holbrook & Fessenden imported a set of stereotype plates to a quarto Bible from England in 1816. From this set the Vermont firm published an "elegant, illustrated" family Bible by subscription for $12.[29]

In 1815, D. & G. Bruce stereotyped and published its own New Testament, further cutting into part of Carey's business. And as further evidence of the increasingly competitive Bible marketplace, Carey's New York colleagues Whiting & Watson became more critical of his output. In June, that firm requested on exchange a large quantity of Carey's works, including a thousand fine paper New Testaments and a selection from his list of Bibles and other works totaling twenty-five hundred volumes. In November, with only part of the order fulfilled, Whiting & Watson wrote concerning problems with what had already arrived, including missing sheets, the wrong sets of illustrations to the Bibles, and numerous signatures to books that were damaged in shipment. Moving books between Philadelphia and New York before the advent of railroads was, as William Charvat and others have documented, never without potential pitfalls.[30]

Whiting & Watson wrote again in December of that year, pressing Carey further on his Bible costs as well: "Your terms for your 4to [quarto] will never do. We could now sell 100, but cannot consent to do business for nothing." And, later in the same letter: "We submit to you, whether it is good policy to destroy the predilection of the community in this state leastward for [i.e., with regard to] your Bible, by denying to the Dealers who must be the medium of its diffusion, liberal terms; especially at a time when one Stereotype 4to is almost ready for publication, and the facility of stereotyping bids fair to put Bibles of all denominations upon the footing of the common books."[31]

Whiting & Watson was fully aware that Collins & Co. was about to cast multiple sets of stereotype family Bible plates. Carey's near monopoly on this work in the United States was about to end. By early December 1815, every bookseller in New York would have been aware of this impending change in the Bible business and seem to have welcomed it. Collins & Co. had issued a trade circular for its own stereotype quarto Bibles early in 1815. It used Mathew Carey's model of numbering each variant available: with or without the notes, Apocrypha, and plates; on four different kinds of paper; and with several different binding options (see figs. 8 and 9). All told, 106 possible quarto Bible

STEREOTYPE EDITION
OF
COLLINS'S QUARTO FAMILY BIBLE,
With Canne's Marginal References.

In a former Circular we gave notice of our intention to procure a set of Stereotype plates for our Quarto Family Bible; and remarked, at the same time, that great success had attended this mode of printing, both in France and England. To accomplish our object, we have employed John Watts, who introduced the art into this country about two years since, after having received complete instruction in the business from his brother Richard Watts, and from Andrew Wilson, of London, who alone (with the exception of the founders employed at the Universities in Great Britain) possess the art in perfection.

We have now the satisfaction of stating that a great proportion of the work is already finished, and that the whole will be completed in a few months: shortly after which, our first edition from the plates will be printed. The Small Pica type of our late edition of the Bible has been chosen as the model for our Stereotype Plates; having, however, been much improved in the Roman, and a new Italic introduced. We have enriched the work by inserting Canne's copious and highly esteemed Marginal References. Great attention is bestowed to render this Stereotype edition free from errors; which, when accomplished, will recommend it to every reader of the Sacred Volume. By the union of correctness in typography, with beauty of type, we hope to gratify all our friends; and we shall reflect with pleasure, that we have used our utmost endeavours to produce a volume claiming general approbation throughout the United States.

We cannot more clearly point out the advantages of Stereotype Printing, than by presenting an extract from the advertisement of A. Wilson, of London, whose experience of nine years has fully proved that this art promises the most extensive and important advantages to modern literature. Among many unanswerable arguments in favour of this mode of printing, he states that, " The Stereotype Art possesses a *security against error*, which must stamp every work so printed with a decided superiority of character. If, after all the care and attention that competent and industrious editors can bestow, some inaccuracies should still escape observation in a first edition, it is a pleasing satisfaction to know that these may be corrected as they are discovered, without any injury to the plates, and with such perfect nicety that the most acute eye cannot discern where an alteration has been made. Thus in all Stereotype books, the *imperfections*, if any, of a first and small impression, may be easily and speedily rectified; whilst its *perfections* remain undisturbed in all future impressions; and of course all *accumulation* of error in each succeeding edition is entirely precluded. And what an important security it is, that the numerous train of incidental mistakes which are continually occurring in the printing of works by moveable types, *and to which every new edition superadds its own particular share of error*, may thus be completely remedied by the Stereotype invention. In Stereotype, every page of the most extensive work has a separate plate; all the pages, therefore, of a work, must be *equally new and beautiful*. By the old method, the types of each sheet are distributed, and of the distributed types the succeeding sheets are composed; so that, although a few of the earlier sheets of a volume may be well printed, the last part of the same volume, in consequence of the types being in a gradual state of wear as the work proceeds, must be executed in a very inferior manner."

We annex our terms to the trade for the work, bound and in sheets. On purchases the net amount of which is $50 a 100, a credit of three months will be allowed, from 100 to 200, 6 months; on all exceeding 200, 9 months. A discount of ¼ will be made from the printed retail prices on all purchases exceeding 50 dollars net, with credit above mentioned.

COLLINS & CO.

New-York, First Month, 1815.

SUPERFINE MEDIUM.

	Prices in Sheets.	Retail Bound.
No. 1 Old and New Testament	$3 50	$7 50
2 .... with Apocrypha	4 07	8 50
3 .... Apocrypha and Concordance	4 32	9
4 .... with Concordance	3 85	8
5 .... with Notes	4 10	8 50
6 .... with Notes and Concordance	4 45	9
7 .... Notes, Apocrypha and Concordance	5 02	10

12 Maps and Plates 100 cts.

COARSE MEDIUM.

No. 37 Old and New Testament	$1 62	$3 50
38 .... with Apocrypha	1 90	4
39 .... Apocrypha and Concordance	2 14	4 50
40 .... Concordance	1 86	4
41 .... Notes	1 93	4
42 .... Notes and Concordance.	2 17	4 50
43 .... Notes, Apocrypha and Concordance	2 45	5

20 Maps and Plates for the coarse copies, 50 cts.

FIG. 8 Trade circular for Collins & Co.'s family quarto Bible, 1815, p. 1. From *Stereotype Edition of Collins's Quarto Family Bible, With Canne's Marginal References* (New York: Collins & Co., 1815). John Watts, printer. Printed broadside. SY1815 no. 43, neg. #90171d, New-York Historical Society. Photography © New-York Historical Society.

PRICES OF THE STEREOTYPE EDITION

OF COLLINS'S QUARTO FAMILY BIBLE,

With Canne's Marginal References,

ON SUPERFINE WOVE MEDIUM PAPER.

In handsome strong Sheep Binding.

No.		D. C.
1	Old and New Testaments	7 50
2	with Apocrypha	8 50
3	Apocrypha and Concordance	9 00
4	Concordance	8 00
5	Ostervald's Notes	8 50
6	Ostervald's Notes and Concordance	9 00
7	Apocrypha, Ostervald's Notes and Concordance	10 00

Same Binding with Maps and Elegant Historical Engravings.

8	Old and New Testaments	9 00
9	with Apocrypha	10
10	Apocrypha and Concordance	10 50
11	Concordance	9 50
12	Ostervald's Notes	10
13	Ostervald's Notes and Concordance	10 50
14	Apocrypha, Ostervald's Notes and Concordance	11 50

Handsome Calf Binding without Maps and Engravings.

15	Old and New Testaments	8 50
16	Apocrypha	9 50
17	Apocrypha and Concordance	10
18	Concordance	9
19	Ostervald's Notes	9 50
20	Ostervald's Notes and Concordance	10
21	Apocrypha, Ostervald's Notes and Concordance	11

Same Binding with Maps and Elegant Historical Engravings.

22	Old and New Testaments	10
23	Apocrypha	11
24	Apocrypha and Concordance	11 50
25	Concordance	10 50
26	Ostervald's Notes	11
27	Ostervald's Notes and Concordance	11 50
28	Apocrypha, Ostervald's Notes and Concordance	12 50

Elegant Calf Gilt, or Red Leather Gilt Bindings, with Maps and Elegant Historical Engravings.

29	Old and New Testaments	11 00
30	Apocrypha	12
31	Apocrypha and Concordance	12 50
32	Concordance	11 50
33	Ostervald's Notes	12
34	Ostervald's Notes and Concordance	12 50
35	Apocrypha, Ostervald's Notes and Concordance	13 50
36	Contains the same as in No. 35, but bound either in Russia, Morocco, or Extra Calf.	18 50

ON COMMON MEDIUM PAPER.

In strong Sheep Binding, without Maps or Engravings

37	Old and New Testaments *(not lettered)*	3 50
38	Apocrypha *(not lettered)*	4 00
39	Apocrypha and Concordance	4 50
40	Concordance *(not lettered)*	4 00
41	Ostervald's Notes *(not lettered)*	4 00
42	Ostervald's Notes and Concordance	4 50
43	Apocrypha, Ostervald's Notes and Concordance	5 00

Same Binding, with Maps and Historical Engravings.

44	Old and New Testaments	4 50
45	Apocrypha	5 00
46	Apocrypha and Concordance	5 50
47	Concordance	5 00
48	Ostervald's Notes	5 00
49	Ostervald's Notes and Concordance	5 50
50	Apocrypha, Ostervald's Notes and Concordance	6 00

FIG. 9   Trade circular for Collins & Co.'s family quarto Bible, 1815, p. 2. From *Stereotype Edition of Collins's Quarto Family Bible, With Canne's Marginal References* (New York: Collins & Co., 1815). John Watts, printer. Printed broadside. SY1815 no. 43, neg. #90171d, New-York Historical Society. Photography © New-York Historical Society.

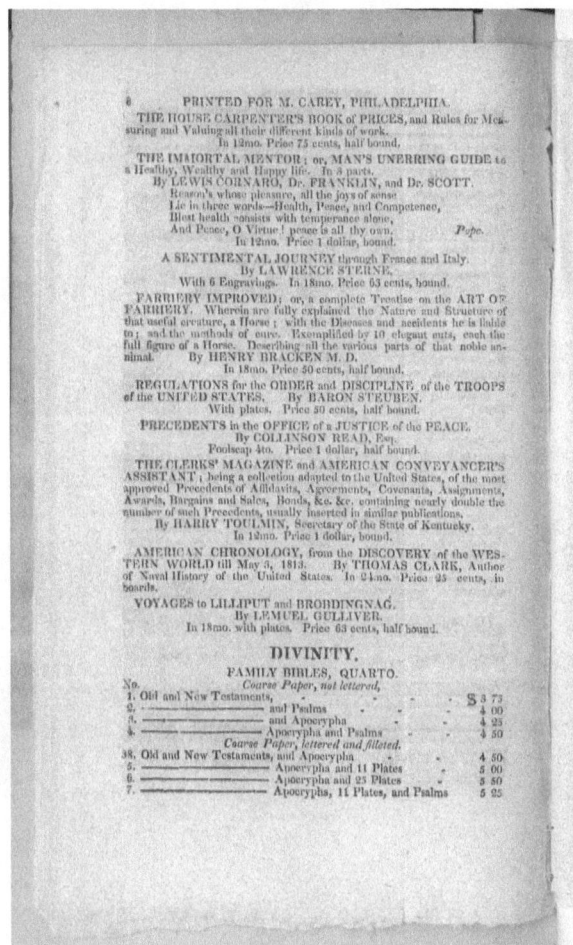

FIG. 10   Mathew Carey's Bible list, March 1816, p. 1. From Mathew Carey, *Modern Publications, and New Editions of Valuable Standard Works* (Philadelphia: Mathew Carey, 1816), 8. The Library Company of Philadelphia.

variants were offered to booksellers and the public at prices ranging from $1.62 for a coarse edition in sheets to $18.50 for a superfine wove paper edition with the full complement of additional texts and engravings in gilt calf, and with Russia or Morocco bindings. Collins & Co.'s prices slightly undercut Carey's family Bible options for most of these variants (see figs. 10 and 11). Carey's dominance in the family Bible marketplace was now seriously challenged, and the rapid changes taking place in typefounding and bookselling in New York

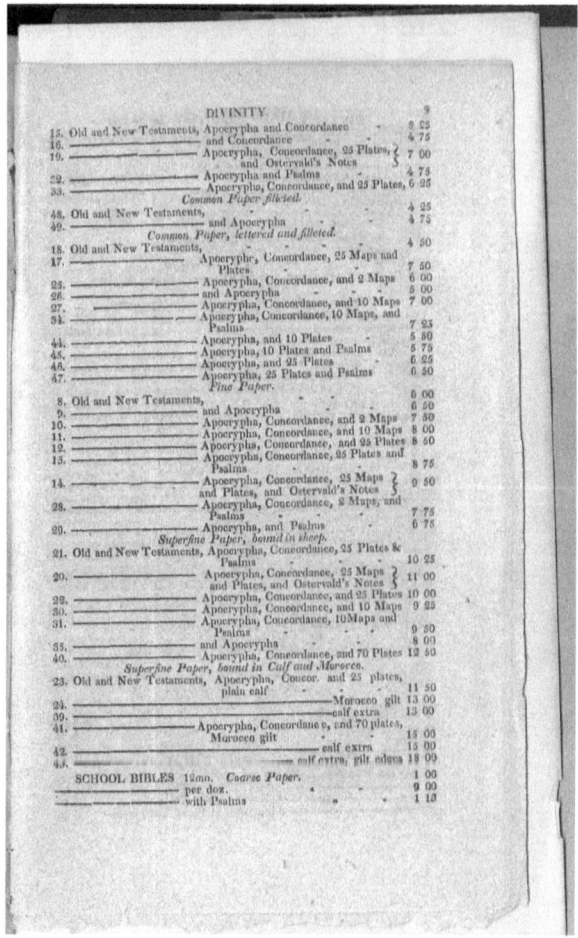

FIG. 11 Mathew Carey's Bible list, March 1816, p. 2. From Mathew Carey, *Modern Publications, and New Editions of Valuable Standard Works* (Philadelphia: Mathew Carey, 1816), 9. The Library Company of Philadelphia.

now made Philadelphia seem very far away from the center of innovation in the American printing trades.

SELLING THE NEW TESTAMENT PLATES

Mathew Carey never printed from the 336 New Testament plates he purchased in the fall of 1814. His 1814 New Testament printed from standing type was the last edition of the New Testament he would ever print. Carey made an agreement with the New York printing and bookselling firm of T. & W. Mercein in the summer of 1816 to sell his New Testament plates, offering them at cost ($756), one-third of which was payable in copies of Mercein's edition of Lemprière's *Classical Dictionary* and the remaining two-thirds in stock of the New Testament that Mercein would then print from the plates.[32] Carey benefited in several ways from this arrangement. He had already embargoed his set of plates in Philadelphia for eighteen months, thus preserving his hold over the Philadelphia market for stereotyped New Testaments during this early period. As we have seen, he was also able to print one final New Testament impression from standing type before sending the old type to the Bruces as partial payment for the plates. And by 1816, he had used his investment in the plates as capital to procure more stock and a large quantity of newly printed stereotype New Testaments that would carry him forward for several years.

Carey's business decisions show his evolution as a publisher who was confronting the new landscape of stereotyped works in the United States. For widely reprinted works like the New Testament for which no copyright could be held, the advantages of owning a set of plates were minimal. By establishing a relationship with a New York printer who did own the plates, Carey could obtain new stock on exchange whenever he wished, without the worry of tying up a $700 investment, either in standing type or in plates. He could treat the owner of the New Testament plates as a job printer, and the work would be accessible anytime Carey needed a new quantity struck off. He did maintain an early advantage by owning a set of plates as he established market dominance between 1814 and 1816. But after that period, Carey could control reprintings as needed by making the proper arrangements with the new owners of the plates for jobbed or jointly published editions.[33] Later in the century, issues of reprinting would be handled quite differently by Mathew's son Henry C. Carey for works that were under copyright protection. The younger Carey arranged multiyear copyright agreements with authors such as Washington Irving and James Fenimore Cooper and had plates cast of their works. After allowing sales from the first impression of each title to pay for the cost of the plates, Henry Carey then made a steady full profit on all later impressions made and sold during the period in which he held the copyright.[34]

Mathew Carey's agreement with Mercein, however, did not proceed smoothly. More than a year after their initial agreement, late in 1817, Carey was forced to make arrangements with D. & G. Bruce to commission repairs to the New Testament plates the Bruces had cast for him three years before. Carey wrote to the brothers in November, "We put our Testaments into the hands of a miscreant to print, who has most grossly abused it. We wish it repaired completely & send you a copy of it for examination, that you may be able to state at what terms you w^d make the necessary repairs."[35] The Bruces replied a few days later, "We would willingly bestow a few days work on your plates without charge; but if they are grossly abused it may be a tedious and costly operation to correct them. We shall charge you however no more than a reasonable compensation for the time bestowed upon them." Mercein, with no prior experience printing from plates, had evidently misjudged their height on the press and crushed parts of the type surface. In the same letter, D. & G. Bruce also made Carey two new offers:

> About two years ago we introduced an improvement into our stereotype business by which our plates are produced of a uniform thickness, and consequently can be printed from without overlays. We have a set of New Testament plates on the same type as yours, with three lines more in a page and making but <u>thirteen</u> sheets, which, with 12 blocks, we would be willing to exchange for your set with 24 blocks if you will add $250 at 6 months. We have lately stereotyped for the American Bible Society a Minion 12mo Bible, of which we enclose a proof. It makes <u>thirty-five</u> sheets. We have a set of it for sale, with 24 blocks; for which we would take $2100 at 6 months.[36]

The offer to exchange his damaged plates for a new set for only $250 was probably tempting, but Carey insisted that repairs to the damaged set of plates proceed instead. The offer of a duodecimo school Bible in plates to Carey, as a commercial publisher, and made from the same setting of type as the plates the Bruces had made for the nonprofit American Bible Society would have further complicated the market for cheap Bibles in the United States. Carey, who already owned a standing-type duodecimo Bible, and who would have been aware of the large quantities being printed for cheap or even free distribution by the American Bible Society, wisely declined the offer.

When they received the damaged plates in early January 1818, the Bruces were dismayed at their condition, telling Carey that they were in a much worse state than he had intimated. The corrector they employed likewise expressed doubts as to whether they could be repaired. "We shall do what we can to serve you," they wrote, "and hope that you will be satisfied in that respect. But we will hardly be able to forgive ourselves for engaging in so unpleasant and unprofitable a business as the rectification of three hundred battered plates, which, had they been our own, would certainly have been condemned to the pot."[37] Months later, in the autumn of 1818, Carey was still waiting for the repairs to be completed, and by this time was probably regretting his decision not to exchange his damaged plates for the Bruces' new set. In late November, Carey informed the Bruces that he had sold his New Testament to another printer "& the purchaser is impatient to receive it."[38] The repairs were still not complete by the end of the year. From the end of 1814, when he first took possession of his set of New Testament plates, until their final sale in early 1819, a published edition was never made from them. This incident shows the risks involved in owning a set of plates when most printers in the United States were not experienced in printing from them. After losing time and money on these ill-fated plates, Carey ended up cutting his losses and disposing of them without ever having seen a printed impression from them.

COMMISSIONING A STEREOTYPE FAMILY BIBLE

While his dealings with the Bruces proceeded in 1817–18, Carey was also negotiating with Collins & Co. and its stereotyping partnership, Collins & Hannay. He inquired in January 1817 about the availability of "stereotype woodcuts" for Bibles, and Collins wrote back that it had some on hand that it could sell him for ten dollars each. The firm sent Carey two woodblocks for examination at his request. Carey replied brusquely in February, "The cuts are not worth a Dollar. I shall return them."[39] Might Carey have been testing Collins & Co.'s skill at reproducing images via the stereotype process? This exchange occurred two years after the introduction of Collins's family Bibles, and we may read it as a dismissal of Collins & Co. for the price and quality of the firm's merchandise after it had backed out of a printing job with Carey because of his prices. Or perhaps Carey deliberately wanted to cast some doubt on the quality of Collins's printed Bible illustrations while he continued to offer his own Bibles printed from standing type with accompanying engravings. Collins wrote back on 15 February, having received Carey's terse dismissal of its cuts: "We are surprised @ your famous <u>Printers</u> have not ingenuity sufficient to Print the Stereotype Cuts sent on; — <u>We</u> can take off impressions without any difficulty & so will, that 'tis not easy to distinguish between those & impressions from the Wood cuts, & as a proof of this the impressions sent on with the Stereotype Cuts were taken from those very cuts in our office a few minutes before we sent them to you."[40] After this exchange, the correspondence between Carey and Collins stopped for several months, which is unusual as they tended to correspond several times a month for the purpose of exchanging stock.

Their correspondence resumed in the autumn of 1817 with a more substantial offer. Collins wrote on 7 November:

> We are offering @ 6000 dollars for our set of Quarto Bible Plates—including old & new test—apoc, tables, say 1144 Plates & Brown's Concordance—Blocks & Boxes, also complete—but as it would raise another competitor in the Bible Printing, We should prefer selling them to you & would take your standing Bibles, as type metal, at 20 cents p. lb.—our Plates are none the worse for wear as you may observe by examining our Royal Quarto Bible at E. & R. Parkers or Thos. DeSilvers store—we have not printed any Bibles since.—Another Bible in Phila would no doubt interfere somewhat with thine & if 'tis an object to accept our offer please write us same.—We paid 6000 dollars in Cash for our Plates.[41]

This offer essentially repeated Collins's first offer in 1815 of a stereotype family Bible, which Carey had refused. With Collins's family Bible for sale in at least two Philadelphia bookstores in addition to the New York market, why would the firm be offering to sell Carey its nearly three-year-old plates, at cost? Collins & Co. either needed to raise capital or was planning to cast new sets of plates. Carey responded three days later with a refusal: "We cannot conceive how the idea c^d ever occur to you, that we w^d sacrifice our quarto Bible to the furnace, when it is but a fourth worn. We are so far from such an intent, that we w^d not exchange it for the stereotypes, without at least 3000 dollars difference & hardly that. If you sell in Phila we cannot help it. You have a right & we must meet the rivalship as well as we can."[42] And there the matter ended for several months.

Nine months later, in August 1818, Benjamin Collins wrote to his brother Isaac that a letter had arrived from Mathew Carey inquiring about a set of plates for a Pica Bible. Carey wanted to know how long it would take to cast, and "will you engage to cast but one set?"[43] Carey offered Collins half the cost in his own quarto Bibles at a one-third discount off the trade price. Benjamin

Collins answered each of Carey's initial questions in his letter to his brother. He wrote that it would take about four months to cast a Bible, and Carey could take delivery of it in parts to print from as the plates were made. Collins & Co. would keep its own set of plates and would not give Carey an exclusive set. Collins would take his Bibles as partial payment, but only at a 50 percent discount. The price for the Bible would be $4,500 for the Old and New Testaments and Apocrypha. Benjamin also wrote, "Your contract with Watts was $6 per page for a single set. At this rate it would cost more than $6000."[44] If Watts was doing the casting, as he had for the previous sets of plates, the cost for this Bible, in two copies, represented a substantial savings in the unit cost of making a plate, down to about $4.50 from $6.00 in only three years.

After refusing Collins & Co.'s existing set of quarto Bible plates, and with nine months to think about it, Carey at last seemed interested in acquiring a complete stereotype Bible. Carey received the details of Collins & Co.'s offer and wrote back to inquire about the schedule for delivery of plates. He also wanted to keep the negotiations open "until next Wednesday, till the return of our H.C.C.," meaning Henry C. Carey, by this time Mathew's partner in the firm of Carey & Son.[45]

The deal was agreed to. Beginning in September 1818 and continuing for several months, Carey's frequent correspondence with Collins is concerned only with the specifics of the Bible's setting and production. Carey gave Collins exacting instructions for setting up this work, specifying typefaces, sizes, and the layout for each part of the book. His opinions would become even more exacting as page proofs begin to arrive in Philadelphia for examination. Carey was concerned with the headers and how notes and references within the book were treated; he complained about the number of lines on each page and how the layout would not fit his standard paper stock. He conceded to giving up catch words in the book to save one line per page, as Collins thought them costly and of little use, especially for their tendency to become more quickly damaged when a plate was stored and then removed from its box. To most of Carey's criticisms, Collins & Co. patiently explained the rationale and noted how certain types of changes would be impossible owing to the difficulty of correcting plates once they were cast; additional lines of text, Collins said, could not be added to a plate so it would print evenly.[46] By the 1820s, correcting stereotype plates would become a more common practice.

By late October 1818, the first 250 plates had been cast. On 8 December, the first shipment of finished plates left New York on a ship bound for Philadelphia. Twelve boxes were sent, containing one-fourth of Carey's quarto Bible, along with a bill of lading for $1,100. This would amount to about twenty-four plates housed in each box.[47] The second shipment left New York on 9 February 1819. A third shipment of twelve boxes of plates left on 5 March, with the final shipment of twelve boxes of plates sent on 1 May 1819. Carey paid cash for all four shipments, including boxing and shipping, for a total of $4,535.75.[48] Carey was taking some risk in paying so much for a set of plates, especially as they only gave him a duplicate text of his own standing-type family Bible. But by owning the "Philadelphia set" of Collins's new Bible, he was able to prevent a third publisher from competing in the family Bible business, and the work was composed to his own standards. Collins's earlier family Bible was already for sale in Philadelphia bookstores. Publishers at this time claimed that stereotype editions had a greater degree of textual accuracy, even if this was not usually the case, and there was greater interest in them as being newer and more innovative. Carey could now claim that his Bible plates were the newest and the most accurate on the market, surpassing Collins & Co.'s older edition that was then being sold in town.

After committing to purchase the Bible, Carey was naturally concerned about any new challengers to the Bible business. Early in 1819, he asked Thomas Kirk, a bookseller in New York, to quietly make inquiries on the state of the Bible business in that city, especially concerning rumors that another stereotype Bible was being commissioned by the bookseller Daniel D. Smith. Kirk wrote back that he had made inquiries and was convinced that Smith had not commissioned a set of plates. Kirk noted that he had spoken with the foreman of the stereotype foundry, and that the project with which Smith was rumored to be associated had not been undertaken.[49] Smith was a general-interest publisher and sold schoolbooks, Bibles, New Testaments, and other steady sellers. He had published an edition of Walker's *Critical Pronouncing Dictionary* in 1818 that had been stereotyped by the New York firm of E. & J. White. Consequently, he was in a good position to know whether New York stereotypers were beginning to produce more sets of plates. And, in fact, Kirk's message to Carey was incorrect: Smith did publish a quarto Bible in 1820 from plates made by E. White that directly competed with both Carey's and Collins's editions. The New York Bible business was increasingly crowded, and Carey, in Philadelphia, could not muster the correct intelligence from so far away to maintain his former competitive advantage.

By 1820, the United States Bible marketplace was booming. That year, as noted above, the Brattleboro, Vermont, firm of Holbrook & Fessenden, general publishers and booksellers and early adopters of stereotype printing with its

$12 subscription Bible in 1816, published a trade circular listing its own family Bible, now available in fifteen different variants on the Carey and Collins model: on coarse, fine, and superfine papers, and ranging from $3.50 to $18, with additional options for adding the Psalms and Ostervald's *Notes* to each set, for a total of fifty-one possible variants.[50]

Carey visited New York in the summer of 1820 and spoke with the Bruces about stereotype plates to editions of Horace and Cicero. They wrote to him in Philadelphia soon after his visit, quoting a price of $3,467 for both works, boxed and with blocks on which to mount them for printing. They also noted their own innovations to these sets: "It is proper to inform you that these works have been remodelled; and the notes, which formerly interrupted the text are now entirely to the bottom of the pages. By this alteration, and something in the proportions of the pages, a considerable saving is made. Horace, with an Index of 60 pages of Nonpareil, makes but one sheet less than your editions without the indexes. Cicero, with the same matter, makes 144 pages less than the old editions."[51] Carey did not immediately agree to the offer, and by August, on his recommendation, the Bruces sold the Cicero to Thomas A. Ronaldson of Philadelphia. Carey held off on the Horace, asking for proofs before making any commitments. In September, Carey agreed to buy a set of plates to Virgil's works from the Bruces for $3,400, boxed and with blocks and copperplate engravings. The Bruces also noted that they had had an impression of 750 copies of the Virgil just printed, except for title pages, which they could also offer. Carey agreed to buy the 750 printed copies as well, for $585, or seventy-eight cents each, on 9 September 1820. In October, he asked the Bruces to create a stereotype plate for the title page to his new Virgil and to print 250 copies of it, to be added to his edition. This would have satisfied Carey's immediate need for 250 copies under his own imprint and given him time to either print up title pages for the remaining 500 copies or sell them to another bookseller.

Also in October, Carey struck an agreement with the Bruces to have plates made of the Psalms to add to his quarto Bible. A set, in Bourgeois type (about nine point), was made for him for $180. The decision to purchase the Horace in plates was delayed until 1821. On 9 April, the brothers wrote to Carey that they had 750 copies of the Horace printed, fifty of them bound, together with the set of plates to it, which had not yet sold and which they would value at $2,800. They added, "This is less than 3000 copies of the same book would cost in the common way of printing and must be desirable property to those who would wish to publish the work."[52] Carey quickly agreed to the purchase price on 11 April. The Bruces agreed to his suggestion that they could receive partial payment in old type. Carey initially offered half but settled for one-third in old type, to which the Bruces agreed. Carey asked that they ship the plates in three or four vessels "so as to divide the risk."[53] The Bruces shipped the plates to Philadelphia on 2 May 1821. Mathew Carey now owned the stereotype plates to four books: Murray's *English Grammar*, his family Bible, a Virgil, and a Horace. Counting his now sold New Testament, he had owned five works in plates up to this point, one of the largest collections by a publisher in the United States.

In March 1821, almost two years after receiving his final shipment of family Bible plates, Carey wrote to Collins & Hannay, "On examining the Stereotype plates of the Quarto Bible which we purchased from you we find there are no Blocks with them, which is usual, we presume you intended to send. We request you will be so good to supply this deficiency as soon as possible."[54] Carey had been warehousing the fifty boxes of stereotype plates to his quarto Bible since the spring of 1819, and they apparently remained unexamined. He continued to negotiate with Collins & Hannay throughout the spring about the blocks and the lack of an index to the Bible, which he also assumed was included with the plates. An indication of greater problems occurred in June, when Carey requested six to eight pounds of Pica type from Collins & Hannay "to correct the text of the Stereotype Bible which appears to have been very carelessly packed."[55] One week later he increased his request to thirty pounds of type, "there being sundry battered & defective letters in it. We are informed that some errors have been discovered in the Bible furnished Collins & Co.—pray let us have immediate information of this that we may have them corrected before the Edition is worked off."[56] Collins & Hannay replied that it had taken proofs of every plate before boxing and sending them on, so had no knowledge of any improper fabrication. Henry C. Carey had visited the New York foundry when the Bible was being cast and had stated that the plates he saw were of good quality and were not found wanting, so the firm did not believe there was any reason for complaint.[57]

Carey had been thinking about printing from his Bible plates at least as early as March 1821, when Collins had written to him that the firm was putting a new edition of the quarto Bible to press from a newly cast set of plates. Carey wrote to Thomas Kirk in New York about his ideas in March and April, attempting to enlist Kirk's assistance as an agent for procuring subscriptions. Later that summer, in negotiating Kirk's commission, his plan became clear:

"We find we cannot afford a commission for procuring subscribers higher than 12 1/2 Dols. & the same for supplying them. You will be pretty well convinced of this if you make a few calculations. The Binding alone of the 50 Dollar Bible is to be 18 Dollars. This with 12.50 for procuring subs it will leave but 19.50 for plates, paper, printing, etc. You will have the best of the Bargain."[58] Carey went on to say that his profits from the first edition would be negligible, but he would be willing to offer 33.33 percent commissions on future editions. Carey's proposed edition, priced at an astronomical $50, would have been more than twice the price of his previous most expensive edition, and more than twice the price of Collins's or any other family Bible available at this time. Joel Barlow's *Columbiad*, the most elaborately produced book published in the United States to that point, sold for $20 when it was published in 1807, and was not at all a best seller.[59] Carey must have thought there was a market for such a new luxury product, even in a country still recovering from the economic downturn caused by the Panic of 1819. Was he making one final attempt to control the high end of the family Bible marketplace, even if this elaborate and costly edition would only pay for itself and not generate significant profits? Kirk, who was an experienced subscription agent, selling Carey's editions of Lavoisne's *Atlas* and a set of common law reports for him in New York, agreed to Carey's terms and awaited a specimen to show potential New York subscribers.

In September, Carey sent out prospectuses for two different stereotype Bibles, his $50 "Splendid Bible," as it was now called, and a more modest one. But one month later Carey changed his mind and abandoned the prospect of a $50 Bible. Kirk wrote back to him, agreeing that the new, scaled-down version "presents a better prospect of success."[60] Kirk then sent a fateful letter to Carey on 27 November about the state of subscriptions for the Bible and Lavoisne's *Atlas*. He said that subscriptions had been less than he expected: "To almost every application to subscribe for the Bible the answer has been, by some, that the pretense of the times would not permit the expense and of others, that they already had several Bibles and some of them sufficiently elegant."[61] The family Bible market, especially for deluxe editions, appeared to be saturated.

After Carey published his trade circular announcing his new stereotype family Bible, J. & J. Harper of New York, newly established job printers and not yet publishers, wrote to Carey inquiring about their printing it for him. The Harpers stated that they had the most experience in New York printing from stereotype plates, and had even printed Collins's family Bible, which was cast from the same setting of type as Carey's, thus making them the best firm for the job. Tellingly, and perhaps remembering the stories surrounding Carey's experience with the inexperienced T. & W. Mercein company, which had damaged his New Testament plates in 1816, the Harpers concluded, "Should you think proper to favour us with the Printing of your Bible, we will expect to return you the Plates free from <u>Bruises</u>, one evil which inexperience so often meets with."[62] In the end, and after further delays, Carey would turn down their offer and instead print his Bible in Philadelphia. J. & J. Harper would grow and flourish, incorporating stereotyping into their printing work from the start, and would become one of New York's largest publishers by the 1830s.[63]

As Carey began to make further preparations for bringing out the deluxe Bible, he discovered that the plates had become damaged at some point. He sent a long, aggrieved letter to William Collins in January 1822, laying out Collins's responsibility for making reparations for his damaged plates: "a very large portion of the plates which we have rec^d are unmerchantable.... The injury we suffer from the delay which accrues out of this affair is very great."[64] Collins agreed to send replacement plates where needed and to allow a third party to examine them in order to ascertain their state of repair. These negotiations went on through the spring and summer of 1822, further postponing the publication of Carey's Bible. Collins and Carey sparred during this time, each accusing the other of breaking verbal agreements and promises that the other claimed not to remember. At the lowest point in the negotiations, Collins wrote a long, anguished letter to Carey itemizing all their disagreements and concluding, "We cannot pass over your letter of the 3rd without indignation. That you should remark opposite 90 plates '<u>Very Bad</u>' & insinuate in a subsequent remark that they are so bad as to be irreparable is too insulting to our feelings to permit it being passed by in silence."[65]

Three days later, Collins sent a more temperate letter, agreeing to waive some of the disputed charges and to make the necessary repairs to the plates. William Collins also sent a personal note of apology on behalf of his brothers, stating that proofs for the required replacement plates would be made from Collins's own set and then replaced in Carey's set.[66] The repairs were made and the replacement plates delivered to Carey that spring and summer. The experience of correcting his damaged Bible plates caused Carey a delay of one full year in his plan to bring out his first stereotype family Bible. Carey finally published his edition in 1823, four years after taking ownership of the plates. It would be the only stereotype Bible printed by Carey & Son and its successor firms. Carey & Son would also print one final impression of the family Bible from standing type in 1824, after the stereotype edition. By this time, the United States family Bible market was completely different from the one that Carey had dominated earlier in the century. Many competitors across the country were now publishing similar or cheaper editions, and the American Bible Society was successfully carrying out its mission to distribute inexpensive copies of the Bible to all parts of the United States. Carey & Son would abandon the Bible business entirely in 1824.

Mathew Carey's experiences in negotiating the newly emergent marketplace in stereotype plates for this one product, the quarto family Bible, illustrates some of the risks and rewards that were possible for an early adopter of this new technology. Success required choosing the correct works to be cast into plates, the right typefounder to work with, and printers who could print expertly from plates. Even so, delays in shipping, production, and textual correction made moving from standing type to stereotype printing possible for only a small number of bold, well-capitalized publishers in the 1810s. As an experienced publisher, Carey managed on several occasions to delay an inevitable loss of market share for a few years as this new technology became more commonly employed, but ultimately the family Bible marketplace grew larger than one publisher could control.

CHAPTER 3

 The American Bible Society and the Possibilities of Large-Scale Printing

In the spring of 1829, the American Bible Society (ABS) took an inventory of its assets in anticipation of setting an unprecedented new goal. The society already operated the largest publishing house in the United States, and its plans for the construction of Bible House, its new offices and manufacturing headquarters on Nassau Street in lower Manhattan, were proceeding apace. The primary mission of the society, to "furnish a supply of correct and well-made Bibles and Testaments for the use of our own country," had by all accounts been successful, year after year, to the extent that the ABS reported the total issue from its presses as 1,767,736 volumes since its founding in 1816, thirteen years earlier.[1] In response to an inquiry from its board of managers, Daniel Fanshaw (1789–1860), the society's printer, reported that his eight power presses and staff of twenty could print 291,000 Bibles or a combination of 398,000 Bibles and New Testaments per year at the current capacity. Four more power presses had already been ordered. When installed, they would increase Fanshaw's production capacity to 421,200 Bibles or 580,000 Bibles and New Testaments per year.

The secretary of the standing committee of managers, a group of five members of the board charged with the care and oversight of the society's property and assets, later reported, "Mr. Fanshaw has now in operation 8 power presses and by the 1st of August will have 8 more. 16 power presses in addition to these must be provided in order to obtain the maximum of work in the proposed new building." With thirty-two power presses, the ABS would have more under one roof than anyone else in the United States. With the anticipated sixteen presses, Fanshaw further estimated being able to produce 518,400 Nonpareil Bibles or 680,000 books of scripture per year.

With thirteen years of publishing experience, the ABS had the production and distribution infrastructure in place to attempt something unprecedented in the spring of 1829: what its managers called a "General Supply" of Bibles to the nation. They resolved "to supply all the destitute families in the United States with the holy Scriptures, that may be willing to purchase or receive them, within the space of two years."[2] The technological revolution that Tocqueville witnessed taking place in the early Republic would be employed in the New York printing and publishing world to further the evangelical aims of the ABS, whose managers were confident that they could put a Bible into the hands of every family in the land, regardless of income.[3] "While other ambitious men and women of letters worked 'to build a new Athens in America,'" Michael Paulus writes, "theological authors effectively exploited innovations in the production and dissemination of printed materials and looked for the establishment of a new Jerusalem."[4] The ABS was in the best possible position to meet this unprecedented goal. By the end of the 1820s, "the society's New York operation was one of the largest and most highly-capitalized publishing houses in the country, virtually monopolizing the production of inexpensive Bibles in the United States," according to David Paul Nord. In the two years following the ABS's announcement about providing a general supply of Bibles, the society increased its total fifteen-year output to 1.3 million Bibles—this in a nation of only about three million households.[5]

This chapter explores the publishing practices of the ABS as it employed new technologies to print Bibles and New Testaments in the years leading up to its "general supply" initiative, especially as it commissioned and amassed stereotype plates to augment its presses and other assets. The ABS innovated in other ways as well. It purchased the first rubber inking rollers for its handpresses, was an early purchaser of domestic machine-made paper, and financed the first use of steam-powered printing in New York City. The society's managers, a group of the city's professional and mercantile elite, were not hesitant to harness new technologies to further their civic and evangelical aims. By looking closely at their decisions to employ new technologies in their printing work, we can better understand this second period of growth in stereotyping and its widespread adoption in the United States, the new challenges they faced as early adopters of new printing technologies, and the ways in which the ABS's calculated growth and innovation served as a model for the large-scale commercial publishers that would emerge by midcentury.

The American Bible Society was founded in 1816 in a coordinated effort by local and regional Bible societies to amalgamate into a national organization for more effective evangelization. Its founders had several models on which to draw. The British and Foreign Bible Society, founded in London in 1804 by William Wilberforce, was a correspondent and active supporter of the ABS's early work. The Methodist Book Concern, founded in New York in 1789, was the first publishing house in America to "initiate the systematic printing and distribution of evangelical books."[6] Its Bibles, hymnals, medical advice books, and shorter tracts were printed and successfully distributed across the nation, inspiring other denominations and organizations to do likewise. The first local and regional Bible societies in the United States were founded after 1808 and operated primarily as local charities, purchasing Bibles and New Testaments and distributing them at a modest cost or even for free as a "tool of evangelization."[7] At least two "African Bible societies" had formed by 1816, in Philadelphia and Newark, for the purpose of supplying the scriptures exclusively to poor African American communities. The African Methodist Episcopal Church was organized in 1816 and founded its AME Book Concern, the first Black-owned publishing house in the United States, in 1817. The AME Book Concern published three titles in its first three years: two editions of its book *Doctrines and Discipline* and a hymnal.[8]

Many evangelical groups gained a deeper sense of purpose following Jefferson's election to the presidency in 1800, as fears that Jefferson's deism and the residual effects of Thomas Paine's influence on him would shape national policy and the country's spiritual orientation. To counter the threat of secularism, evangelicals, many of whom had conservative Federalist leanings, pushed to create private religious associations and initiatives. Through their efforts to centralize the production and distribution of religious literature in challenging times, their work would effectively launch the first forms of mass media in the United States.[9]

In 1812, four years after its founding and after three years of serious intent and fundraising, the Philadelphia Bible Society ordered a complete set of stereotype plates to the Bible from the British and Foreign Bible Society's typefounder in London, having raised $3,500 for the purchase. The plates arrived in the United States in October, four months after the outbreak of war with Great Britain. An edition of 1,250 copies was quickly struck off, making this edition the first Bible printed from plates in the United States.[10] The Philadelphia society, one of the largest Bible societies in the country, recognized early on that stereotype plates would allow it to print as many copies of the Bible as were needed at any one time and would last for years, if not decades. By 1816, it would claim to have printed more than fifty-five thousand Bibles and New Testaments from multiple sets of acquired plates.[11] While raising funds for their first set, the officers of the Philadelphia society purchased Bibles for distribution to the needy in Pennsylvania and Maryland, and even supplied Bibles to ships bound for Canton, China, and, in small quantities, for distribution among literate enslaved people in Virginia.[12] Following the Philadelphia model, new Bible societies quickly sprang up in American cities and towns. By 1816, there were more than a hundred independent societies in the United States.[13] The Baltimore Bible Society, founded in 1810, determined in 1814 to "procure from London, as soon as the relations of amity between this country and Great Britain shall, through divine goodness, be restored, a set of octavo stereotype plates of the Bible for the use of the society." Two years later, the Baltimore society succeeded in owning its own set, which it would later sell to the ABS. The New York Bible Society decided in 1809 not to commission and import a set of plates from Britain because of "delay, expense, and uncertainty," instead ordering two thousand Bibles from a Hartford printer. It would acquire its first set of plates, cast in New York, in 1815, which it would then offer to the ABS the following year.[14] Individual Protestant denominations also maintained their own publishing businesses, the largest being the Methodist Book Concern. Nord notes that of the hundreds of denominational Bible, missionary, and tract societies that sprang up in America after 1800, "by 1815 their leaders had begun to dream the dream of mass communication—that is, they imagined placing the same printed message into the hands of everyone in America."[15] The casting of stereotype plates, which was first successfully accomplished in the United States in 1813, was the perfect vehicle for this sort of large-scale uniform mass media production and distribution.

The idea of amalgamating regional and city Bible societies into a national organization was not without its critics. When the delegates from thirty-five regional societies met in New York in May 1816 to discuss this idea, representatives of the Philadelphia society and several others chose not to attend, arguing that any national organization would prevent local decision making on issues of both production and distribution. Despite this reservation, the delegates to the convention were enthusiastic about forming a national body. The driving vision of its organizer, Elias Boudinot, founding president of the New Jersey Bible Society and former president of the Continental Congress, came to pass as twenty-two vice presidents were chosen from across the country, among them many of the country's most influential citizens. John Jay of New York, Charles Cotesworth Pinckney of South Carolina, Isaac Shelby of Kentucky, and Bushrod Washington of Virginia all agreed to serve. Also present at the founding were James Fenimore Cooper (representative of the Otsego County Bible Society), Connecticut preacher Lyman Beecher, and Jedidiah Morse, the Massachusetts theologian and geographer.

The treasurer, Richard Varick, was a former mayor of New York and speaker of the state assembly. DeWitt Clinton, governor of New York, also agreed to serve. The society's board of managers, separate from the more symbolic group of vice presidents, was populated locally with a representative selection of thirty-six members of the rising New York mercantile class, businessmen and lawyers who saw the work of the society and their own work as joined together for a common purpose. In their involvement in public life through the work of an interdenominational Christian charity like the ABS, these men saw themselves as uniquely qualified to advance social reforms in the country and their communities while also doing God's work.[16] The focus on producing and distributing Christian scripture also provides evidence of what Candy Gunter Brown calls a confluence of the religious and commercial culture of the early Republic, a part of the market revolution that was enacted in the nonprofit sphere. The aims of organizations such as the ABS provided a "close connection between religious and commercial meanings" found within Protestant evangelical circles at the time.[17] Nord situates organizations like the ABS, and later groups such as the American Tract Society and the American Sunday School Union, firmly in what historians call the "market revolution" of the United States after 1815, but with a nonprofit orientation. These groups were national in outlook, "wedded to commerce and infatuated by new technology."[18] As the anonymous author of "Review of the Character and Claims of the American Bible Society" remarked in 1847, "For as things now go, we are continually in the leading strings of a spiritual machinery, and made to go and act according to its bidding, instead of the old fashioned method of doing noiselessly and without solicitation, what our judgment approved of and conscience dictated."[19] As religiously oriented publishers, these organizations saw themselves as "countering the errors of the secular press and rival religious denominations by proclaiming pure gospel truth" through this "spiritual machinery."[20]

Locating the headquarters of the newly founded ABS in New York City was never in question. Elias Boudinot wrote at the time that "New York is fast becoming the London of America, and already possesses facilities for correspondence with and transportation to all parts of our own and other countries." New York was also "the American incubator of technological innovation in the art of printing. For Bible work, the most important innovation was stereotyping."[21] New York was already the largest city in the United States by 1810 and was quickly becoming its commercial center. In the 1820s, all the technological advances that would take place in the printing trades were put to their first successful commercial applications in New York, so much so that the members of the ABS, when looking back at their initial successes of that decade, considered it the work of Providence that they were guided to organize themselves and their work when and where they did.

The ABS took a deliberately ecumenical stance, at least between the several Protestant denominations of its founding membership. Written into its constitution was a mission to "encourage a wider circulation of the Holy Scripture without note or comment." And while most attendees of the founding convention came from established mainstream Protestant denominations, small numbers of Quakers, Baptists—and one Methodist—were represented as well.[22] As a sign of encouragement, within the first year of its founding, letters of support arrived from the General Assembly of the Presbyterian Church in America and the General Convention of the Baptist Church as well.[23]

One of the primary motivations for the delegates who gathered in New York in the spring of 1816 to form a national body was the potential for large-scale production of Bibles made possible by the new technology of stereotyping. Other regional Bible societies took notice of the example of the Bible Society of Philadelphia and were already attempting to obtain their own sets of plates. The successful work of the British and Foreign Bible Society (BFBS) was a clear model for a similar American organization. As Leslie Howsam has written about the BFBS, "These merchants, lawyers, and businessmen did not hesitate to risk an untried technology" to accomplish their goals.[24] The same was true for the leaders of the ABS. Because of the significant costs involved, it made perfect sense to amalgamate into a national organization with centralized production that would leave distribution up to the regional auxiliary societies. The vote to incorporate passed without incident. In the United States, religious publishing bodies such as the ABS would be among the earliest adopters of advances in papermaking, printing technologies, and centralized mass production. By applying a commercial mindset to the work of evangelizing, religious organizations like the ABS, using earlier models from the Methodists and the BFBS, were able to take commercial form as nonprofit businesses.[25]

At the society's third meeting, and before it had even drafted a constitution, the ABS received a letter from Albany printer and publisher E. F. Bakus, "offering to the Board a set of stereotype plates for an octavo edition of the Bible which was referred to Messrs. J. E. Caldwell & D. Bethune."[26] John Caldwell and Divie Bethune, both New York businessmen on the board of managers, were charged to follow up with Bakus about his terms. They reported that the Bible on offer from Albany contained 1,171 pages, including the Apocrypha, and was priced at $3,911.40, or about $3.34 per plate. Caldwell and Bethune concluded that the type size was too small and that the book would be more useful if it were one size larger. The Apocrypha were not needed but could not be removed to lower the cost. They thus made further inquiries in New York and reported that a "skillful stereotype founder" had made them an offer for an octavo Bible in the larger type size that would run to only 960 pages, and for a lesser price than Bakus's.[27] As the Apocrypha and other added parts such as commentaries, historical notes, maps, and illustrations were not in accord with the ABS's mission to spread the word "without note or comment," this alternative was considerably more attractive as a candidate for the society's first purchase of a set of plates. The typefounder in question, Elihu White, also managed to save two sheets of paper per copy even with the larger typeface, thus saving the ABS substantial amounts of paper and presswork over time. In their report to the board of managers, Caldwell and Bethune wrote:

> It is further to be observed, that if the Board contemplate having more than one set of plates it would be a great saving to have them done at the same time. If, for instance, two sets of plates are to be cast, they would each cost upwards of $600. less than one; & if there are three, each would cost upwards of $800. less per set than one. An impression of a page, from a plate cast for the purpose accompanies this report. Three sets of plates for the Bible, of which this is a specimen, would cost, each set 2,500 Dollars, one or two of them might be sold to the trade for 33 to 3400 Dollars each.[28]

With these knowledgeable recommendations in hand, the managers declined Bakus's offer and set aside a fixed sum of $7,500 to obtain new sets of octavo Bible plates in New York instead. Even at this early date, the society was thinking about questions of scale and the efficiencies of having multiple sets of plates from which to print. The businessmen who were the managers of the society also saw potential profit in commissioning and selling additional sets of plates to other publishers. There were three firms in New York City able to cast stereotype plates at this time: D. & G. Bruce, typefounders and stereotypers; Collins & Co., printers and typefounders; and Elihu White & Co., the firm that made Campbell and Bethune the offer described above. All three would remain in close contact with the ABS in the years to come, competing with one another for the society's business.[29]

At the same meeting, the ABS managers directed the secretary for domestic correspondence to reply to a request for Bibles from the New York Female Auxiliary Bible Society. As the ABS was only two months old, he was directed to decline the request on the grounds that the society's attention and funds were first being directed to "procuring good stereotype plates & that therefore it will not be in the power of the Society at present to furnish them with Bibles."[30] Rather than begin to purchase Bibles wholesale for distribution to its auxiliary societies around the country, the ABS, in its first year of work, focused exclusively on securing stereotype plates to begin its own publishing operations. The large number of impressions that could be made from plates made them ideally suited to the ABS's large-scale production goals. The scale at which the new ABS wanted to produce Bibles was unprecedented, surpassing by far the total output of the Philadelphia Bible Society, which in its first four years of owning a set of Bible plates managed to print only 55,000 volumes. In correspondence with the ABS, the secretary of the BFBS wrote confidently, "It is considered and found by experience that good plates will work 200,000 copies."[31] The society's work and growth would continue apace. By the end of its third year, the ABS owned eight sets of stereotype plates and was printing 70,000 Bibles per year on eight handpresses. By year eight (1824), it owned twelve sets of plates and had published 265,000 volumes.

At its fifth meeting, on 15 July 1816, the society passed the following resolution: "Resolved, that this Board will proceed without delay to carry out into execution the great object contemplated by the Convention which founded this society, viz., 'To furnish great districts of the American Continent with well executed Stereotype plates for the cheap & extensive diffusion of the Scriptures, through regions which are now scantily supplied at a discouraging expense.'"[32] This resolution appeared in newspapers throughout the country to inform the US public of the society's formation and intentions, from Hallowell, Maine, to Columbia, South Carolina, and west to Ohio and Kentucky.[33] The founding convention discussed stereotyping extensively as the means that would allow the new society to best fulfill its mission. In addition to centralizing production of scripture in New York, the ABS in its earliest years would also experiment briefly with sending sets of its plates to outlying areas of the country, thinking that some branch production would help offset the shipping costs and the risk of sending large amounts of printed materials over long distances into rural America.

Before they rented meeting space and eventually built their own headquarters, ABS members often met in New York's city hall, an indicator of the ABS's status as one of New York's—and the nation's—most socially and politically well positioned philanthropic organizations. Soon after its founding, the society leased a dedicated meeting room at the New-York Historical Society. Initial fundraising was strong, an encouraging sign. In addition to founding gifts from the many individual members tapped as officers—the regional vice presidents—and gifts from newly joined regional auxiliary Bible societies, the ABS received a donation of £500 from the BFBS as a show of support. The BFBS also offered the ABS a set of stereotype plates to a French Bible, which the members discussed taking on in their first meetings. In their earliest discussions of which forms of scripture to offer to the public, the society considered offering a separate New Testament and a Spanish Bible if it could, but placed its greatest emphasis on obtaining a complete English Bible, without Apocrypha or commentary.

During this first summer, the society declined several other requests for shipments of Bibles from auxiliaries. It also received a letter of support from a Reverend Dr. Griffin recommending that the ABS procure a set of plates to produce a Bible in Spanish. In his correspondence with the regional Bible societies, the secretary was directed to state consistently that the ABS was devoting all its energies to having several sets of English Bible plates made first and then printed from itself. At the July meeting, the board authorized contracting with Elihu White to produce three sets of octavo Bible plates, at a cost not to exceed $7,500.

Just after this recommendation was made, a subcommittee of the managers charged with investigating other options for stereotype plates reported that

> a letter of the 19th July last from Messrs. B. & I. Collins Stereotype makers addressed to Saml. Boyd, Esquire, was handed to them. In this letter Messrs. Collins offered to this Board "to cast from three to six sets of plates on any type from Long Primer to Pearl inclusive, at fourteen hundred dollars a set; the page of any size wanted; & to give security that the plates

should be executed in a style equal to any that can be procured, & furnished in as short time as can be done in any foundry whatever." Shortly afterward Messrs. D. & G. Bruce, Stereotype Makers of this city offered to the Committee to make three or more sets of plates for a less sum than that proposed by Messrs. Collins.[34]

Word had clearly gotten out about the intentions—and the assets—of the newly formed society. The typefounding trade in New York, while the largest in the United States, was still modest in size and concentrated within a few square blocks in lower Manhattan. There were only twelve typefounders in New York in 1816.[35] The number of those that could also cast stereotype plates was smaller still, probably just the three firms that corresponded with the society in its earliest days: D. & G. Bruce, Collins & Co., and Elihu White & Co. The typefounders and stereotypers of New York were about to compete for a significant and lucrative new commission. A stereotyping race was on. Pausing a bit over this new information, the committee decided to send a circular letter to the three establishments setting out its requirements for the project and inviting each firm to respond. Two responses came back. D. & G. Bruce offered to complete three sets of plates of any size Bible between Long Primer and Nonpareil by 1 May 1817 for $4,000. Collins made an offer for three sets between Long Primer and Pearl type priced at $1,400 per set. If White's initial offer of $2,500 per set still stood, the Bruces' offer was the low bid by $200.[36]

At its monthly meeting in August, the society reconsidered its resolution authorizing the subcommittee to contract for three sets of octavo plates and instead authorized the managers to increase the contract to three octavo *and* three duodecimo sets. Elihu White would supply the octavo Bible plates and D. & G. Bruce the duodecimos. An octavo Bible could be used as a modest family Bible, and the smaller duodecimo would be a personal or pocket Bible. Having assessed what types of books could be produced and their estimated production time, the ABS now began the process of obtaining subscriptions for Bibles from the various societies and affiliates around the country in anticipation of being able to print from the newly commissioned plates by late spring or early summer of 1817. Many affiliate Bible societies at this point were sending money to the ABS, either as start-up gifts for operations or as loans to be held in trust, bearing interest for the ABS, to be repaid in the form of Bibles at a time when the society was able to supply them. The Burlington Female Auxiliary Bible Society of New Jersey, for example, sent a gift of $50; the Charleston,

South Carolina, Bible Society gave $500; and the Georgia Bible Society gave $1,000, of which $500 was a gift and the remaining $500 a payment for the future delivery of Bibles to Georgia. The amount of support given to the ABS's work from around the country was significant, and this gave the managers reassurance that there was a very real regional need for scripture that they could fulfill.

This initial process of organizing the society's first works was speeded up considerably by an opportunity that unexpectedly arose the following month. At its 19 September meeting, the society considered a joint offer from the New York Bible Society and the New York Auxiliary Bible Society to transfer as a gift to the ABS their joint interest in a set of newly cast stereotype plates to a Bible. This was a set of plates to a duodecimo Bible that the two societies had jointly commissioned from E. & J. White but that had not yet been printed from. The New York societies commissioned the plates in the fall of 1815 and issued a circular at that time announcing the forthcoming project, anticipating that their plates would begin arriving in the spring of 1816, fortuitous timing for the newly formed ABS.[37] The managers were clearly delighted at this prospect, as it allowed them to carry out their objective of publishing their first books months earlier than anticipated. They accepted the offer and immediately charged a committee with seeing that ten thousand copies were printed from the plates and bound for distribution. At the same time, the society turned down an offer from the publisher William D. Allen & Co. of Newburyport, Massachusetts, to supply the ABS with a large quantity of Bibles for distribution, arguing that it would not be purchasing Bibles as it was just beginning to print its own from its first set of plates.

The society contracted with New York printer Daniel Fanshaw for its first imprints. Fanshaw would continue to operate as the printer of record for the American Bible Society for thirty years. Fanshaw had been an apprentice with D. & G. Bruce when the Bruces operated their printing business from 1806 to 1816. He was a witness as they developed their stereotype casting process between 1812 and 1814. When the Bruces quit their printing operations to focus on typefounding and stereotyping, Fanshaw bought half the printing business and set up his own shop as a master printer. Having worked for the Bruces during their period of stereotype experimentation, he was one of the few printers in the United States who had direct experience working with stereotype plates. Historians of New York publishing have noted that "Fanshaw's name appears perhaps more frequently on title pages of Bibles than any New York printer" of the early nineteenth century, and he continued to work for the ABS through 1844.[38] Fanshaw would also complete contract work for the newly formed American Tract Society beginning in 1825, choosing to keep his own independent business rather than be employed full-time by the societies, even though evangelical commissions made up the vast majority of his printing jobs. On several occasions, Fanshaw turned down a set salary offered by the ABS, preferring to contract out all his jobs instead.

Fanshaw, too, was continually interested in using new advances in printing technology in his own work. He was the first printer to use power presses in New York, installing his first in 1826. Before that, he was the first to use rubber rollers instead of inking balls for his handpresses.[39] He acquired his first mechanical inking device, an apparatus mounted to the bed of a handpress, in September 1817, shortly after the innovation was brought to market, having persuaded the ABS to fund this acquisition, as the society's meeting minutes reflect: "It having, also, been ascertained to the satisfaction of this Committee that Rollers for blacking the types can be used without additional expense, and with less injury to the plates and can be worked independently of this combination; therefore Resolved that the Chairman and Mr. Collins be authorized to purchase the patent right for _five_ sets of Rollers and cause them to be put in operation without delay."[40] The American Bible Society was one of the first purchasers of paper made from the new automatic Fourdrinier papermaking machine first set up in the United States in Connecticut in 1829. Amos Hubbard, a Connecticut paper merchant, acquired paper from the mill and, being an auxiliary Bible society officer, arranged for the ABS to acquire some of this domestic machine-made stock for its operations.[41] Fanshaw himself married Mary Ramage, the daughter of Adam Ramage of Philadelphia, the first printing press builder in America, which put him in an ideal position to take advantage of technological innovations in his work for an organization equally interested in new advances in printing technologies.[42] His presses, with the newly acquired set of stereotype Bible plates, began working off their first book in November 1816, with an initial press run of ten thousand Bibles.[43]

Also in November, the ABS received a letter from the Kentucky Bible Society "on the subject of locating a set of Stereotype Plates of the Bible at Lexington."[44] The Kentucky society had also written directly to Elias Boudinot in New Jersey to inquire about the possibility and cost of sending a set of stereotype Bible plates to Kentucky. With multiple copies of the same Bible plates about to be cast, would it be in the society's best interest to share production and distribution in two locations, or to concentrate it solely in New York?

The ABS standing committee recommended that one of its sets of Minion Bible plates be sent to the Kentucky Bible Society, at cost and when ready. The plates were to be housed in Lexington and Bibles printed from them would be bound and distributed throughout the far West in partnership with the ABS. The managers agreed, and the motion passed. Centralizing all western printing operations in Kentucky would help solve the cost issue of sending printed Bibles there and, especially, would free the ABS from having to accept devalued western currency back in New York. Not long afterward, in March 1817, the Utica Bible Society in upstate New York sent a donation and a request for a set of stereotype plates. Similar requests were made of the ABS during its first year from Bible societies in Baltimore, Pittsburgh, Cincinnati, and Charlestown, Massachusetts, but only the initial Kentucky request was granted. The number of requests from regional Bible societies across the country that had presumably seen the ABS's newspaper announcements is clear evidence of the interest in stereotype printing throughout the United States in 1816 and 1817. The technology was known and proven in New York, though stereotype founders and the quantities of cast plates circulating in the publishing industry were still small in number. The regional Bible societies, many with the same innovative spirit of the national body, wanted to embrace stereotyping as a mark of evangelical progress.

The ABS also accepted an offer from the British and Foreign Bible Society to acquire a set of plates to a French Bible at cost. Thus, in its first six months of existence, the ABS had one set of Bible plates in hand, was under contract for six additional sets, had secured an alternative printing and distribution agreement in Kentucky, and had secured a set of plates to a French Bible, each accomplishment a major step toward realizing its goals, and much sooner than anyone had anticipated. Under the transfer agreement, the French Bible plates were to be used to distribute Bibles not only in Francophone Canada but also potentially in France under the auspices of the ABS, making it a true multinational publisher. The committee charged with debating and deciding this issue recommended that Albert Gallatin, the US minister to France, be contacted so that he could make inquiries with the "Consistories of the Lutheran and Reformed Protestant Churches in Paris" to secure distribution agreements.[45]

The society continued to keep up good relations with its British counterpart, and the correspondence files of the ABS are full of news reports and information shared between the two organizations. In a letter of 4 October 1817 about the society's work, BFBS secretary Joseph Tarn reported on the state of printing in London and included this note on the first experiments with cylinder presses using curved plates: "A variety of Schemes are at present afoot in London to accelerate the progress and ease the labour of printing; some of which are at present in action, and others in preparation; the most simple and least expensive one that I have seen is that of Mess[rs] Applegath and Mitton, Nelson Square; which prints about 700 sheets per hour, printing both sides as it passes through the Machine. It is, however, only adapted to Stereotype as the plates are bent by a precision process, round a large cylinder."[46]

In March 1817, the ABS committee charged with commissioning stereotype plates reported that it had contracted with David and George Bruce in October for three sets of a duodecimo Bible in Minion type, to be completed by 1 June, for $4,000, or about $1.50 per plate. The plates began arriving in increments in March, twenty-four to a box. The previous November, the ABS had contracted with Elihu White for three sets of plates to an octavo Bible in Long Primer for $4,300, to be delivered in increments in March, April, and May. By March, White had delivered one complete set comprising 920 plates and was working on the remainder. The total cost came in just under the estimate, at $4,236 for the plates and $70 for blocks, boxes, and bonnet paper. The ABS also purchased a set of brass stereotype blocks from Collins & Co. for mounting its duodecimo plates to type height, thus employing all three New York stereotypers at once.[47] The standing committee would administer the publishing operations of the society, and it proceeded with businesslike vigor, overseeing printing, corrections, and supplies, and keeping an eye out for new developments in the printing trades and potential uses for new sets of plates.[48]

With a set of Bible plates now in hand, the society turned its attention to textual accuracy, something that would occupy and frustrate it for years to come as its new and used sets of Bible plates continued to grow. The founders were aware of the need for textually accurate plates to print from, and they even included the position of "Proof-reader" as article 32 of their constitution, the incumbent being "responsible for the integrity of the text" of the society's printed output. The proofreader was to "examine the printed sheets with minute care, and thus ascertain the state of the stereotype plates, and cause them to be corrected and repaired if necessary."[49] The consistent output of textually accurate scripture was a constant concern, especially once the ABS began printing from multiple sets of plates cast by different foundries. Because different sets were used, close comparisons and some textual compromises had to be made. The correction of plates would occupy a significant amount of time and money after the initial cost of commissioning them. After the ABS's first Bibles were printed and distributed, ministers from across the country pointed out errors in the texts, even after proofing and correction. In addition to paying a proofreader to identify errors and a typefounder to correct them, the society had to purchase extra type from D. & G. Bruce, at a cost of $100, in June 1817, for use in making the corrections.[50] (See appendix B for the society's instructions for repairing stereotype plates.)

At its 7 February 1817 meeting, the ABS created a committee "to examine & revise the Stereotype Plates belonging to this Society for the purpose of making them accurate."[51] The ABS proofreader compared proofs from the new Bible from Elihu White's set of plates from the New York Bible Society to an edition of the King James Bible published by Collins & Co. in 1791 in Trenton, which was thought to be the most textually accurate American Bible in print at the time. On 21 April, the committee reported that the three sets of octavo plates were now all delivered and proofed, and it recommended that a set of corrections be made to the plates before printing from them.

In the meantime, the New York Bible Society's set of Minion Bible plates, given to the ABS in September 1816, were lent to Daniel Fanshaw and impressions were struck off. By March 1817, 8,493 copies were ready, printed on four different paper stocks (fine American, good American, fine French, and fine Italian), with another fifteen hundred copies in press, enough to meet the initial contract run of ten thousand copies.[52] The cost of printing the Minion Bible amounted to about 18 cents per copy, with binding in plain sheepskin also at 18 cents. Paper costs averaged 49 cents per copy, bringing the average unit cost, printed and bound, for this initial printing of eighty-five hundred Bibles to 85 cents, or about one-fourth of the retail price of the most basic family Bible offered by Mathew Carey or Collins & Co. in Philadelphia or New York.[53] The paper was acquired from several sources and the binding work was divided between four firms: B. F. Lewis in Newburgh, New York, and B. Leland, Thomas T. Reynolds, and James Olmstead, all in New York City. As each group of Bibles from this first impression were finished, they were immediately sent out to the local Bible Societies that had requested them, beginning in November 1816. They were sent in quantities ranging from four copies to 336, but mostly in groups of twenty or one hundred. The New Hampshire and Long Island Bible Societies requested that their copies (five hundred and one hundred, respectively) be delivered in sheets; the ABS managers granted these requests, though they later stopped sending out unbound copies because of the higher potential for damage in shipping and the shorter life span of an unbound work, once they learned that many unbound copies would never be bound. The initial distribution of Bibles stretched from New Hampshire to Norfolk, Virginia, with a concentration of initial fulfillments coming from upstate New York.

Given the quantity of requests for plates from auxiliary societies, at the board's 5 June 1817 meeting, one year after its founding, the ABS appointed a committee of five managers to "report to this Board a general plan for the location and management of the Stereotype plates belonging to the A.B.S."[54] The society was now responsible for seven sets: one given to them, two sets of three that were commissioned, and one more soon to arrive. Fundraising had been a great success: the society raised more than $35,000 from individuals and auxiliaries in its first year, and it clearly needed a management plan for the safe housing and administration of its major capital investment.[55]

To publicize its activities, the ABS appointed a committee to contract with newspapers in Boston, Philadelphia, New York, Baltimore, Charleston, and Lexington, Kentucky, to publish ABS documents and reports on a regular basis, thus informing the nation of its activities and keeping the regional auxiliary associations involved in its work. As John Fea, a historian of the ABS, remarked in a 2016 interview, "Over the two hundred years of its existence, the ABS has been both a ministry and a business. Until recently, the ABS was in the business of selling Bibles and often measured its success based upon the numbers of Bibles sold and distributed."[56] Publicity and marketing were critical to maintaining active auxiliary societies around the country and raising funds for additional printing work.

The issue of what languages in which to print scripture continued to evolve during the society's first decade. Plates for French and Spanish Bibles were acquired early on, while repeated requests from auxiliaries to print Bibles in German, Welsh, and Gaelic were either deferred or rejected as impractical. A committee also explored costs for a small Spanish New Testament in Bourgeois duodecimo. There was a desire to distribute Bibles to Native Americans, but the relatively modest populations of each tribe and their distinct languages and dialects posed challenges. In July 1817, a committee charged with reporting on the prospects for translating the Bible into Native American languages recommended that the society do so, beginning with two languages, Delaware and Mohawk. The committee reasoned that these tribes had the greatest immediate need for scripture as they were the most likely to abandon hunting and take up farming as their landholdings diminished. Their small settlements would grow and become permanent Christian communities. It was thought that the Delaware translation would be of use to other Iroquois nations and even to tribes farther west, as the Kickapoo and Miami were likely to understand the dialect. For the Mohawk version, the Tuscarora, Wyandot, and Huron tribes could also benefit. A Cherokee translation was considered, but the committee recommended no action. No effort was made to reach tribes in the far West, or indeed those substantially west of the Mississippi. The society also agreed in those early days to acquire from the BFBS five hundred Welsh Bibles and five hundred in Gaelic to satisfy the requests of auxiliaries.

At the same meeting in July 1817, the stereotype plates management committee, weighing requests for plates from auxiliary societies, reported that plates, "if judiciously located & placed under proper regulations, cannot fail of being powerful instruments in spreading the knowledge of the Scriptures; but on the other hand should local jealousies be excited by the distribution of the plates, or should they, by an inconsiderate location, interfere with the issue of Bibles from the depository at New York, they would counteract that great principle of unity of effort on which the American Bible Society is founded, and from which its fairest hopes of success are derived."[57] Centralized control over publishing operations was still the best option, the sole exception being the set of plates in Kentucky. The committee took as its guiding principle the address of the ABS convention to the people of the United States, which stated that the society "should furnish great districts of the American continent with well executed Stereotype plates for the cheap and extensive diffusion of the Scriptures throughout regions which are now scantily supplied, at a discouraging expense."[58] The committee concluded that the society was bound to keep the set of plates given it by the New York Bible Society, plus at least one set each of the three sets of octavo and duodecimo plates it had commissioned. The Kentucky Bible Society had already been promised one duodecimo set, leaving one additional duodecimo and two octavo sets to potentially place elsewhere. Keeping the octavo and duodecimo sets together seemed practical, as outlying auxiliaries would appreciate the variety of having two Bibles of different sizes available for distribution. The committee noted that most people preferred the larger type of the octavos over pocket duodecimos. It recommended that Kentucky receive one set of octavo plates as well, leaving one remaining pair to be placed. This recommendation was passed by the society at its August meeting. Selling the final sets could generate a modest profit, but it could also potentially undercut the ABS's own market, so these final sets essentially became warehoused backups to be rotated into use when the first production set was fully worn down and beyond repair.

In drawing up a transfer agreement for its plates to Kentucky, the ABS did not transfer ownership outright. Instead, it lent them to be printed from freely as the auxiliaries estimated demand in their district. As part of the agreement, the plates could be recalled by the ABS at any time. Any Bibles printed from the plates were to remain only in their specified districts and not sent elsewhere. This allowed the ABS to exert central control over the distribution—and revenue—from Bible production. It was also a safeguard against plates being used in ways that undermined or worked against the central mission of the society. For example, the ABS was not interested in entering the commercial market by publishing elaborate family Bibles, and by imposing these conditions it could prevent the regional Bible societies from attempting to publish and sell higher-priced editions to subsidize their inexpensive editions.

Because of the ABS's very public incorporation and publicity campaign, printers and publishers across the United States quickly recognized it as an influential force for the production and distribution of Bibles. Publishers of higher-end scriptural products did not for the most part feel threatened by this work. They were certainly attentive to and possibly wary of the scope and reach of the society and its rapid growth, but by their own admission they had carved out one segment of the commercial Bible marketplace that remained steady in the first decades of the nineteenth century.[59]

For its first eighteen months, the society had only printed complete Bibles from its plates. On 7 January 1818, the standing committee took up the question of whether a freestanding New Testament should be printed; at its following meeting, this committee agreed to proceed. There was concern that printing only the New Testament from a complete set of Bible plates would cause undue wear to the plates over time, so that a later impression of a complete Bible would look uneven and mismatched. An increasing need for Testaments from the growing evangelical denominations in the United States also meant that the society needed to explore commissioning separate sets of New Testament plates.

In its first years, the ABS wanted to have one building suitable for housing its entire operations that would include a printshop, a bindery, a depository for storage of Bibles and stereotype plates, and meeting and office space for the officers of the society. All its printing jobs had been contracted out individually, and its Bible depository, paper stock, stereotype plates, and other assets were scattered across several rented spaces in lower Manhattan. With a new headquarters, the officers also wanted to hire a manager to supervise the printing and binding operations, purchasing of paper, "correction and safe keeping of the Stereotype plates," and other on-site management. Daniel Fanshaw, the ABS's printer, still operated his own shop and bookstore at this time. The society estimated that its printing "annually will not be less than from thirty-five to forty thousand" Bibles, and that it would "be requisite to keep at least eight printing presses constantly in operation." The ABS now possessed "upwards of seven thousand and three hundred plates," and a Spanish New Testament was about to be commissioned. But more work had to be done to all the received plates to render them ready for printing. "The greater part of the Octavo and duodecimo plates executed for the Society, are yet to be examined and corrected," according to the minutes of a January 1818 meeting, "and the corrections revised before they can be used. The process of doing this is laborious, and requires considerable care, minute accuracy, and a competent knowledge of the subject. Of the six sets of plates executed for the Society, only the first two sets of the Octavo have been corrected at all, and these two are not yet in a finished state."[60] The society had complete sets of these newly commissioned plates in its possession for at least eight months but had not yet printed from them. It was still only printing from the set given by the New York Bible Society.

> The other set of the Octavo and the three sets of the Minion plates (12") are all still to be examined and corrected.... The French plates are likewise said to be incorrect, and in several instances whole words left out. It will be proper to have them all read and revised.... All the plates are liable to receive injury by accident or carelessness. When repaired they should be carefully examined. The work is too important to be confided entirely to the ordinary fidelity of mechanics. The keeping of these plates in good order, requires no little care, under all the removals to which they are necessarily subject, when used; and when they are transported to a distant place, a still greater care must be exercised, to have them properly packed up and forwarded, together with the necessary tools, type and furniture accompanying them.[61]

From this point through the late 1820s, the society would continuously employ correctors on contract, often more than one at a time, essentially paying for one full-time position to proof new plates. The resulting corrections to the plates required additional time and expense, increasing the initial cost by roughly one-third.

In 1824, when considering the offer of an octavo Bible in plates, a subcommittee of the standing committee commented that the text should belong "to the authorized version of the English Bible" now in circulation: "They are also of the opinion that, whenever a Quarto Bible is procured, great pains should be taken to secure the accuracy of the text, so that said Bible may form a standard for future Bibles and Testament plates to be secured by the Society. The committee are led to make this remark, in consequence of there being a considerable difference between the Bibles and Testament plates now owned by the Society, especially as to punctuation, which has arisen from their being completed from different copies of the Scripture in which such variances from each other existed."[62] As the society's stereotype inventory grew from multiple sources, the problem of textual accuracy became increasingly acute. In 1828, the ABS acquired a Spanish Bible in plates that came with the Apocrypha. The society affirmed that the Apocrypha should not be included in any Bible it produced and had those plates destroyed.

For a full year, from the late spring of 1818 through May 1819, the society paid a proofreader, Joseph Osborn, to read through proofs of its Bibles at $3 for eighteen sheets. The corrector, Francis Urban, was paid $10 per week to work on mechanically correcting the Minion Bible plates, cutting and soldering new pieces of type into the plate to ready it for printing. The ABS then moved on to the octavo Bibles and Bourgeois New Testaments, followed by the Spanish New Testament. Periodically, Urban would be reimbursed for solder, type, and other supplies necessary for correcting the plates.[63] Later on, no doubt on the basis of this laborious and time-consuming experience, the society signed a contract with D. & G. Bruce to commission a New Testament that would be delivered on the condition that the society would read proofs of it and the Bruces themselves would make the necessary corrections to the plates as requested, all as part of the initial purchase agreement. This contract was made in October 1818 for a complete New Testament, with boxes and twelve blocks for printing, for $500.[64] Together with other working supply requests, the society paid $177.43 for "Boxes, to contain the Stereotype Plates, and repairing Brass Blocks, and new Boxes &c." The managers also purchased a set of foundry tools, "for Stereotype Plates sent to Kentucky," so that future corrections could be made on-site in Lexington.[65]

In November 1817, the society sent a request for proposals for a Spanish New Testament set in Bourgeois duodecimo to the three major stereotype founders in New York. Responses arrived within two weeks, with D. & G. Bruce offering to supply it for $700, B. & I. Collins for $650, and E. White & Co. for $625. The standing committee voted to accept White's low bid.[66]

At the end of 1817, the society took an inventory and valuation of its assets for insurance purposes. The plates and valuations were listed as follows:

> 1 set Brevier 12mo, 1088 plates, value $2000
> 3 sets Minion 12mo, 2520 plates, cost $4500
> 3 sets Long Primer 8vo, 2760 plates, cost $4800
> 1 set nonpareil French, 12mo, 996 plates, value $2000
>   7364 plates $13,300
> 4 Sets Brass blocks
> 6 sets wooden blocks
> 5 sets Rollers, for blackening types
> A qty. of Type for Minion & long primer plates
> Boxes to contain the plates, tools, &c. $700
>   Total value: $14,000[67]

One set of octavo and one set of duodecimo Bible plates were held at the store of William Walton Woolsey on Pearl Street for safekeeping, with the remainder either at the ABS's depository, at White's foundry for correcting, or at Fanshaw's printshop. Woolsey (1766–1838), a member of the standing committee, was a prominent New York merchant and civic official who would become chair of the standing committee the following year.[68] With more than seven thousand stereotype plates in numerous locations in and around lower Manhattan, the rapid successful expansion of the society in just over a year necessitated new conversations and plans to build a centralized headquarters.

In April 1818, breaking from its previously announced plans, the society agreed to print an edition of the Gospel of Saint John translated into Mohawk in a slim eighteen-page edition of one thousand copies. This was its only deviation from printing Bibles and New Testaments, and the work was not stereotyped. The source text was a copy of a work published by the BFBS that was distributed in Canada.[69] While numerous similar requests had come in over the years, many of them supported by Elias Boudinot, this edition was the only one taken on as a project.

That same month, the society also resolved to have five thousand copies of the New Testament printed up and bound for distribution. This, the ABS's first New Testament project, was printed from a set of its Bible plates, as the society did not yet have a separate New Testament. This must have caused some concern, because in October a committee investigating the acquisition of New Testament plates gave its report to the managers. The report stated that the society now had Bibles in Minion, Brevier, and Long Primer type. The first two sizes were too small to use in printing stand-alone New Testaments, and the last, Long Primer, was too large "for general use," despite entreaties from Boudinot to print a Testament in larger type for older readers. "The Bourgeois letter is better adapted to the purpose" of printing the New Testament, the report concluded, "and will, it is thought be preferred by a great proportion of those to whom New Testaments will probably be distributed." If printed as a duodecimo, it would cost less than the octavo New Testament then being printed from Bible plates already owned by the society. As to the question of how many copies to print, if the same present need continued, the subcommittee concluded, then the Bible plates from which it was currently being printed would wear down more quickly than the rest of the Bible. The difference between the Old and New Testaments would then "become so apparent as to be a material blemish to the whole."[70] But the committee also offered a solution. A Bourgeois Testament in duodecimo was currently on offer within the trade, fully corrected, including boxes and twelve printing blocks, for $500. The committee recommended that the ABS purchase this set and received authorization from the managers to do so, thus solving their greatest long-term printing problem.

By late 1818, the society's output was about four thousand published Bibles and New Testaments per month. It had printed and distributed two annual reports of five thousand copies each and had advertised its activities in newspapers across the country. The ABS's work was written about in American and British newspapers and periodicals. In two short years, the organization had gained command of the American Bible marketplace for cheap editions of scripture. The finance committee report of October 1818 included a proposal to raise funds to print "Anniversary Speeches, Newspaper and pamphlet publications," and it suggested "publishing a legal form of Bequest on the cover or front page of the Annual Reports of the Society."[71] The body of the whole agreed to the drafting of a legal bequest form only, and not to raise funds for additional types of publications. The American Tract Society, founded in 1824, would eventually help fill the need for additional evangelical publications.

The Panic of 1819 affected orders for Bibles and caused the society to pause and again take stock. In June 1819, despite worsening national economic conditions, it was reported that since the previous autumn, demand had grown for more Bibles, so the managers instructed Fanshaw to increase his number of presses from nine to twelve. He did so, increasing his production proportionately. But later that year, as the effects of the economic slowdown were felt, the number of Bibles on hand was 15,296, together with 10,557 New Testaments. Payments from the auxiliaries were slow in arriving, so production likewise needed to slow down. Elias Boudinot suggested in June that the ABS contribute to publishing a "small harmony of the life and proceedings of Christ" in the Delaware language by the Female Auxiliary Missionary Society of Bethlehem, Pennsylvania, "which was deemed inexpedient" at the time and was declined.[72] By mid-July, the society was forced to slow down production and curtail expenses owing to the effects of the recession. The managers requested that their agent, essentially the business manager of the production facility, supply Fanshaw with paper sufficient to keep only eight of his twelve presses working.

Fanshaw had to let his foreman and other workers go. Still needing to pay off the loan for his four new presses, Fanshaw asked the society for a loan either to cover their expense or to purchase them directly for him. The ABS managers agreed to lend him $1,500 to pay off the loan for his presses, from which he could deduct the loan in printing work done for the society. During this time, the managers continued to express confidence in Fanshaw as someone whose interests were closely aligned with theirs, and whose workmanship and attention as a printer were highly valued.

While the New York operations were well managed, the Kentucky printing experiment was proving more problematic. A complete Bible in stereotype plates was sent from New York to Lexington in September 1818 in six boxes, along with one box of brass blocks for mounting them. To reach Lexington, the parcels traveled from New York to Baltimore, and thence to Pittsburgh and Maysville, Ohio, before arriving at their destination. More than six months later, in May 1819, the Kentucky Bible Society struck off its first impression of two thousand Bibles from the plates. The Kentucky managers sent samples of their work back to New York, but the results were not well received. The standing committee reported to the managers:

> The Committee are of the opinion that the edition of the Bible now issuing by the Kentucky Auxy. Bible Society is very badly executed. The paper is not good, and costs as much money as the finer paper used in N. York. The printing is badly done being more faintly impressed on one place than on another. The register is so incorrect, that in binding the volume a part

of the printing must inevitably be folded in, or hidden, and a part cut off; and there is great reason to fear that the binding of the volumes will be so poorly finished, for want of proper workmen, as to render them much less desirable than the Bibles issued at the Depository of the A.B.S.[73]

As a result, the managers insisted that the Kentucky society not supply any Bibles outside its own territory. All the other auxiliary Bible societies in the West were to order their stock directly from New York until the problems were solved. The ABS managers also decided not to send the additional set of plates (to an octavo Bible) to Kentucky that they had once promised. The report concluded, "They also believe, that experience will convince the Am. Bible So. that both the manufacture and sale of Bibles from their own Stereotype plates, ought to be confined to their own Depository."[74] This first experiment in lending plates to an auxiliary society to save time and the expense of shipping Bibles a great distance clearly did not turn out as expected. The ABS was increasingly convinced that it needed to centralize all production and distribution operations in New York.

More than a year later, the Kentucky experience still stung. The ABS standing committee, studying pricing for printing jobs and stewardship of the society's plates, stressed in July 1820 the importance of not committing the society's investments to "unskillful or careless workmen," because more injury would be sustained than could be offset by cheaper printing costs. This had already happened, as a set of plates, "after having a large number stricken off, without apparent injury, ha[d] been ruined in printing two editions of about 2,000 books each."[75] Kentucky continued to press for more support to expand its own operations and also requested that its printing costs be subsidized by New York, to which the managers were united in opposition, instead debating whether Pittsburgh might be a better site for hosting western operations.

In contrast to the damage to the Kentucky plates wrought by unskilled handlers, the New York sets were holding up admirably under Fanshaw's stewardship: "From the Brevier Stereotype plates belonging to the Society upwards of 46,000 Bibles were printed by Mr. Fanshaw; the plates then underwent a revision and repair and the whole expense to the Society was only $12.50 and the Minion Plates after 47,000 Bibles were printed, were revised and repaired and the expense to the Society was only $18.18 and both sets of Plates are now very little less valuable than when new."[76] Ultimately, the Kentucky Bible Society would print only three impressions of two thousand Bibles each during its tenure holding a set of stereotype plates. The Panic of 1819 caused a currency crisis, further devaluing western bank notes in the East, so it was deemed expedient to let Kentucky continue selling and distributing its Bibles locally for the time being.⁷⁷ Sending the damaged plates back to New York and shutting down the Kentucky operation would have been even more disastrous during the panic and recession. Despite the results, local enthusiasm in Kentucky remained high, but New York was unconvinced. As late as December 1822, one agent in Kentucky noted that "the wisdom of the Parent Society in locating plates in this place is still evident, and the more zealous and prudent this Auxiliary becomes, that wisdom will also appear more clearly," despite the fact that the ABS managers believed that the Kentucky Bible Society was "in a drooping state."⁷⁸

The first edition of the ABS's French Bible was ready for distribution, and the ABS was also becoming interested in an 18mo English New Testament. Once this interest was shared with the trades, proposals came in from all the stereotype founders in New York. In July 1820, the ABS contracted with Adoniram Chandler & Co. for two sets of New Testament plates in Brevier 18mo, "for $550, both sets."⁷⁹ Chandler was the former foreman at D. & G. Bruce and had recently started his own stereotyping foundry. By 1820, the number of stereotypers in the United States had more than doubled from only a few years before. Baltimore, Hartford, and Boston also now had foundries.

In April 1821, the Baltimore Bible Society inquired about joining the ABS as an auxiliary society and offered its own set of stereotype plates to an octavo Bible to the ABS for its use. The ABS already had three octavo Bibles in plates from the initial 1816 commission: one set in use and judged good for another ten years; another set in a fireproof store separate from the depository (the security copy in case of fire); and a third, which was "dead property and ought, in the opinion of the Standing Committee, to be sold." The standing committee optimistically estimated that the ABS would not require another set of octavo plates "in less time than fifty years."⁸⁰ By 1821, many American publishers were producing octavo Bibles for retail sale. The society clearly did not wish to enter into the higher-priced portion of the octavo Bible market. As the ABS managers did not want another set of plates, they accepted Baltimore as an auxiliary but declined to purchase its plates. They also declined to commission a German Bible at this time on the grounds that the expense would be too great for too small a potential audience over time.

The society in 1821 was still renting space for its printing and depository operations. The managers appointed a committee to explore acquiring land

and a building, in the process assessing their real property and assets once again. In January 1822, the ABS had 82,552 Bibles and Testaments in sheets, either bound or ready for binding, with a value of $40,422.10. Assets in stereotype plates were valued at $15,198.09. The society started building Bible House, its headquarters on Nassau Street in lower Manhattan, and was moved in by the spring of 1823. Because of this expanded centralization of the business, the managers declined another request to send a set of plates to Pittsburgh and seem to have grudgingly accepted the Kentucky Bible Society's attempts to keep striking off more impressions from its set of damaged plates.

Other offers continued to arrive from around the country, a testament to the ABS's growing success and reputation. The Maryland Bible Society requested the loan of a set of plates, ideally to a Minion Bible. That request was denied, as the managers thought it would establish a precedent for lending plates to additional auxiliaries and create production rivalries that would have to be continually managed. In this discussion, it was noted that of the three sets of Minion Bibles the society owned (one in Kentucky, one in reserve, and one in use in New York), the New York set was "nearly worn out."[81] The society also learned at this time that a Hartford printer with a Bible in standing Nonpareil type, like those held by Mathew Carey in Philadelphia and Isaiah Thomas in Worcester, was offering it to the New Haven Bible Society; would the ABS be interested in acquiring it? After referral to committee, the society declined the offer. It was far more advantageous to possess newly cast stereotype plates than to manage a Bible completely set in forms of standing type.

In addition to the Spanish New Testament, the society decided to invest in a complete Spanish Bible. After making inquiries around the city in late 1822, the standing committee reported to the full board of managers that a set of octavo Bible plates in Spanish could be procured for between $2,300 and $2,800. The board told the committee to act on this proposal, and in early 1823 the society solicited proposals from the New York foundries. The solicitation, which asked for pricing for one, two, and three sets of plates, resulted in offers from four stereotype foundries:

	1 set	2 sets	3 sets
D. & G. Bruce	2800	4000	5200
Trow	2702	3982	5262
A. Chandler	2474	3612	4750
Hammond Wallis	2274	3270	4260

Hammond Wallis's offer, which guaranteed that the work would be completed within four months, was accepted, but for one set of plates only.[82] Wallis was a young New York stereotyper who had just made a set of plates to a Greek New Testament for Hartford publisher Oliver D. Cooke. He also made a set of plates to an English schoolbook for the New-York Free-School Society.[83] He occasionally published titles under his own imprint, jobbing the printing out. While his business and Christian credentials seemed sound, the society's work with Wallis would prove frustrating. Wallis did not offer samples of his work in advance, despite repeated requests. Later in the year he wrote to the managers that his "sureties" had backed out of the project, leaving him in a bind. He offered as an act of good faith not to accept any payment for himself until the end of the contract, requesting only expenses for casting the plates if an amendment to his contract was drawn up. The managers agreed on the condition that Wallis deliver "two perfect sheets" to them by 17 October. Wallis failed to deliver. On 18 October, he sent thirty-two plates to the society "in an unfinished state, not regularly following each other, but taken from all parts of the Bible."[84] The standing committee was uniformly dissatisfied with the work and told Wallis that it was recommending that the ABS break all contracts with him at that point. Wallace wanted to continue and offered his house as security, but having made inquiries into the true owner of his property, members of the subcommittee learned that Wallis was in no position to make such a guarantee. Concluding that there was no chance that the project could be completed, they canceled his contract in late December, losing one year's time on the project.

This incident illustrates the volatile commercial landscape of the first stereotype founders in New York. The contracts into which they entered for casting large, complex works such as complete Bibles involved large sums and required enormous amounts of time, skill, and labor. Wallis, just starting out in business on his own, risked a year's employment on a project he underbid and did not have the skills or resources to complete successfully. Older, more established, better-capitalized firms such as D. & G. Bruce or Collins & Co. could shift time and resources more easily between jobs, especially when, like the Bruces, they had a sister firm that specialized in the steady business of typefounding, regularly supplying type to most New York printers. As an 1874 career guide remarked, "Stereotyping requires a quick eye, sharp criticism, carefulness, rapidity of motion, and in some departments of it considerable physical strength, especially in the shaving of plates."[85]

Wallis tried to salvage the project by soliciting notes from Collins and Bruce as guarantors on the Spanish Bible project. Both the Bruces and the Collinses agreed, but the ABS subcommittee said no. Adoniram Chandler, the second-lowest bidder on the project, offered to complete the plates for ninety cents per thousand ems of type, and a new deal was struck. Chandler would also be commissioned later that year to produce an octavo Pica New Testament for the ABS, with boxes and blocks, complete for $500. Wallis continued to press his case. He asked the managers in January 1824 to at least purchase the type he had acquired for the project (about 530 pounds' worth, purchased from D. & G. Bruce) and the 120 plates that were already cast. The standing committee agreed to accept the 120 partially completed plates for the cost at which he was to have been paid for them, provided they were "conformable to the requisitions of said contract and approved by the persons Therein named to examine them." Fanshaw, whose shop was composing the Bible for Chandler's foundry, agreed to take about four hundred pounds of type. In this agreement, and in the sureties granted to Wallis by his competitors Bruce and Collins, one can see how the printers and typefounders of New York worked together informally to advance their trade and maintain their reputations as honorable businessmen working for a charitable cause.[86]

Wallis persisted in his entreaties. In April 1824 he offered the society a set of plates to a quarto Bible he was just beginning to cast. While some members of the standing committee were interested in a quarto or "family" Bible, they declined Wallis's offer. By 1824 the family Bible market was saturated, with several publishers offering multiple variants at many price points, and such a work would not fit well into the ABS's publishing model. Wallis never completed this set of plates, but he did stereotype a Greek New Testament that was published by Collins & Hannay that year, a Greek and Latin lexicon also published by Collins & Hannay in 1825, a New Testament in 1826, and other works in the later 1820s. By the 1830s, he had moved over exclusively to publishing with his firm Wallis & Newell.

In November 1823, the ABS standing committee directed a subcommittee to acquire a set of Pica New Testament plates for not more than $560, along with a set of plates to a "Pocket Bible ... as soon as possible."[87] John Nitchie, the society's agent and accountant, wrote to stereotype founder Jedidiah Howe, a former New Yorker recently relocated to Philadelphia, concerning the pocket Bible. Having seen his recent work—a Bible Howe had cast for the New York publisher D. D. Smith—Nitchie inquired, "Did you cast more than one set, if yea, have you any for sale and for how much, if no, what would you be willing to cast just such a set for, only making it better as there appears to be room for improvement."[88] Howe wrote back that he cast only one set of plates for Smith, for $2,500, and that after printing only two or three thousand copies from them, he had bought them back. He could offer the set to the ABS for $2,400. He was beginning to cast an octavo Bible for Smith instead and enclosed a proof, stating, "I can do but <u>one set</u> like it—but can overrun it into a different form or leave off the notes & cast an extra set without coming in contact with my agreement with him."[89] In other words, Howe was willing to use the same setting of type but would adjust the forms to cast a new set of plates to an octavo Bible sufficiently different from Smith's copy that it would not break his exclusivity agreement. Receiving no immediate answer, Howe wrote again six months later about his pocket Bible, stating that upon examination, the engravings are "much more worn than I had an idea of—& that, with a desire to dispose of the plates, to a <u>safe</u> purchaser," he now could reduce the price to $2,250, inclusive. In both letters to Nitchie, Howe was careful to ask that no mention of this possible sale, or its price, be made to anyone outside the ABS.[90] In the end, the ABS did not acquire any plates from Howe.

As the stereotyping trade in the United States expanded, more offers of new and used plates continued to flow to the American Bible Society, along with requests from auxiliaries to borrow sets. Nearly all of these requests and offers were declined, including an offer of sample plates for a new quarto Bible and a request for a loan of plates to Meadville, Pennsylvania, in April 1824 and a gift offer of plates to a pocket Bible from the BFBS in February 1825. As noted above, the ABS had no need to compete in the quarto Bible marketplace, which was crowded with commercial publishers producing many different variants by 1824. The managers' decision to decline the gift of plates from their British counterpart on the grounds that the BFBS's assets were better used in Britain and Europe *was* new, however, and it reflected the ABS managers' confidence in the society's stability and assets. If it wished to have a pocket Bible, it would commission and pay for its own set without foreign assistance. The ABS did in fact acquire its own set of pocket Bible plates later that year for $2,400 (but not from Jedidiah Howe), and it bought a set of plates to an octavo Bible from the Baltimore Bible Society in 1827, also for $2,400.[91]

During these decades, the ABS was not alone in printing Bibles for charitable distribution in the United States. The Philadelphia Bible Society had always operated independently, using its own sets of plates, going back to 1812. Baltimore had published Bibles from its own plates for several years. The New

York Bible and Common Prayer Book Society commissioned a set of Bible plates for its own use in 1826, even though its predecessor organization had given its first set of plates to the ABS in 1816. By the mid-1820s, stereotyping had spread among American typefounders and publishers to the extent that secondhand sets of plates were just beginning to appear in the marketplace, and additional offers from typefounders and publishers continued to come in. In the fall of 1826 alone, the ABS declined an offer of a used set of quarto Bible plates from New York printer John Evans and considered a new set of plates to a Long Primer New Testament in duodecimo offered by New York printer George Mather. Complete with boxes for $175, the price was cheap, but an examination of the plates revealed that more than $100 worth of repairs were needed to bring them up to good printing quality, and the standing committee declined to pursue it.

Printing firms in several cities and towns in upstate New York had been printing and publishing Bibles from plates from the early 1820s, coinciding exactly with the period (1823–29) during which the golden plates to the *Book of Mormon* were allegedly revealed to Joseph Smith. The *Book of Mormon* was first published in Palmyra, New York, in 1830, from set type, not plates. Several scholars, most recently Sonia Hazard, have speculated that the new technology of stereotyping was known to Smith and his associates in the time leading up to its discovery and translation.[92]

Living in what was quickly becoming the center of the printing trades in the United States, the businessmen of the ABS standing committee kept an attentive eye out for new innovations, such as the potential advantages of using new power presses:

> The Committee . . . have examined with much attention the power press invented by Mr. Treadwell of Boston, and which is now in operation in Mr. Fanshaw's printing office, the right to use it in this city being vested in him. The Committee find that very good work [is] done on this kind of press, that the plates are less injured than they are by hand presses, that there is a less loss of paper, and that the labour of girls can be substituted for that of men or boys, and that of the power by which it is moved is favourably located and well regulated, there will not be more interruptions than is usual in hand presses; and they are of opinion that four presses, moved by a single horse or an Engine of equivalent power, would do as much printing as the Society now find necessary, and that an extension of the work should it be required, could be provided for, by adding two

or four presses, connected with power which moves the four presses first erected.

The Committee have with a reference to this plan of printing examined the rooms in the rear building and find them well adapted for this purpose, and believing that this mode of printing has advantages over printing done on hand presses, they lay before the Board propositions made by Daniel Fanshaw for performing the printing work of the Society.[93]

In November 1827, Fanshaw reported to the society his conversations with Daniel Treadwell of Boston, the power press manufacturer. Fanshaw had four power presses, purchased the previous year, and had been offered four more. Treadwell was going to Philadelphia to conclude a deal for four presses, and Fanshaw hinted to the ABS that the Philadelphia Bible Society was the commissioner, so he wanted to persuade Treadwell to supply him with presses first for the ABS. It would take about ten months for delivery, so Fanshaw requested a loan for the initial deposit and payments. The cost was about $5,000, due on delivery, for all four. The ABS managers agreed to lend Fanshaw the funds for the additional presses. Their need was so great, in fact, that they purchased five additional handpresses in January 1828 to use until the power presses arrived later that year. Initially, they asked Fanshaw to acquire the handpresses himself, but he refused. By this time, he was only interested in power presses for his own use. And "although the original plan called for a horse in the basement of the rear building, a steam engine was actually installed" in 1827.[94] Running four additional presses from one steam engine was entirely possible, but that quantity of power could not be supplied by only one horse.

The society continued to innovate, using the latest trends in binding as well. Early on, it decided not to distribute Bibles and Testaments in sheets, knowing that the auxiliary Bible societies and the eventual recipients of the books would probably never have them bound, thus significantly decreasing their life span. They contracted with several binders in New York at first, and then set up a contract binding operation in an arrangement similar to the printing arrangement with Fanshaw. ABS bindings were basic undecorated calf- or sheepskin until 1827, when a resolution in the standing committee minutes notes that "the price of the Non Pareil Testament bound in Cloth be 12½ Cents."[95] Cloth bindings had been successfully introduced in Great Britain in 1822 by the publisher William Pickering and were quick to catch on for their inexpensive but relatively sturdy construction. Lowering the binding unit cost by choosing cloth for smaller items was another important innovation that improved the cost-effectiveness of the ABS operation.

In May 1826, James Reed wrote to the society from Boston, notifying it of his new venture, the Forthill Stereotype Foundry, and soliciting inquiries for work. George Mather wrote from New York the same month enclosing specimens taken from a set of stereotype plates to a New Testament that he owned and wished to sell for $300. Mather wrote again on 5 September, lowering the price to $200. George Bruce wrote in May offering the society a quarto Bible in plates, with Apocrypha, marginal notes, and tables, for $2,500, plus another set without marginal references or tables for $2,000. H. H. Phinney of Cooperstown, New York, wrote in October 1826, enclosing samples of his recent quarto Bible. S. Walker in Roxbury, Massachusetts, wrote in October 1829 offering a set of quarto Bible plates in 1,385 pages for $2,638.08. John Evans wrote from New York in 1829 about a quarto Bible in plates he had taken on but found "too heavy a work for me, at present, to sustain." In nearly all these instances, the managers declined the offers without further consideration.[96]

G. W. Mentz in Philadelphia wrote to the society in November 1829 that he was finishing up a set of plates to a duodecimo New Testament in German and a full German Bible that he could offer to the society at fair prices: Bibles for $1 and Testaments for twenty-seven cents per plate. When he failed to get a reply by the following March, he dropped the price of his New Testament to twenty-four cents. The society then purchased both sets. Complete books cast in stereotype plates that had been rare commodities when the society was founded in 1816 had become commonplace by the late 1820s.

By 1829, as it began planning for the "general supply" idea, the ABS had such a large stock of plates on hand that it completed an extensive inventory and condition report (see appendix C). A few years before, noting that their first sets of plates were almost a decade old, the managers had begun paying closer attention to their condition and making preparations for their eventual replacement. The 1829 inventory notes the condition of a particular set of plates and the number of impressions that had been made from it, providing a window into the ways in which the society used its most important assets. The inventory was discussed and used as a planning document for increasing production for the general supply. "The demand running more on the Minion and Nonpareil Bibles than on any other sizes," they noted, "and the Soc. having only one of each and those partly worn," it made sense to attempt to acquire new replacement sets of each, as both sets would likely be worn out by the time replacements could be procured. If two sets of each Bible could be acquired, one could be put into reserve as a backup, and at a lower unit cost. They estimated a set of Minion Bible plates would cost about $1,900, with a duplicate set at $900, and a Nonpareil Bible to be about the same price. The board also asked the standing committee to make inquiries about an octavo Bible in Pica type, "intended for aged persons," thus reconsidering Elias Boudinot's recommendation of a decade earlier for a larger-type edition.[97] The lowest estimate for a Pica edition was $3,500, and $450 for a New Testament.

Of the many religious publishers in the United States in 1829, the ABS had the best potential to succeed in offering a General Supply of scripture to the nation. The Philadelphia Bible Society had continued to publish with its sets of plates but kept its distribution primarily regional. Other organizations were new, among them the American Sunday School Union, founded in 1824 (which also employed stereotyping from the start), and the American Tract Society, which did likewise from its founding in 1825. Older groups, such as the Methodist Book Concern, lagged behind and only turned "to stereotyping and power printing as part of a modernization effort in 1828–29."[98] The New England Tract Society, cofounded by Jedidiah Morse in 1814, likewise only began to invest in stereotype plates in 1824. In comparison, commercial publishers such as Harper & Brothers, which was founded in 1818 and would become the largest publisher in the United States by midcentury, were also early adopters of stereotyping, but they did not invest in steam power for their presses until 1833. In 1829, Harper & Bros. had only one horse-powered press at its printing shop.[99]

Nothing close to a "general supply" had ever been attempted in Great Britain, despite the longevity and stability of the British and Foreign Bible Society. As Nathan Hatch has written, "Religious print became much more a popular medium and agent of change in America than in Great Britain. There, the flood of religious print after 1800 was largely the product of elites working to shore up an ordered religion." In the United States, new evangelical denominations were able to harness printing to differentiate themselves and their aims from the older elite, state-sanctioned Protestant denominations. "The religious press in America, by contrast," Hatch writes, "sprang from an explicit faith in reason and popular opinion." This ethos also deliberately struck out against a Christianity that was tied to aristocratic eighteenth-century privilege.[100]

If early national Christian faith in the United States had strong republican underpinnings, its natural reliance, like that of its Puritan forebears, would have been on emphasizing the Word of God as contained in scripture "without note or comment," as the American Bible Society explicitly stated. Gordon S. Wood has written, "The Scriptures were to democratic religion what the Constitution was to democratic politics—the fundamental document that would bind all the competitive American Christian sects together in one national communion."[101] The general supply of a Bible to every US household, the product of more than a decade of expansion and the perfecting of a business model for distributing scripture, would be the culmination of this republican evangelical movement that had its first stirrings with the founding of the first Bible society in Philadelphia.

While the ABS's technological innovations and New York administration were in place and ready, the speed with which its managers wished to accomplish their general supply was overly ambitious. In the first two years after the announcement, they had managed to print only 480,000 Bibles. Production had the capacity to be scaled up further, had they wished, but doubts arose about the ability of the auxiliary Bible societies scattered across the country to canvass rural America with the "systematic organization" required for success. After two years of concentrated effort, thirteen states and territories were considered fully supplied, but many areas in the West had not been canvassed at all. Western auxiliary societies defaulted on both their pledges and their payments for books, and the sheer size of rural America proved daunting.[102] A true general supply might not have been possible in 1829–31, but in conjunction with the other interdenominational evangelical organizations that would be formed in the antebellum United States, some forty million Bibles had been printed and distributed by 1850. In 1855 alone, three organizations—the American Bible Society, the American Sunday School Union, and the American Tract Society—would together publish 2.4 million volumes, 15 percent of all books published in the United States.[103]

CHAPTER 4

❧ Material Texts
Trade Sales, Reprinting, and the Book Trades

After a work was stereotyped, its plates were housed in small wooden crates, about twenty-four to a crate, and securely warehoused, to be brought out and printed from as needed. A work no longer had to be composed anew from type when more printed copies were required. For the first time in the history of the printed book, works of authorship became, quite literally, material texts. They were objects of capital investment by publishers, objects that had intrinsic value for their potential long-term, high-volume use to generate future profit. Books-in-plates also had the added advantage of mobility. As sources of capital, they could be bought, sold, used as collateral, and owned by different publishers after their initial creation. As Alexis Weedon notes, speaking of Britain but applying equally to publishers in the United States, "Stereoplates and electroplates were often the embodied form of the publisher's intellectual property. Deeds of transfer of copyrights between publishers frequently revolve around the transfer of ownership of stereos, electros, and books in sheets."[1] The life cycle and reproductive potential of many works extended long after their copyright, if there was one, had expired. Inevitably, a market for used stereotype plates developed.

The widespread manufacture and trade in stereotype plates began at a point in the early nineteenth century when the American publishing industry itself was in a prolonged period of significant growth and change. Small, localized printers were beginning to become publishers in the modern sense, with a greater national interest and orientation. The growth of the printing trades in Philadelphia, Boston, and especially New York in the first decades of the nineteenth century created new opportunities for job printers, typefounders, engravers, and new stereotype foundries. And while there was no real regulation of the printing industry at the national level, as there was in many European countries, several nascent attempts at a nationally organized system of book trade and distribution were made by American publishers during this period. The adoption of stereotyping intersected with and affected all of these areas.[2]

As we have seen in the example of Mathew Carey, who acquired and then sold his New Testament plates in the 1810s, publishers realized early on that owning a set of plates to a certain type of work could give them an advantage in the marketplace. As stereotyping grew more common and a wider variety of genres and titles were cast in plates, a new national marketplace in used sets of plates began to develop. Buying a newly cast set of plates initially cost more than twice the standard composition costs of having a work set up in type. As firms dissolved, changed ownership, or went bankrupt, plates were liquidated in order to pay creditors. Publishers like Carey parlayed their investments in plates to acquire new printed stock on exchange or to publish joint editions. Publishers could also simply sell their own plates to raise capital for other projects. All these varieties of exchange would have occurred as singular transactions, and the relative paucity of early nineteenth-century American publishers' records (with the exception of Mathew Carey's and Isaiah Thomas's) presents challenges to researchers who seek to reconstruct the entire scope of the sale and movement of plates from publisher to publisher.

By midcentury, several organized alternatives for buying and selling used plates were available to publishers in the trades. Occasional advertisements for individual sets of plates for sale appear in the 1850s in newly established trade papers such as *Norton's Literary Gazette and Publishers' Circular* and its successor, the *American Publishers' Circular and Literary Gazette*. For example, an ad announcing the sale of the plates and copyrights to Charles Follen's *German Grammar* and *German Reader* first appeared in *Norton's Literary Gazette and Publishers' Circular* in January 1852. The same ad appeared regularly in subsequent issues; the plates remained unsold for almost three years. It appeared for the last time in November 1854 under the new headline "for sale very cheap."[3] The last edition of Follen's *Grammar* had been printed from those plates in 1849 by the Boston firm of Phillips, Sampson, and Co. The same firm printed Follen's *Reader* from its set of plates during the 1840s, and it, presumably, was the seller. Follen, the first professor of German at Harvard University and a Unitarian and Transcendentalist fellow traveler, first published his *German Grammar* in 1827 and his *German Reader* in 1831. These works were no longer the only German-language textbooks available in the United States in 1852, as they had been when they first appeared. Superseded textbooks, outdated reference works, and older editions of scripture that had been extensively printed from over many years constituted a substantial proportion of the first used plates offered for sale. A purchaser seeking to turn a profit faced the additional impediment of paying royalties to the author when used plates came with a copyright attached. As that was the case with Follen's works, perhaps it is no surprise that these two German textbooks took so long to sell. But even thirty years after being produced, the plates still could be useful in some downgraded segments of the market, and they eventually did sell. An edition of Follen's *Grammar* printed from the 1827 plates was published in Boston by James Munroe in 1858, and an edition of his *German Reader* from the 1831 plates was printed in New York by Leypoldt & Holt as late as 1867.

Advertisements for individual sets of plates were still anomalies. By far the most effective means of buying and selling used plates in the United States was the newly organized publishers' trade sales. In the 1830s, the regularization of multiple auction sales within the printing trades several times a year shows both a greater national organization in the trades and an increased market for new and used books throughout the country. Held twice a year in Philadelphia and New York and once a year in Boston, with later sales also taking place in Cincinnati, trade sales offered publishers a chance to sell both new and older stock directly to booksellers from across the country. Smaller regional booksellers could, in turn, preview and purchase new titles from multiple publishers at once. This regularity and direct contact also had the advantage of giving publishers insight into which types of books were popular in certain markets and geographic areas. The stock that booksellers acquired at these events, by sale and by auction, was often lower in cost than direct sales through traditional channels. By the 1840s, the spring New York trade sale had grown into the major North American sale, a two-week extravaganza attracting booksellers and publishers from throughout the United States and Canada. Other events included ancillary sales, hosted dinners and banquets, and extensive press coverage, making them "old home weeks" of sorts for publishers and a self-fulfilling celebration of the importance of the American publishing industry.

Prior to each sale, trade newspapers often included advertisements for larger sales or liquidations of publishers' stock and stereotype plates, either as part of a large invoice of plates at one of the trade sales or at a separate auction held in conjunction with the trade sales around the same time.[4]

In addition to publisher-to-bookseller sales of printed stock, organized auctions of stereotype plates were featured as separate lots. Generally held on the final day of the sale, lots of stereotype plates were sold from publisher to publisher. Listings of plates appeared in the published trade sale catalogs, with unusually large groupings of plates from a retirement or liquidation often warranting a separate advertisement and notice in trade papers like *Norton's Literary Gazette*, the *American Publishers' Circular*, and, later, *Publishers' Weekly*.[5] In the interest of keeping up the appearance of growth and progress in the trades, occasional articles in the trade journals reported on some of the more notable prices realized at the sales. While some sets of plates sold in the $1,000 to $2,000 range, a rough equivalent of their production costs, these are generally anomalies; most sets of used plates sold for much less than the cost of their manufacture. And despite the regular presence of secondhand sets of stereotype plates, the main purpose of the trade sales was to move publishers' stock to retail booksellers.[6] As a proportion of the total items changing hands, plates made up a modest part, about 10 percent of the catalog copy, with occasional exceptions.

ORGANIZING THE TRADE

Before the trade sales provided a regular form of sales and exchange, several attempts were made to organize the book trades in the United States around a European national model, but none achieved any real success. Throughout the nineteenth century, the US book market was the largest unregulated marketplace in the world, with no national organizations or state-sponsored bodies providing oversight over production, distribution, sales, or resales. In the United States, free markets and deregulation ruled.

Mathew Carey helped organize the Company of Printers of Philadelphia in 1794, the first American attempt at an organized trade body, but that organization lasted only two years. In 1801, Carey also proposed an annual book fair modeled after the fairs in Frankfurt and Leipzig. After some negotiations, a "literary fair" took place in New York the following summer, with New York printer Hugh Gaine presiding over the organization and Carey serving as secretary.[7] This fair was intended to connect publishers and booksellers, help regulate book prices throughout the country, and discourage the import of foreign titles that were already being reprinted by domestic shops. The fair committee had two representatives each from Philadelphia, New York, and Boston and can be seen as the first national attempt at trade regulation. The committee's work, and its literary fairs, ended by 1806 owing to the limited output of American book production during a period of strong foreign imports.

Carey later argued, in his *Address to the Booksellers of the United States* (1813), that smaller editions and more frequent press runs would be better for a national publishing industry and for the consumer than large editions that took four to six years to sell out. Smaller press runs would be almost as cost effective for the publisher, and they would be more responsive to market needs. Notably, smaller-sized editions would also avoid large overstocks of printed matter that would eventually be sold at a discount at auction. Given that he was aware of the potential advantages of stereotyping by this point, Carey's argument also favored publishers who invested in sets of plates and continued to bring out smaller impressions of a work from them as needed, according to demand.

In 1824, Carey's son Henry, in one of his own innovations in publishing, organized the first book trade sale by and for Philadelphia booksellers, modeled on the Frankfurt book fair. Everyone in town was invited, but the only sellers were his own firm of Carey & Lea. This model met one need: it enabled publishers to get their stock to booksellers more efficiently than postal delivery allowed. The following year, a more open trade sale was held in New York, and a Boston sale began shortly thereafter. As noted above, these sales, along with a new sale in Cincinnati, generally occurred twice a year (once a year in Boston) for several decades in their respective cities, bringing publishers and booksellers together to exchange new and old stock and, eventually, sets of stereotype plates.

While commerce at the trade sales was initially conducted directly between firms, as they expanded, professional auction houses began to take over their management. The auction house conducted all of the sale administration: publishing catalogs, collecting fees and payments, and warehousing and shipping the books sold, thus becoming de facto bankers and distributors for the printing trades. When the Boston firm of Ticknor and Fields sent shipments to the 1856 New York trade sale, the auction house of Leavitt and Delisser charged consignees a 9.5 percent commission on books, plus fees for cataloging and shipping the new stock to purchasers. Plates were presumably charged at this rate or at an agreed-upon fixed price and were more than able to make up that expense in the higher purchase price.[8]

As we will see below, the variety of works in plates that were being brought to auction at the sales did not represent the newest segments of the publishing marketplace. Many sets of plates listed in the trade sale catalogs were to superseded textbooks, older editions of Bibles, and other examples of potentially worn-out stock without substantial market value. Older and presumably heavily used plates to Walter Scott's Waverley novels and Shakespeare's plays also appeared with some regularity. If trade sales were primarily held so that publishers could sell new and existing stock to booksellers, the marketplace in plates was and would remain a distant second or third in importance, after the general socializing and networking that took place there. More often than not, stereotype plates were offered at trade sales as a result of bankruptcies, liquidations, and receiverships, or because a literary work had declined in popularity. Formerly valuable sets of plates, now decades old and worn down, were sold at modest prices to increasingly down-market publishers who intended to bring out cheap reprint editions as long as the plates held up. Many of these publishers, especially as markets expanded after the Civil War, had little interest in maintaining high production standards or the textual accuracy necessary to publish a new edition of, say, a schoolbook or grammar. For them, a cheap reprint of an older work could also be made profitable and would find its audience.

Prices realized for plates at the sales also present a problem in documentation. While a few auction catalogs that have survived are annotated with results, the new printing trade papers tended to print only a selection of prices from some of the more notable sales, often to point out a particularly slow sale and the bargains to be had there, or to note high prices from a particularly large or notable sale of plates.

STEREOTYPE PLATES AT THE TRADE SALES

The earliest cost book ledgers of the Philadelphia firm Carey & Lea note a separate trade sale price for books that was lower than the standard wholesale price. The trade sale price never goes below 10 percent of wholesale. For publishers, a 10 percent discount at trade sales would have been mostly offset by increased sales volume.[9] This discount would have been in addition to the seller's premium paid to the auction house. Some publishers argued against the trade sale model for this reason: that it allowed steadily lower wholesale prices to develop, creating an expectation among potential buyers, especially for new stock, and thus severely undercutting profits and profit margins for new works. This, in turn, could influence publishers' decisions about the profitability of potential new titles and whether they should be published at all. One result was an extremely varied set of prices for new books paid by different booksellers, even in the same city, that depended on how and where they obtained their stock: through direct purchase or exchange or via the trade sale, where sales and auction prices could fluctuate depending on the day, the seller's needs, or the purchaser's available credit.

The first recorded instance of used sets of stereotype plates offered for sale that I have identified appears at the August 1833 New York trade sale. Among several lots of plates, including editions of Herodotus and Goldsmith's *Vicar of Wakefield*, was *Mental Treasures*, a 130-page octavo compendium of short essays, including Washington's Farewell Address, that was stereotyped in Philadelphia in 1826. Unlike the sales of Follen's *German Grammar* and *German Reader*, which took place decades after their first printings, this was a short turnaround time from the initial creation of its plates to their sale. Afterward, the plates do not appear again on the market in any later trade sale catalogs, and no new edition was ever published from them. The title and the plates simply disappeared. Publishing historian Daniel Sheehan has written about the trade sales, "After the books had been sold, each trade sale devoted at least one day to an auction of stereotype plates. This part of the proceedings introduced a different set of buyers, the publishers themselves.... In contrast to the book auctions, which at their height brought prices permitting a reasonable profit, the disposal of plates under almost any circumstances involved a considerable sacrifice. In 1862, for example, stereotypes valued at $360,000 were sold for 15 percent of their cost."[10] *Mental Treasures* had either quickly repaid its publisher the initial investment and any likely opportunities for reprintings, or, more likely, it was a forced sale to raise money to pay debts or for other projects, and may not even have sold.

While most plates were offered on the final day of the sale, together with miscellaneous lots of stationery and fancy goods, at the March 1835 Philadelphia sale, fourteen sets of plates owned by Lilly, Wait & Co. of Boston were sold in the middle of the sale proper. The Philadelphia auctioneers chose to include printed stock from the plates alongside the plates themselves to generate interest. The Boston trade sale in June 1836 included twelve sets of stereotype plates, all of which were included within the single invoices of their consignees, about five different publishers, and were also dispersed throughout the catalog and sales calendar instead of clustered at the end. This also occurred with some plates during the 1838 Boston sale, though on the last day of that sale a separate auction of thirty-two plates from the liquidation of the American Stationers' Company stock of plates also took place.[11] Compared to Philadelphia and New York, the appearance of stereotype plates at the annual Boston sale was much less frequent, and perhaps can account for the different order in which they appeared at auction.

Other intriguing items appear in some of the early trade sale catalogs. The April 1834 New York sale had two separate lots of plates to the *Beauties* of Washington Irving offered by different consignors. Some of the early catalogs list plates intermixed with their own publisher's book stock as placeholders for the last day's auction to draw attention to their presence and then repeat the listing at the end for the final sale group. The final catalog page listing often provides the page number of the main publisher's listing in the catalog, where some additional narrative or copyright information about the plates, the presence of illustrations, or the initial cost may be found. One also sees occasional lots of stereotyped illustration blocks or plates for sale in sets separate from the book to which they belong, especially sets of plates for illustrated Bibles. The owner of a set of Bible plates could be interested in a set of illustrations to it to expand the range of their variant Bible offerings. Other copied illustration blocks could be reused in multiple books, periodicals, and newspapers, as needed.

Stereotype plates, the most expensive single items, were primarily held until the final day of the sale as the main publisher-to-publisher sales event. The auction house knew that publishers would be more willing to make larger purchases on new sets of plates if they had had a good sales week. There was also a symbolic importance to grouping the majority of sets of plates on the final day of the sale. As the culmination of the week's events, the plates of American authors, some of which still had copyrights attached, were significant markers of both American literary output *and* advances in mechanical production. As US publishers became increasingly celebratory about their contributions to American culture and the rise of a literate American citizenry that they had helped create, these sales offered fitting conclusions to busy weeks of literary commerce.

By midcentury, the sales had become established events on North American booksellers' and publishers' annual calendars. In 1851, the fall New York trade sale began on a Wednesday in early September and continued for four days. The final day, Saturday, was reserved for stereotype plates, along with stationery, writing implements, and one hundred thousand rolls of wallpaper.[12] Within a few years, the New York spring sale had grown to ten days, with auxiliary sales and other events taking place around it, making it the major literary and book trade event of the year. *Frank Leslie's Illustrated Newspaper* covered several trade sales for its national audience and described the work of publishers and booksellers, in a high tone of serious purpose, as the honorable and deliberate spread of civilization via literary commerce. The trade sales became both a curiosity (and occasional a spectacle) and a source of national pride that combined American manufacturing innovation with literary and cultural achievement:

> To their auction rooms, twice a year, have the booksellers of the Union wended their way, congratulated each other, formed new friendships and cemented old ones, purchased their books, and again departed to their several homes. It is a pleasant feature, that the streams of literature are circulated under auspices so favorable, and that about the business associations of the mind there is so much that is genial, elevating, and humanizing. We cordially recommend strangers who take an interest in the literary matters of our country, visiting the city at the time of the annual sales, to pay them a visit. It is something to see all publishers together, for they are the men whose united labors circulate the mental wealth of the country, who take the ideas of the authors and stamp upon them the form that facilitates their currency, and to a very great extent give the great public its ideas of their value.[13]

The sales days themselves were long, as the size of surviving catalogs attests. Publishers were expected to be present when their consigned lots came up for sale to field questions and generally drum up interest. John Keese, a former publisher and the principal auctioneer at the firms of Lyman & Rawdon and, later, Leavitt & Company, was a voluble presence at these sales, and did much to make them both profitable and entertaining. At the auction podium, Keese appears in several nineteenth-century literary memoirs as a wit and raconteur, adding life and spontaneous humor to what might otherwise have been the tedious recitation of long lists of book titles. The venerable New York bookseller, publisher, and editor Evert Duyckinck remarked, "Few who attended his 'Sales' did not carry away with them some recollection of his sparkling genius."[14] As a literary man steeped in printing and publishing, Keese displayed wit and astuteness that was highly valued on the auction platform. He kept the trade sales running with enthusiasm, providing entertainment along with the steady business of selling books. In a memoir of his father, Keese's son remarked, "It is no wonder that people flocked to the evening sales; and I have heard many say that to go there was as good as a play."[15] "If John Keese should quit the auction business, I should die of ennui," Keese's son remembered one bookseller saying.[16] In another anecdote meant to show Keese's sharp wit at the podium, when a bookseller bid twenty-five cents for a copy of a history of the Battle of Waterloo, Keese shot back, "There was no quarter at Waterloo, my dear sir."[17] The publisher James T. Fields mentioned Keese in one of his punning trade sale poems, written on the auction floor and recited during the Publishers' Association banquet: "But all were gay, and every one / Before the feast agrees / That, when he wants for food or fun, / He'll shake a bunch of KEESE."[18]

With a circulation of four thousand at its height, *Norton's Literary Advertiser* was the largest printing trade publication in the antebellum United States. *Norton's* covered the trade sales during the 1850s, publishing advertisements from the auction houses announcing the dates and terms of sale for each of them, along with ads from individual publishers noting their offerings, including stereotype plates. Its editorials and reports provide one of the few looks into this aspect of the book trades during this period. On 15 July 1851, *Norton's* reported on a Philadelphia trade sale held by a new firm, M. Thomas & Sons, which did a brisk business, apparently to the surprise of the *Norton's* editorial staff. Thomas had taken over the Philadelphia trade sale business from the firm of George W. Lord, who held the sales throughout the 1840s. A highlight of Thomas's first sale was the stock of stereotype plates owned by Thomas Davis, the surviving partner of M'Carty & Davis, one of the first Philadelphia publishers to commission stereotype plates back in the 1820s. *Norton's* saw fit to list the "most important" plates sold and their prices:

> Purdon's Digest, balance of editions, copy right and stereotype plates, $1,118.25.
> Sergeant & Rawle's Digest, balance of editions, and do., do., $6,143.05.
> Bacon's Abridgement, do., do., $12,596.40.
> Pike's Arithmetic, copyright and stereotype plates, $1,025.00.
> Key to do., do., do. $200.00.
> Franklin's Works, do., do. $1,200.00.
> Brown's Commentaries, do., do. $1,350.00.

Byerly's Spelling Book, do., do. $340.00.
Shakespeare, stereotype plates, $1,400.00.
Hume, Smollett & Miller's History of England, 4 vols., do. $1,100.00.[19]

Of particular interest here, in addition to the substantial prices realized for Sergeant & Rawle's *Digest* and Bacon's *Abridgement*, is one of M'Carty & Davis's sets of stereotype plates to its collection of Shakespeare's plays, which was first published in 1823 and cast in New York by the typefounder Jedidiah Howe. These plates were among the earliest to arrive in Philadelphia, years before anyone was casting plates in the city. M'Carty and Davis were later able to persuade Howe to come down from New York and set up his foundry in their city as Philadelphia's first stereotyper. This set of plates was their first commission and one of their strongest steady sellers as an eight-volume duodecimo set and a two-volume quarto edition, brought out as a jointly published venture with Mathew Carey. From a single setting of type by Howe, two different sets of plates were made, with different orientations: an eight-volume duodecimo first, and then a two-volume quarto edition. At some point in the late 1840s, Davis sold one of his two sets of Shakespeare plates to a "persistent publishing firm in Boston" for $1,500, this set being the other, which he kept until his retirement.[20] At this sale, American works under copyright were noted as such in the catalog and sold for prices as high as other sets of works not under copyright.

In its February 1852 issue, *Norton's Literary Gazette* (the successor to *Norton's Literary Advertiser*) provided a brief report of the most recent Philadelphia trade sale. More than two hundred members of the trade were present, many traveling great distances from the Northeast and the South. *Norton's* also hinted that the next New York sale would be the largest ever held in the United States and promised a full report. As the primary organ of the trade, *Norton's* almost never failed to be upbeat about the growth and positive prospects of the American book trades. At this sale, one publisher's listing even included plates consigned from two London booksellers. Plates from British publishers are rarely found listed under their own lots in the trade sale catalogs. As a transatlantic system of plate distribution and exchange began to form, British-produced plates were offered by American publishers for sale with increasing frequency.[21]

By 1853, booksellers in the United States had several options for obtaining new and older stock over the course of a year. Advertisements on the same page of the February 1853 issue of *Norton's* announce the upcoming fortieth

Philadelphia and fifty-seventh New York trade sales on 9 and 21 March, respectively. With the Cincinnati sale also taking place on 21 March, booksellers could choose where to go to obtain their stock. The larger publishers had to expend considerable amounts of time preparing their lots and traveling to the sales. Multiple sales in the same season also encouraged competition between publishers to place their stock—and representatives—at all the sales in order to reach every regional bookseller who could only attend one.

In this busy spring season, the 15 April 1853 *Norton's Literary Gazette* reprinted a two-page article on the trade sales that originally appeared in the *Boston Transcript* and described how the spectacle of the sales was becoming of interest even to the greater public: "All the new books, all the old books, all the literature that can be gathered together, centre in one spot for the space of ten or twelve days." The article reports five or six hundred gentlemen in the audience, "with their huge octavo catalogues spread out like maps of the great literary voyage they are about to undertake for the year."[22] Sales took place between 8:30 in the morning and often ran to 11:00 at night. In New York, lunch was provided for buyers and sellers in special dining rooms within the auction house, and the article reports that authors often used the occasion to meet with their publishers and observe the sale of their books. Such newspaper accounts made special note of the air of conviviality at the sales. Meals were served, toasts were made, and the proprietors of each publishing establishment would often come up on stage when their lots appeared, so as to encourage their colleagues to purchase more items.

The New York Book-Publishers' Association formed in 1855. The following year, it sponsored a new trade sale exclusively for its membership, thus "attempting its right to manage the trade sales."[23] Harper & Brothers, the largest publisher in New York, chose not to join, and continued to participate in the existing New York trade sale, which ran parallel to the Book-Publishers' Association sale for several years. One of the association's membership clauses prohibited its members from offering their stock at any but an association-sponsored trade sale. Consignees at all the previous sales were permitted to withdraw or multiply their contributions at any time, which many thought led to unfair manipulation of the auction market above and beyond what had already been listed for consignment, an abuse the association was trying to counter. This apparent manipulation of prices and quantities of stock by larger publishers who could afford it placed smaller publishers at a clear disadvantage, which the association wanted to reform. Its new sale format, with strictly fixed quantities and prices, was an attempt at a more regulated environment.

By the mid-1850s, the volume of stock exchanged at the sales had become considerable. At the March 1854 sale, despite suffering a damaging warehouse fire the year before, Harper & Brothers sold more than a hundred thousand items.[24] A long report on this sale appeared in the *New York Tribune*, which extensively covered literary New York and the book trades at this time. The publisher George Palmer Putnam hosted a dinner for authors and booksellers at his home during the sale and a second dinner for all participants at the Astor House Hotel on the night before the final sales day. The New York Book-Publishers' Association also helped make its New York sale a highlight of the year's cultural calendar, and was the closest thing the United States had to the Frankfurt book fair in Germany.

Stereotype plates from the large firm of Putnam & Co. were sold at this sale, and the *Tribune* reporter waxed lyrical on the promise of a wider dissemination of literary works across the country: "Through the indefatigable exertions of Messrs. Barnes, we shall soon see the 'Handbooks of Science and Art' gladdening the eyes of the woodcutter's son on the banks of the Mississippi, and the planter's cabin in the wilds of Texas. From the great variety of channels into which this immense stream of literature has been changed, we can but hope that many portions of our land will be enriched that have heretofore been neglected."[25] What is particularly striking in this passage is its allusion to a form of literary manifest destiny—to the potential of the book trade, through the sale of plates and copyrighted American works, to achieve longevity and purposeful existence in new markets across the United States. The life, or afterlife, of literary property had been extended because of the trade sale format, and its method moved capital from owner to owner so that more books could be printed domestically and sent out across the country to (white) American citizens as they occupied new lands. The publishers and booksellers of the United States, never humble in their self-congratulatory rhetoric of promoting Western civilization and American values, were publicly praised in passages like this for their collaborative efforts at the sales.[26]

A short list of eleven sets of plates, with their prices and the names of their purchasers, appears in this article. Some works went for fairly high prices. Putnam's *Homes of American Authors*, presumably a steady seller, sold for $2,000 to Appleton & Co. Andrew Jackson Downing's *Landscape Gardening* went for $2,050 to J. C. Riker, including copyright. Four volumes of Goldsmith's works sold for $1,660 to Leavitt & Allen, and Hawthorne's *Mosses from an Old Manse* was a bargain at $290, sold to Ticknor, Reed and Fields, and subject to copyright. Ticknor, Reed and Fields was surely glad to be able to consolidate the older works of Hawthorne, including his copyrights, under its own roof so as to be able to eventually bring out a collected edition of his writings. From this sale of plates, Putnam realized about $75,000.

One month later, the 1 May *Literary Gazette* printed the entire Putnam list of plates and their purchasers, though it did not include prices. Ninety-nine separate titles were listed, with purchasers from Philadelphia, New York, and Boston. No publisher acquired a disproportionate number of plates. D. Appleton & Co., which owned the largest retail bookstore in America, purchased nine sets of plates for its publishing arm, the largest quantity by any one publisher. Following the Putnam sales results were the titles and purchasers of seventy-five sets of plates belonging to long-standing Philadelphia publisher Abraham Hart from the same sale. From this group, Appleton acquired five sets of plates, while the leading purchaser, the Philadelphia firm Parry & McMillan, acquired seventeen sets.

As the largest and most economically robust sale organized by the publishing industry in the United States to date, the March 1854 New York sale occasionally lapses into mythology in later publishers' memoirs. Given the popular press coverage of the time, this sort of self-congratulation seems almost inevitable. At the grand Astor House banquet held for members of the New York Book-Publishers' Association during this sale, the Boston publisher James T. Fields was called upon to speak. He chose, as was his wont, to read a poem he had written that day in the salesroom:

> Why will you call for one whose soil
> No fruitful harvest yields,
> And waste your precious time to-night
> On unproductive FIELDS?
>
> Brave plenty spreads her ample board
> At PUTNAM'S generous name,
> And though he sold his *plates* to-day,
> He feeds us just the same.
>
> . . . .
>
> When ANNERS balances his books –
> (Good fellow, all have known) –

And PRATT, whose church is finished now,
Is going, going, gone!

Let this be said in sober truth,
Engraven deep and fair –
*They lived like brothers here below.
And now they're happy there!*[27]

The idealized conviviality of the trade comes through in these lines, together with Fields's proclivity for making playful puns of his fellow publishers' names. The final stanzas promise eternal heavenly reward for the good works done by the members of the association, with the promise of the same conviviality in heaven. It was easy to be convivial when business was uniformly good for all and the markets strong. A report in *Norton's* gave the revenues for these two New York sales at "about $350,000."[28]

The first Cincinnati trade sale was held in October 1838. The fifty-fourth and final sale was held in October 1877.[29] By the late 1830s, Cincinnati had become the fourth-largest publishing center in the country. Cincinnati publishers and stereotypers supplied schoolbooks for many markets, even on the East Coast, and books for the emerging western book trade. The Cincinnati trade sales were advertised early on in newspapers across the entire country, from Boston to New Orleans and St. Louis. Cincinnati publishers such as U. P. James regularly contributed lots to the New York sales in the later 1840s and 1850s and traveled to New York to acquire new stock. By midcentury, Cincinnati was no longer so far away from the coastal centers of commerce in the United States, but the perils of distance in the era before railroads, combined with the substantial volume of stock exchanged at the sales, did cause occasional problems. In 1857, James purchased books and stereotype plates at the March New York sale, paid his invoice on 17 April, and then complained to Leavitt and Company, the auctioneers, on 29 April that he had not yet received shipment of his goods. By 7 May, an incomplete shipment of books had arrived in Cincinnati, but it did not contain the plates he had purchased. The plates finally arrived in late May, but some were missing and others badly damaged. Two additional boxes of books that James had not purchased also arrived, for which he was billed an additional $2 in freight charges.[30]

As the trade sales grew in importance and the New York spring sale began to dominate the annual calendar, the existing trade sale model was also increasingly criticized for its varying sale prices for new books rather than more uniform pricing. An editorial on the need for reforming the trade sales first appeared in a trade paper in March 1855.[31] It argued that the time and expense of contributing lots to the sales was simply a more expensive way of doing normal business, and that the largest firms benefited most by being better able to offer their stock for smaller firms to buy. This debate continued, one result being the newly formed New York Book-Publishers' Association. One of the association's new rules fixed the quantity of stock offered by publishers at each sale. No overages or side deals after the sale were allowed, something that the larger publishers generally enjoyed, as once they found an interested buyer they could set a price with him and then amend the quantity above and beyond what was being formally offered at the sale. As noted above, Harper & Brothers chose not to join the association and held sales of its stock at another New York auction house (Bangs Brothers), essentially setting up a parallel trade sale under the old rules.[32] Harper's main argument was that the sales needed to be bona fide auctions, where publishers could sell as much stock—even new stock—as they wished at a price any individual bookseller was willing to pay. Fixing the price and quantity of the merchandise ahead of time would only limit a publisher's ability to sell its stock and would inhibit future growth as well. Harpers also favored the "withdrawal" plan, in which a bookseller could remove unsold stock from the sale, or decrease quantities of stock offered, depending upon demand. The new requirements stipulated that every book offered at the sales be sold at the sales, a further tightening of regulations. For a time in the mid- to late 1850s, New York held two trade sales in the spring hosted by the two auction houses. A number of smaller publishers followed Harper and did not join the association, and they were able as a result to fill out the catalogs of publishers' offerings at the Harper-led sale held at Bangs Brothers.

The *American Publishers' Circular* reported favorably on the first trade sale held by the New York Book-Publishers' Association at the auction rooms of Leavitt and Delisser in 1856 and provided an extensive list of the final day's sale of stereotype plates.[33] Titles and prices were noted for some of the sets, including a list of fifty-seven titles. The prices realized for these sets were fairly modest. A duodecimo 404-page edition of Michelet's *History of the Roman Republic* brought $70 and was noted to have cost $360. Likewise, Michelet's *Life of Luther* realized $65 but cost $234. Two novels by Lady Georgiana Fullerton—*Ellen Middleton* (328 pages, duodecimo) and *Grantley Manor* (329 pages, duodecimo) sold for $60 (but cost $245) and $80 (cost $237), respectively. An eight-volume pocket edition of Shakespeare, complete with forty steel engravings and totaling 3,693 pages, sold for the very attractive price of $480. The Booksellers' Association, which sponsored the sale and the *Circular*, was clearly interested in keeping up interest and momentum for its own sales. Putting a positive spin on a list of fairly poor prices realized was an inducement for members of the association to actively take part, or join if they hadn't already, and obtain some true bargains.

At the 1857 New York fall trade sale, all the plates belonging to the firm of Miller & Curtis were sold following the firm's bankruptcy and liquidation. The *New York Daily Tribune* reported that the competition for Miller & Curtis's plates was between a mere four publishers and also "the authors, two or three of whom were represented" at the sale.[34] A clause included in many book contracts at this time gave authors an option to buy back the plates to their own works at cost, either after a certain amount of time had passed, or as a contingency if the publishing firm broke up. In rare cases, such as Longfellow's, in which an author could afford to pay in advance for the production of his stereotype plates, he could usually argue instead for a higher initial royalty or a "rental fee" to the publisher for use of the plates in printing.[35]

Famously, Herman Melville faced the bankruptcy purchase option at this sale. In 1857, after years of steadily declining book sales and several publishers, Melville's publisher at the time, Dix, Edwards & Co., dissolved, the same year it published *The Confidence Man* and the year after *The Piazza Tales* came out. In his contract, Melville had the option of purchasing the stereotype plates to these works for 25 percent of their initial cost as a contingency. Dix, Edwards was acquired by the firm of Miller and Co. (which became Miller & Curtis after 1 June), but attempts to salvage the firm apparently failed completely in August of that year.[36] Both of Melville's new works were being continually advertised for retail sale nationally by booksellers during this time, along with the rest of the Dix, Edwards trade list. The Curtis of Miller & Curtis was the author George William Curtis, who was making occasional forays into publishing at this time. As the new partner in the firm, Curtis wrote to Melville on 4 September that the two sets of plates to his works would have to be put up for auction at the fall trade sale as the firm was going to liquidate all of its remaining assets. Melville thus had the right to purchase them back before that happened.[37] In a letter to Curtis on 15 September, Melville wrote that he could not "at present conveniently make arrangements with regard to them [the plates]." Melville continued, "It strikes me, though, that under the circumstances (copyright &tc) they can bring but little at the Trade Sale, or any other sale. Whereas, if held on to for a while, they might be transferred to me to the common advantage of all concerned.... Do with the plates whatever is thought best."³⁸ Rather than have the plates—and his copyright—exposed to the free market and an unknown purchaser at auction, Melville, writing from his farmhouse in the Berkshires to Curtis in New York, was suggesting that Curtis hold on to the plates himself until they could be used under a new firm, led by Curtis.

The plates to *The Piazza Tales* and *The Confidence Man* were offered in the catalog of the Miller & Curtis inventory for the fall 1857 New York trade sale, but the *Daily Tribune* reported in September that "two volumes by Herman Melville were withdrawn."³⁹ Curtis had agreed to Melville's request and pulled the plates, perhaps hoping that something could be made of them after the firm was reorganized, or that Melville might eventually purchase them back. A few weeks later, Melville wrote Curtis again with dimmer prospects: "I will try and do something about the plates as soon as I can. Meantime if they bother you, sell them without remorse. To pot with them, & melt them down."⁴⁰ In 1857, after a succession of novels that sold poorly, Melville could not afford even the liquidation price of 25 percent of the cost of the plates to his two most recent books, both of which were still in print and one of which had just been published. Melville clearly did not purchase the plates back from Curtis, and subsequent correspondence between the two authors makes no further mention of them. Neither work was reprinted from its original set of plates, and their fate, like that of many plates, remains unknown. Melville biographer Herschel Parker speculates that Curtis probably sold them as scrap metal shortly after this incident, not anticipating any reprints.⁴¹

On one rare occasion, an author leased his stereotype plates back to a struggling publisher, to their mutual benefit. George Palmer Putnam's business had just emerged from bankruptcy in 1857 and was in need of revitalizing. Washington Irving allowed Putnam to lease his plates for new editions of Irving's works. This act essentially repaid Putnam for his faith in Irving in 1848, when Irving had been out of print for several years and his old Philadelphia publishers had no interest in bringing out new editions of his works. Putnam had just set out in business at that point and made Irving a generous contract for royalties for the exclusive right to publish his works for a period of years, to their mutual benefit.⁴²

At the same trade sale, George William Curtis himself was faced with a situation similar to Melville's, for a five-volume set of plates to his own works was also being offered for sale by one of his former publishers, and with a 12.5 percent copyright attached to it. The plates to each volume started at $100 and were bid up to $205 and sold, reported the *Tribune*, "to a gentleman who purchased them in behalf of the author."[43] Curtis, more than Melville, had wealthy New York patrons upon whom he could call for assistance. Other sets of plates sold at that sale were less successful: *Twice Married: A Tale of Connecticut Life*, with an attached 10 percent copyright, was sold for $20 to the only bidder, Dick & Fitzgerald, even though the plates themselves cost $133. Like low published auction estimates today, the production costs of a set of plates were frequently listed in the trade sale catalogs as a benchmark indicator of value and an inducement to buyers seeking a bargain. Several other works at this sale sold for between 10 and 20 percent of their cost, sometimes even less. The *Tribune* saw fit to print a somewhat embarrassing list of works sold off for their value as metal alone, all at less than 10 percent of cost.

In summing up the results of this sale, the *Tribune* reported it "probable that not one of the volumes had paid for itself, so that Miller & Curtis were like to be exceeding temperate if their only wine was to be drunk out of the skulls of authors."[44] If Miller & Curtis purchased the remains of Dix, Edwards & Co. at a bargain price, paid its creditors, and sought to make a profit from the liquidation of its assets in stock and plates, this plan was clearly not successful.

THE REPRINTING HISTORY OF SOLOMON NORTHUP'S
TWELVE YEARS A SLAVE

Given Melville's experience with his final two novels, it may be helpful at this point to look at the role of stereotype plates on the secondhand market through a series of transactions relating to the plates of one work of nineteenth-century literature, and to trace them through several sales and subsequent owners. Solomon Northup's memoir *Twelve Years a Slave* was jointly published in 1853 by the Auburn, New York, firm of Derby and Miller, its Buffalo branch, Derby, Orton, and Mulligan, and in Cincinnati by Henry W. Derby. In subsequent impressions, the publisher was given as Derby, Miller and Osgood and Miller, Orton & Mulligan. *Twelve Years a Slave* was the first narrative of an enslaved person published by a commercial publishing house; all previous narratives of enslaved persons had come to print under the auspices of the antislavery societies. Derby and Miller was a general-interest publisher of schoolbooks, popular histories, and literature in upstate New York. That same year, it published the best-selling *Fern Leaves from Fanny's Portfolio* by the popular author Sarah

Payson Willis (Fanny Fern).[45] Northup's work was published simultaneously in England by the established London firm of Samson Low, Son & Co. Textually, the first London edition matches its American counterpart exactly. As the setting of type is exactly the same between the two editions, two sets of stereotype plates to it were made in the United States, one of which was sent to England and published there first, so as to secure the British copyright. Only three years later, its publishers noted the twenty-nine-thousandth American impression. All of these impressions of the work came from the same set of stereotype plates.

The plates to *Twelve Years a Slave* were offered for sale at the spring 1859 New York trade sale—not by its original publishers but in a large lot of forty-two sets of plates offered by another firm, Campbell & Smith, which had not published an edition of it under its own imprint. These plates presumably sold at the sale, as an edition of *Twelve Years a Slave* printed from the same set of plates appeared later that year under the New York imprint of C. M. Saxton.[46] Saxton, interestingly, was known primarily as a publisher of agricultural and horticulture books and the journal the *Plow*. He presumably saw a bargain at the trade sale for a steady seller about plantation life for his primary audience that could bring a modest return, despite the tens of thousands of copies already in circulation in the United States over the previous six years.

The next edition of *Twelve Years a Slave* was published just after the Civil War in Philadelphia by the Keystone Publishing Company. It too was printed from the same set of plates as the 1853 Auburn and the 1859 New York editions. But in this edition, the original two-page editor's preface of 1853, which had appeared in all previous editions and impressions, was replaced with a new two-page publisher's preface that began, "Slavery is now one of the institutions of the past."[47] The same set of plates was used to print the book, including the original table of contents plate, which listed the (older) editor's preface on pages 15 and 16 and had not been corrected to note the new publisher's preface. Keystone chose to cast a new plate for the publisher's preface in order to note the abolition of slavery in the United States, but not to correct the table of contents plate.

One more edition of *Twelve Years a Slave* appeared in the nineteenth century, published in New York by the International Book Company, cheap reprint publishers, sometime around 1890. It too was printed from the same set of plates as the 1853 first edition and all subsequent editions, and it included the postbellum publisher's preface. By this time, the copperplate illustrations used in each previous edition had long since worn out and were not included.

The list of illustrations on the bottom half of the last page of the table of contents is missing from this edition, evidence that the plate itself was corrected to excise the illustration list. Otherwise, the setting of the text is identical, down to the misnamed editor's preface appearing at the beginning of the table of contents for pages 15 and 16, all unchanged from the 1853 edition. After that, presumably worn down from forty years' worth of impressions and at least five different owners, the plates, and the work itself, disappeared from the marketplace.

During the Civil War, northern publishers and booksellers consolidated to some extent to adapt to a smaller market and disrupted distribution areas and networks. Some northern publishers took advantage of the war situation by purchasing the plates of southern authors at trade sales, knowing that subsequent publishers of editions printed from those plates would have no legal obligation to pay the authors their share of any original copyright agreement.[48] A *New York Tribune* article on the 1862 trade sale notes that a "Mr. Scott" purchased the plates to Alabama author Augusta Evans Wilson's novel *Beulah* for $205 after its publisher, Derby & Jackson, went bankrupt and its stock and plates came up at auction, noting, "there is small chance of there being much copyright paid to the authoress hereafter, for she is a rank Rebel, and a nurse in a Southern Hospital."[49] The plates then changed hands from Mr. Scott to the New York firm of Carleton, who brought out a new edition of *Beulah* in 1863.

Wilson understood her awkward situation in the literary marketplace and worked to regain the best possible advantages for her later works. For her subsequent book, *Macaria*, a southern novel about women's work during the war written while she was serving as a Confederate nurse, Wilson managed to send an early copy of the manuscript to the New York publisher J. C. Derby by a blockade runner via Cuba, in much the same way that one would send an advance copy to a British publisher to secure a first printing in Great Britain and thus preserve a copyright "internationally" by first securing a northern edition.[50] This strategy worked, as *Macaria* was published in 1864 in both New York and Richmond authorized editions. Wilson's contract with the Richmond publisher West and Johnston (claiming copyright under the laws of the Confederate States of America) brought her notoriety in the South but little money, while her contract with J. C. Derby in New York provided her and her family with much-needed support for the duration of the war.[51]

Wilson's first novel, *Inez*, published anonymously by Harper & Brothers in 1854, also became a contested literary property during the war, stemming in part from the success of *Beulah* and contemporary wartime interest in novels of southern life. New York publishers Bradburn and Doolady purchased the Harper-made stereotype plates to *Inez* at an 1862 trade sale and began advertising their forthcoming edition of it in January 1864, noting that it was "by Miss Evans, author of *Beulah*," to capitalize on *Beulah*'s success and also to hint, misleadingly, that it was a new southern novel about the war. Bradburn and Doolady clearly felt no obligation to negotiate new copyright terms with Wilson after her original Harper & Brothers agreement had ended.[52]

At the same 1862 fall trade sale, it was reported that the sales value of stereotype plates relative to their cost of production was about 15 percent. One article speculated that three years earlier, before the book trade was interrupted by the war, most plates would have brought twice that amount. But, as a positive example of the briskness of the trade (most such articles insist on positive speculation for the trades, even in hard times), it concluded that some publishing houses clearly had extra capital to invest in plates, despite the tough times of war, which raised paper costs alone 20 to 25 percent in just two years: "The plates which have changed owners are to be laid away in vaults until the troublous times are past, and commercial skies brighten."[53] Plates were clearly seen as a form of long-term capital investment, to be used to advantage at the proper moment.

At the same sale, the stereotype plates to Fanny Fern's *Ruth Hall* (1854), which had sold some seventy thousand copies in the previous decade, went for only $25, as did the plates to her *Fresh Leaves* (1857). Works by nonliving writers such as Jane Austen, Hannah More, and Ann Radcliffe did only slightly better, selling for about $50 per volume, and a duodecimo *Pilgrim's Progress*, a steady seller with a solid market value, was bid up to $137.50. A reporter for the *American Publishers' Circular* remarked, "The standard ancient classics in 8vo. brought only $44, and a pretty series of modern classics $12, both of which were dog cheap at twice the money." Likewise, another investment property was secured for a modest sum: "Mary Forrest's *Women of the South Distinguished in Literature*, which glorified her heroines on steel and in long-primer, to the tune of $3,250 was started at $50, and dragged on and hung, until Hazard of Philadelphia, with an eye to the future, bid an even $100, and got the plates."[54]

After the Civil War, the trade sales continued for another decade but became less advantageous to publishers. Jobbers—middlemen who sold stock to booksellers—became increasingly prominent, eliminating one of the main rationales for the sales. Publishers who needed quick infusions of cash could still sell at auction, but as the large firms grew even larger, they found less need to sell stock and plates this way. Charles Madison writes that James R. Osgood & Company in Boston was "chronically in need of cash" after the war and contributed more stock to trade sales in order to raise funds than any other publisher. An unfortunate cycle continued for several years in which Osgood was forced to sell new stock at reduced prices at the sales to maintain his business and publish even newer stock. According to trade notices and articles in *Publishers' Weekly*, his large spring 1876 liquidation sale of plates to works by European authors was designed to shift his focus to American literature, but it was also an attempt to break out of this cycle of dependency. Madison calls it a "distress sale" in which "each sale thus chipped away a sizable chunk of his fine list."[55] Osgood's plan worked, at least in the short term, as he raised $110,000 from his lots of nearly five hundred plates and printed stock. The following year, he sold an additional 130 titles to the firm of Houghton and Mifflin: plates, copyright, and stock. He also sold off the *North American Review* to right his business, to no avail. James R. Osgood, a much better editor than businessman, was forced to merge his firm with Houghton and Mifflin in 1878 to form Houghton, Osgood and Company.

By 1875, the regular trade sales were replaced by a series of book fairs organized by the American Book Trade Association, formed in 1855 as the successor to the New York Book-Publishers' Association.[56] The American Book Trade Association had since grown into a national trade association, continuing through the war years, and was the longest-lived book trade association in the United States to date. Its book fair ceased being an auction and became a fixed-price semiannual sale of new stock by publishers to booksellers. In January 1876, *Publishers' Weekly* announced the introduction of a new "remainder sale" at the spring New York book fair to take the place of the now defunct trade sale auctions.[57] This was the beginning of the modern practice in which publishers offer remaindered editions for sale, primarily to dealers who specialize exclusively in remaindered stock. The same issue included a full-page advertisement from George Leavitt & Co., the former trade sale auctioneers, announcing and detailing the formation of the Booksellers' Exchange and Clearing-House in Clinton Hall on Astor Place in New York. The Booksellers' Exchange would host the spring and fall book fairs for the American Book Trade Association. At the close of the fair, a sale would take place that included remainder stock, clearance stock, and stereotype plates. The bulk of the fair was devoted exclusively to new titles. A strict separation was to take place between new stock and the catalog of remainders and plates offered on the final sale day so that no side deals or other trading of them could take place during the sale proper. The association's reforms were intended to curb the wide fluctuations in prices for new stock at the old trade sales and also to prevent new stock from being introduced together with older stock in the same publisher's auction lots.

An editorial in the next issue of *Publishers' Weekly* supported the association line that the previous trade sale system was flawed and unfair because of the price fluctuations.[58] Stereotype plates, as more unusual commodities, were essentially unaffected by this shift in orientation. They would still be sold twice a year in New York at auction, they would be announced in a printed catalog issued just before the sale, and they would be sold on the final day of the fair. In the postwar years, the growth of cheap reprint publishers flooding the marketplace, and the rise of cheap books as retail loss leaders in establishments such as drugstores, had some impact on the attention paid to secondhand stereotype plates as generators of revenue, as can be seen from the postwar reprinted editions of Solomon Northup's *Twelve Years a Slave*. For the right publisher, older, worn plates had some added value as the source of potential cheap reprints. One significant change in the association's membership at this time was the addition of Harper & Brothers, the largest association holdout from twenty years before, when attempts to reform the trade sale system resulted in two parallel trade sales. By the time of the centennial celebrations of 1876, the largest American publishers were all united at last into one book trade organization that agreed on uniform conditions for their operations.[59]

The 25 March 1876 issue of *Publishers' Weekly* reported on the first days of the new book fair in New York while it was still under way. Book sales in general were sluggish because of the economy, and the first day's sales of plates and remainders also went slowly, with most sets of plates selling for the cost of the metal alone. The report ended with speculation about the first large sale of plates from James R. Osgood & Co. the following week, in which plates worth more than $300,000 were to be sold along with $125,000 of Osgood's printed stock.[60] The Osgood collection was the largest group of stereotype plates ever brought up for auction. More than four hundred works were to be sold, including sets of plates to Dickens, Scott, Thackeray, Austen, and other popular steady sellers. British and European literature, travel writing, classical works in English, and children's literature were also included in the sale. The Osgood firm took out a three-page advertisement in the 4 March *Publishers' Weekly* to announce the sale and list the plates to be sold later that month, which would take place as a separate sale following the spring book fair in New York.[61]

"Some publishers take pride in never letting go their hold on any book they have published," read the piece in *Publishers' Weekly*. "Evidently Messrs. Osgood & Co's pride does not take this course, and they have no scruples against disposing of the plates of highly valuable works."[62] In addition to his new focus on American literature, Osgood was experimenting with printing heliotypes, a new illustration process, and used this as another reason for selling off his European works. The grand scale of this auction presented a significant opportunity for newer publishers to invest in solid, steady-selling titles. Just before the New York book fair, on 18 March, a separate sale of plates and remainders from the Philadelphia firm of Hunt & Congdon also took place, in Philadelphia, making the spring of 1876 the high-water mark for sales of stereotype plates in the United States. *Publishers' Weekly* suggested that its readers stop in Philadelphia for this sale on their way to New York. A half-page advertisement for the Hunt & Congdon sale, listing thirty different titles in plates, most of them schoolbooks, appeared in the 11 March issue.

In April, *Publishers' Weekly* reported fully on the round of March sales. At the remainder sale at the end of the trade fair, sixteen sets of plates were offered, with their prices and purchasers noted. None sold for more than $50 per set, and most went for $25 or less. Under the heading "The Estate of H. T. Tuckerman" it was noted, "These plates of the late Mr. Tuckerman's works, it was understood, had been stored in the Messrs. Leavitt's [the auctioneers] cellars so long that their ownership had been forgotten."[63] To close Tuckerman's accounts, a 320-page set of duodecimo plates to the *Thoughts on the Poets* sold for only $15 to a Mr. Jenkins. Likewise, *A Month in England*, a 240-page duodecimo, went for $10, and the *Sicily Pilgrimage*, 188 pages, went for just $5, all to Jenkins. This was not an auspicious start to the most ambitious sales season ever.

The reports from the main fair were similarly not encouraging. *Publishers' Weekly* concluded that the problem was the lack of enough buyers to make the fair viable, not the new format of the fair itself. The trade magazine defended the new fixed-price system, stating that the results would have been even more disastrous had the old system of price auctioning been in place. Fallout from the Panic of 1873 and the resulting depression of the mid-1870s were clearly affecting the printing trades. The one bright spot that spring was the large sale of Osgood's plates, which *Publishers' Weekly* speculated could only strengthen the trade as a whole and justify the remainder sales model.

The Osgood sale took place over two days, 28 and 29 March, following the trade fair. Total quantities approached nearly five hundred sets of plates, with the production cost more than $300,000. The additional seventy-five volumes of stock to be sold were valued at $125,000. *Publishers' Weekly* reported:

> There has been no such offering as this for nearly twenty years, and it is likely that the results will outreach those of any sale ever held in the American trade: the sale of Abraham Hart, in Philadelphia, in the summer of 1854, amounting to something over $80,000; that of G. P. Putnam, in New-York, immediately following, to a few thousands less; that of Phillips & Sampson, in Boston, in 1859, to about $107,000 as nearly as we can get the figures. The present sale, according to Mr. Osgood's own estimate, will aggregate between $105,000 and $110,000, of which the plates brought in the neighborhood of $60,000.[64]

Because of the substantial quantities of plates and stock, along with their subject matter, the sale brought an inordinately large group of publishers and booksellers together: "There were between 80 and 120 buyers present in the auction rooms at any one time. Nothing very lively occurred until the Dickens series was reached, when the entire assemblage seemed to warm up to the work and get, each man of them, personally interested. The sales of the four sets of plates reached the large sum of $14,215, and the 15,000 volumes of stock brought the total nearly up to $25,000."[65]

The high point of the sale was the auction of plates to Thackeray's works on the second day. Harper & Brothers opened with a bid of $360, which was answered steadily by a number of prominent publishing houses, including Hurd & Houghton and Lea & Shepard. "The bidders and a good part of the crowd rose to their feet in their excitement," *Publishers' Weekly* reported, "and one might have supposed that the Gold Exchange itself had sent a delegation to make matters lively at the quiet book-room. . . . Considerable surprise was expressed when they reached the high price of $515 a volume." This was paid by the Philadelphia firm of Lea & Shepard, which also purchased the *Household Dickens*, together totaling about $9,000. Houghton purchased the "Library" Dickens, in a larger format, together with the works of Thomas De Quincey and a set of plates to Scott's Waverley novels, for just over $17,000. The plates to a set of Jules Verne also aroused considerable interest, selling for nearly $7,000. "Those to whom the sale was of most service were, as some one said at the Fair, of three classes: publishers just starting business, or who had but small lists which they wished to extend; the owners of printing establishments which they wished to keep busy, who would naturally seek the plates; and the jobbers and larger retailers who had the capital and custom to handle the stock.... It is rather curious to note that the presence or absence of copyright on a book seemed to make very little difference on the price."[66]

The sale certainly offered the opportunity for a large-scale redistribution of plates across the entire US publishing industry. Osgood was able to raise a significant amount of cash, at least for one more year, and the trades seemed satisfied on the whole.

In another shift away from the trade sale auction format, New York auctioneers Bangs Brothers began to offer a "parcel sale" twice a year beginning in the 1870s that was almost as popular as the trade fair. It was first distinguished by its emphasis on foreign titles and then shifted to supply more remaindered stock. After the trade sales shifted into trade fairs with fixed-price sales, Bangs continued to offer parcel sales in an auction format until 1903. Following this, the Syndicate Trading Company and other cheap book specialists and distributors took control of the remaindered book market in the United States.[67] Bangs attempted to hold a sale of remainders and plates in 1895, which *Publishers' Weekly*—the organ of the association—disapproved of, calling it just another revival of the "old evils of the trade sales."[68] By the turn of the century, the ideal of an organized and united American book trade had still not quite been realized. The marketplace had changed and expanded in new ways beyond what institutions like the American Book Trade Association could have expected or could control. Cheap reprint publishers and book distributors filled some of the earlier roles of the trade sales and secondhand marketplace in books and plates, as the industry continued to expand in size and volume.

CHAPTER 5

꧁ Stereotyping in Language, Literature, and Material Culture

As publishers celebrated what they claimed was increased textual accuracy and authority resulting from casting and printing editions from stereotype plates, a multiplicity of new forms of copying and printing in the antebellum period served instead to challenge notions of authority. While publishers celebrated stereotyping as a positive advance, doubts about mechanical reproduction and the proliferation of new advances in technology in print and visual culture spread subtly outward from the printing trades into broader areas of popular culture. This chapter examines some of the ways in which printing with plates resonated with and affected aspects of nineteenth-century cultural life, beginning with its connections to authorship, its uses in literature, and its role in African American printing and publishing. It will show how some of the new meanings created by the introduction and popularization of stereotyping and electrotyping became infused into the language of everyday life. Concepts of mechanical reproduction that were first used in the printing trades became metaphors used by individuals attempting to understand the implications of technological change, industrialization, new economies, and race relations.

In literary studies, for much of the twentieth century, the standard interpretation of the relationship between nineteenth-century US authors and technology explained that American Romanticism (at least as expressed through the canonical white male authors of the American Renaissance) either expressed itself in opposition to technological advances or was at best ambivalent about them.¹ A work such as Thoreau's *Walden* was seen as the epitome of this argument. If, as Leo Marx argued, the mechanization of American life though industrial advances and the growth of factories spoiled the inherently naturalistic aspects of American thought, life, and aspirations, then the role of the individual, especially as a single authorial voice, was diminished, even crushed. This sensibility, however, was at odds with the widespread and mostly uncritical embrace of technology by the people of the United States throughout the entire nineteenth century. As Klaus Benesh writes, "Given the pervasiveness, and, what is more, rhetorical fervor with which nineteenth-century Americans embraced technology as the new driving force of cultural development, the literary writers of this period were clearly at a loss as to how they should define their professional identity."² Benesh argues that technology not only challenged the autonomy of an American authorial identity but also offered alternatives to the singular vision of individualistic expression, including an ideology that instead favored, at least in part, the replacement of the human body by machines.

Recent scholarship tends to complicate this relationship, seeking to better understand how a multiplicity of American authors of different races and genders interacted directly with technology, actively considered its implications, and saw scientific and technological advances as positive forces. The "question concerning technology," as Heidegger put it, and its role in defining American literary sensibilities is much more complex, and the challenges of technological advances to American identity and authorial perceptions of self and nation continue to be explored in interesting ways.³

Stereotyping, a fully realized component of the printing trades by the 1820s, would have been familiar to many nineteenth-century authors from its outset, and especially to the many authors who had backgrounds in journalism and other direct connections to the printing trades. Edgar Allan Poe's 1845 essay "Anastatic Printing" argues for the great authorial advantages of an even newer process that could bypass stereotyping altogether. Anastatic printing, at least as Poe understood it, could reproduce an author's own hand exactly as it was written on the manuscript page. In this process, a written or printed text was treated with an acid solution and pressed on a zinc plate so that it etched out the empty space, creating a positive plate of the source document. Using anastatic printing, Poe wrote, "anything written, drawn, or printed, can be made to *stereotype itself*, with absolute accuracy, in five minutes."⁴ This technology could allow authors to self-stereotype their work without the intervention of secondary, meddling editors or printing craftsmen, effectively automating the creative process and bringing authors into more intimate contact with their readers through the direct impressions left by their own hands on paper, which would then be reproduced in many copies.

In citing its advantages, Poe noted that authorship had become stale and conventional, as authors were forced to conform to the styles, language, and format that publishers demanded of them. Poe was always wary and critical of magazine and book publishers who exploited authors and abused or negated their copyrights, so this new technology must have seemed a revelation to him.[5] Anastatic printing allowed authors the freedom to create a manuscript exactly as they wished, inserting drawings or diagrams as desired, and then generate the plates themselves, which they could either offer to a publisher or self-publish. These plates, which would not use conventional type in their preparation, appeared to be something like the relief etchings that William Blake invented for his own books half a century earlier.

There were other antecedents to these processes. A form of relief etching on stone—a precursor to lithography—was practiced in France at the turn of the nineteenth century, the etched stone being used as a stereotype plate.[6] Poe argued that textual accuracy would no longer be a concern, and that the scribal profession would thrive as the reading public moved away from the convention of standard printed letterforms. Readers would instead come to prefer the immediacy and connection realized by reading authors in their own hands, technologically reproduced in a finished book. The most important advantage Poe saw in this process was its potential to shift the value contained in a conventionally printed book away from its material value as a unit of publisher's profit back to its more important literary value and the connection between author and reader. Poe noted that when publishers were forced to value works by deciding which were to be stereotyped and which were not, the capital invested in this physical literary property swayed every publisher's decision, often to the detriment of literary value and authorial interest:

> The value of every book is a compound of its literary value and its physical or mechanical value as a product of physical labor applied to the physical material. But at present the latter value immensely predominates, even in the works of the most esteemed authors. It will be seen, however, that the new condition of things will at once give the ascendency to the literary value, and thus by their literary values will books come to be estimated among men. . . . In the new regime, the humblest will speak as often and

as freely as the most exalted, and will be sure of receiving just that amount of attention which the intrinsic merit of their speeches may deserve.[7]

Alas, Poe's democratic vision of authorship, consciously bypassing publishers and speaking directly to readers, never came to pass; anastatic printing never became the force he thought it would. Some echoes of this leveling of speech between the humble author and the powerful publisher can certainly be seen in the mimeo/xerographic revolution of the mid-twentieth century, when new tabletop publishing technologies became widely used by artists, authors, and political groups for self-expression and social change, in contemporary artists' books, self-published genre fiction, and zines.[8]

Like Poe before him, Walt Whitman wanted to control the textual accuracy, appearance, and distribution of his literary output in ways that challenged traditional publishing. Unlike Poe and most authors, then or since, Whitman mostly succeeded. If Poe's vision of technology freeing authors to create a new and more personal bond with their readers was not realized through plate-making, engraving, or lithographic processes, Whitman, throughout his poetic career, was able to find ways to make his work appear to his readers in the singular way he envisioned. The 1855 self-published first edition of *Leaves of Grass* was printed from type, some of which Whitman set himself in the Rome brothers' Brooklyn printshop, in a large-format edition of about 795 copies. But the following year, upon bringing out an expanded self-published edition of the work, this time as a smaller, more conventionally sized volume, Whitman paid to have stereotype plates made of it, surely anticipating multiple reprints over time now that the work better resembled a conventional book of poetry.[9]

Whitman wrote to Ralph Waldo Emerson in August 1856, presenting him with a second-edition copy of *Leaves of Grass*, "Here are thirty-two Poems which I send you, dear Friend and Master, not having found how I could satisfy myself with sending any usual acknowledgement of your letter. The first edition, on which you mailed me that till now unanswered letter, was twelve poems—I printed a thousand copies, and they readily sold; these thirty-two Poems I stereotype, to print several thousand copies of. I much enjoy making poems."[10] Whitman is bragging to Emerson about his print runs and the need to bring out a second stereotype edition, but his reference to enjoying "making poems" clearly has a dual meaning. Like Blake before him, Whitman was both the author and the maker of his poems, the poet/creator as well as the craftsman/artist responsible for bringing his singular vision of how a poem should be "made" and then appear to its readers here via the stereotype plates that

Whitman created, owned, and printed from, truly "making poems" himself in every possible way, both mental and physical. Fowler and Wells, the progressive phrenological publishers who distributed his 1855 first edition, also served as the unacknowledged publishers of the 1856 second edition. They advertised it as a "neat pocket volume," recently stereotyped in an edition of one thousand copies, with themselves acting as agents.[11] Sales of the new edition, however, were not strong, and a reprint was never made from the stereotype plates. Four years later, Whitman successfully negotiated with the Boston publishers Thayer and Eldridge to bring out a more conventionally published third edition, having added still more poems to the book and made textual changes to some of the earlier poems. The fate of Whitman's second-edition stereotype plates is not known. They were textually outdated by 1860, and he probably sold them as scrap metal, the common fate of outdated or worn stereotype plates.

Paths to authorship and the ways in which authors negotiated the expanded publishing landscape in the two decades before the Civil War have been the subject of much recent scholarship, adding depth to our understanding of the multiplicity of antebellum literary cultures and the multiple ways in which men and women from widely different backgrounds became published authors.[12] In printing and publishing during these decades, power presses were introduced, national distribution methods were greatly expanded, and new venues for authorship proliferated, especially in the growing periodical press through reprinting practices. Because of these technological changes, the literary landscape and marketplace of the 1840s and 1850s was vigorous and complex in ways that it had not been a generation before.[13]

Literary works as a genre were initially less likely to be cast in stereotype plates. The potential demand for reprinted novels by even established authors was not guaranteed, and hence presented a much greater risk than stereotyping a steady-selling schoolbook. There were exceptions: Harper & Brothers decided early on, in the 1820s, to stereotype the majority of the new books it published, regardless of genre, reasoning that it would have a greater investment in plates for later use rather than having to pay multiple composition costs, and that the balance of expenditures between reprinted and nonreprinted works favored a greater initial capital investment in plates.[14] Later on, Harper would create contracts with its authors so that many of the production costs, including the casting of plates, came out of the author's royalties. Ronald Zboray has argued that the introduction of stereotyping also caused publishers to commit to long-term relationships with authors and their bodies of work, hoping that readers would purchase new and older works from a publisher's backlist as they discovered them: "Stereotyping and electrotyping encouraged publishers to engage in in-depth, long-term advertising campaigns to boost not only the sales of the particular work but also the author's celebrity, in the hopes of pushing his or her previous works."[15]

By contrast, as late as 1850, the Boston publisher Ticknor and Fields chose to have two editions of Hawthorne's *Scarlet Letter* separately composed and printed from type before finally investing in a set of plates for the book's third edition, despite Hawthorne's already stellar reputation, with a readership that seemed all but certain to purchase multiple reprints of his first novel. Michael Winship speculates that the reason for this ultimately costly decision may be that Ticknor and Fields was expanding its list at the time and may not have wanted the up-front expense of paying for plates (roughly twice the cost) in addition to composition, even though Hawthorne was not at all the typical first-time novelist. Harper & Brothers' early model of making plates for most of its books proved the exception for fiction until midcentury.[16]

Some successful authors, Henry Wadsworth Longfellow most notably, chose to embrace the new opportunities of working with publishers who printed their works from plates. Washington Irving likewise struck a very advantageous agreement with Henry C. Carey in Philadelphia for stereotyping and reprinting rights to his early novels. Other authors, like Melville, found new publishing models initially advantageous but later crippling as their popularity and readership declined with each new book. The dominant publishing model of the early nineteenth century was for a publisher to purchase an author's copyright to a work outright, or for a set number of years, in exchange for a lump-sum payment. A few decades later, a shared-profit model on works was often arranged between author and publisher, in which the author retained copyright but received payment only after the expenses related to publication were met by initial sales. Thus, in the case of a poorly selling work, the publisher could at least recoup much of the production expense, often to the author's disadvantage.

As stereotyping became a viable option for literary works, some publishers allowed authors to pay for the cost of stereotyping out of advance profits, thus allowing them to own their own plates, with which they could then potentially negotiate future reprintings of a work. If there was no demand for a reprint, the publisher was compensated for the cost of making the plates. This model greatly benefited popular authors who could consistently sell new books. Through this method, Longfellow was able to realize an unheard of 18.25 percent royalty, working with his publisher to offer collections of his works at different prices to many sectors of the marketplace, like the family Bibles of the 1810s and 1820s, all of which were printed from the same sets of plates.[17] Melville, by contrast, after the initial success of *Typee* and *Omoo*, found himself losing income as sales of his successive books steadily declined, to the point where he could no longer afford to buy his plates back from Harper, even at a 50 percent discount. And when he finally *was* able to purchase them, Melville found that his plates no longer commanded any real value in the marketplace.[18]

THOREAU AND THE BUSINESS OF ELECTROTYPING

Massachusetts in the early nineteenth century was the center of the nation's pencil-making industry. Because of graphite deposits (then known as plumbago, or black lead) in the eastern part of the state and in northern New England, many experimental shops and several small pencil-manufacturing factories arose in and around Concord. The most famous was John Thoreau & Co., founded by Henry David Thoreau's maternal uncle Charles Dunbar. Dunbar discovered a deposit of plumbago in Bristol, New Hampshire, in 1821 and set up a pencil business in Concord. Henry's father, John Thoreau, came in as a partner and eventually took over the business. Combining the graphite they mined with clay produced a mixture that was better for writing than any other pencil produced in the United States at that time, making Thoreau's pencils competitive with the best European imports, which still dominated the American market.[19]

Henry knew the business well and assisted in its operations while his father was alive, inventing a machine for turning graphite into powder for the electrotyping trade, which had edged out pencil-making by midcentury as the main revenue source of the business.[20] Thoreau's machine produced a finer powdered graphite than any manufactured in the United States. The company was successful enough to provide a steady stream of income for the Thoreau family, allowing John Thoreau to purchase a large house on Main Street in Concord for his family. Orders for the ground graphite first began arriving in the mid-1840s from a Boston and New York firm, Smith & McDougal, whose owners realized that powdered graphite was the ideal substance with which to coat a plate for the newly developed electrotyping process. Electrotyping, first done in the United States in 1841, used a wax mold impressed onto set type or images. The mold was then coated with powdered graphite for conductivity

FIG. 12   "Adding plates to an electrotyping vat." From "Stereotyping and Electrotyping," in *The Great Industries of the United States, Being an Historical Summary of the Origin, Growth, and Perfection of the Chief Industrial Arts of This Country* (Hartford: J. B. Burr & Hyde; Chicago: J. B. Burr, Hyde & Co., 1874), 175. Image courtesy of Special Collections and Archives, Furman University Library.

and immersed in a copper solution bath for several hours with an electric current passing through the tank (see fig. 12). Copper atoms adhered to the surface over time, creating a precise impression as a thin plate on top of the wax form. The resulting plate was then backfilled with type metal and used for printing. Electrotyping's initial advantage was its superiority in reproducing fine-line wood and steel engravings, but by the 1850s it was beginning to overtake stereotyping for book production work as well.[21] Graphite was also a key ingredient in the stereotype process, used to finely coat the plaster molds before the molten alloy was poured in, allowing the mold to break free from the plate without sticking or clogging up small openings. By midcentury, the Boston Type and Stereotype Factory, the largest in New England, needed considerable supplies of graphite to operate, pressuring the pencil industry for a greater share of its raw materials. The Thoreaus' business was perfectly placed to take advantage of this technological change in the printing trades.

Smith & McDougal wished to keep their improved electrotyping process secret and asked the Thoreaus to remain silent about their orders for powdered graphite. In the early 1850s, the Thoreaus were receiving $10 a pound for their ground graphite and selling six hundred pounds a year. Once Smith & McDougal's secret leaked to the printing trades and more electrotypers entered the market, prices dropped, but the resulting rise in additional orders for Thoreau-manufactured graphite kept the family business nearly as profitable as before. By 1854, the Thoreaus were doing business with multiple electrotyping firms in Boston, New York, Philadelphia, and the Midwest, and their pencil-making business had been transformed almost completely into a graphite business for supplying the printing trades. "John Thoreau, Pencil Maker" began advertising "Plumbago, Prepared Expressly for Electrotyping" in major city newspapers.[22] The graphite, which initially came from the mine in New Hampshire, was also sourced in Canada. As late as 1860, Thoreau had 1,068 pounds shipped from a graphite mine near Sturbridge, Massachusetts, to Concord. The graphite business continued to be run by the family after John Thoreau's death in 1859, and by his mother for a short time following Henry's death in 1862, before being sold. The work, which was carried on in the "ell" extension of the family's house, produced such a fine cloud of graphite powder that visitors to the Thoreaus' house observed it resting on the family piano's keys when the lid was opened.[23]

Henry Thoreau was no stranger to stereotyping and electrotyping; indeed, their growth during his lifetime was the primary source of his family's prosperity. Thoreau made several visits to Mount Monadnock in southern New Hampshire between 1844 and 1860, writing about it in his journal. In addition to exploring the area and climbing the mountain, the primary reason for these trips was to inspect a graphite mine on one side of the mountain. Thoreau needed to visit it as a potential source of raw materials for the family business at a time, late in the 1840s, when Smith & McDougal's orders for ground graphite were beginning to increase substantially.[24]

While Thoreau never commented directly on the mechanical processes of stereotyping or electrotyping in his writings, he used stereotyping as a metaphor on multiple occasions. In a letter to Emerson of 17 October 1843, written on Staten Island, where he was spending some months looking for literary work in New York and tutoring Emerson's nephew, Thoreau used the term "stereotype" to mean an unimaginative copy when critiquing a poem Emerson had sent him: "I like the poetry, especially the Autumn verses.... But I have a good deal of fault to find with your ode to Beauty. The tune is altogether unworthy of the thoughts.... 'Remediless thirst' are some of those stereotyped lines."[25] In those lines, where Emerson lapsed into cliché (the French word for stereotype), Thoreau called them stereotyped—with its multiple meanings—as a way to describe something copied over and over again without any original thought.

A few years later, in the "Sunday" chapter of his first book, *A Week on the Concord and Merrimack Rivers*, Thoreau argued for the superiority of poetry over all other forms of writing, stating that, when written by its greatest artists, such as Homer, poetry captures the essence of nature itself: "His more memorable passages are as naturally bright as gleams of sunshine in misty weather. Nature furnishes him not only with words, but with stereotyped lines and sentences from her mint."[26] Here, the stereotype is instead a perfect copy and a positive thing; stereotyping is a metaphor for the poet's ability to perfectly capture the essence of a thing—nature—and reproduce it on the page through the medium of language. The true poet is a medium for mechanically reproducing the complexity of nature to an exacting standard, just as nature copies her own products in her "mint." The stereotyped copy, wielded by one of the great poets, is as close to the original—nature—as art can create.[27] Later in the book, in the chapter titled "Wednesday," in a passage on friendship, Thoreau writes, "A true Friendship is as wise as it is tender. The parties to it yield implicitly to the guidance of their love, and know no other law nor kindness. It is not extravagant and insane, but what it says is something established henceforth, and will bear to be stereotyped. It is a truer truth, it is better and fairer news, and no time will ever shame it, or prove it false."[28] In this passage, about his brother John, knowledge gained from a true friendship is something that should be copied or replicated directly with others. Thoreau may also be hinting that if a friendship is "true," it will hold up to the pressures of being copied many times over, just as a stereotype copy of a text or image can be stereotyped multiple times and printed from without any alteration or degradation in either the original or the copy. The exact fidelity of the stereotyped copy to its original here is so precise as to allow Thoreau to use the term "stereotype" for greater effect, rather than simply saying "a copy."

Finally, in a passage about the nature of poetry in the "Friday" chapter, Thoreau writes, "The true poem is not that which the public read. There is always a poem not printed on paper, coincident with the production of this, stereotyped in the poet's life. *It is what he has become through his work.* Not how is the idea expressed in stone, or on canvas or paper, is the question, but how far it has obtained form and expression in the life of the artist."[29] Here, Thoreau makes a direct reference to Emerson's essay "The Poet," published five years before, in which Emerson states that in artistic sensibility there is poetry, and vice versa. The poet's life itself becomes a poem, both of who he is and of how he chooses to see, live, and write. Simple copying is apparently not enough here to complete Thoreau's metaphor—instead, the poem is "stereotyped in the poet's life." Thoreau's metaphorical use of the term "stereotyping" equates it with a sort of divine copying, occurring at the level of nature or spirit and elevating the concept beyond human ability. These instances show that Thoreau placed great value on the ability of a metal alloy stereotype plate in a printshop to perform exactly as it was intended to, at the same time transcending mere copying and crafting a bridge between body and spirit. Technology, even for someone as skeptical of it as Thoreau was, can be a liberating force. The idea that the technology of stereotyping directly influenced Thoreau's writing about nature provides a new understanding of Thoreau's relationship with technology. There is nothing particularly denigrating here in his choice of words and metaphors, only a sense of refined elevation and reverence for the stereotyper's—and the stereotype's—literal and metaphorical art of reproduction. And with the growing electrotyping trade providing the bulk of his family's prosperity, Thoreau's relationship with technological advances becomes increasingly complicated—and interesting—as a subject for further investigation.

Thoreau used stereotyping as a metaphor again in *Walden* several years later. In the first chapter, "Economy," in the same paragraph that contains the famous sentence "The mass of men lead lives of quiet desperation," this sentence appears: "A stereotyped but unconscious despair is concealed even under what are called the games and amusements of mankind."[30] Thoreau's purpose in *Walden*—to show his readers a better way to live—allows him to use a stereotyping metaphor in a different way than in *A Week on the Concord and Merrimack Rivers*. Here, stereotyping becomes a mechanical form of copying, linking modern technology to modernity in an unfortunate manner, opposed to the elevated transcendence of its use in his earlier writings. In the passage from *Walden*, Thoreau links copying to hiddenness or concealment, arguing against the value of technological progress by linking it to an unfortunate manner of copying. In the "Sounds" chapter, he uses the metaphor differently, this time for exact copying in nature when referring to the sound of an owl. This is more akin to the way stereotyping is used in *A Week on the Concord and Merrimack Rivers*: "I was also serenaded by a hooting owl. Near at hand you could fancy it the most melancholy sound in Nature, as if she meant by this to stereotype and make permanent in her choir the dying moans of a human being."³¹ The owl copies another sound in imitation, but it is also an unsettling and unfortunate sound. Thoreau's final use of the term in *Walden* appears in his final chapter, "Spring," when he discusses the "tonic of wildness" and the human need to experience nature in all its forms, including death and unpleasantness: "Poison is not poisonous after all, nor are any wounds fatal. Compassion is a very untenable ground. It must be expeditious. Its pleadings will not bear to be stereotyped."³² Here, stereotyping is a form of copying that one is ill advised to make, lacking any inherent utility or merit. Compassion's unsuitability to be reproduced honestly makes it an improper candidate for stereotyping. Attempts to reproduce compassion when looking at nature only distance oneself from the natural balance between life and death. This form of stereotyping is an unnatural intrusion and shows its limitations as a mechanical process.³³

Thoreau was not alone in using this new technology as a metaphor. The term "stereotype," used as a synonym or metaphor for an identical copy, appears in print beginning in the 1820s. In 1828, for example, the *Harvard Register* published a "Letter from a Country Schoolmaster," in which the author describes his arrival in a seaside town: "It was on a cold, drizzly morning,—a continuation of a series of days, so gloomy and wet as to beget the idea that this kind of weather had been stereotyped."³⁴ For the schoolmaster, each day in this new town is an exact copy of the previous one; the gloomy weather seems to have been stereotyped and printed from the same celestial plate. Here, the stereotype is something cold and mechanical, and one can see early hints at a negative connotation. A bright, sunny day is never described in print as being stereotyped. In *Dred: A Tale of the Dismal Swamp* (1856), Harriet Beecher Stowe writes of the character Father Bonnie: "Very little of the stereotype print of his profession had he."³⁵ In Melville's *Pierre* (1852), a novel in part about the New York publishing world of the 1840s and 1850s, the title character receives a portentous letter about his past. Trying to convince himself that it is only an invitation to a dinner party or the like, he tells himself to open it: "quick, fool, and write the stereotyped reply: Mr. Pierre Glendinning will be very happy to accept Miss so and so's polite invitation."³⁶ In literary circles, stereotyping by the mid-1850s had already devolved into a metaphor for a sort of unthinking copy, the sort of rote reproduction without human element or emotion that loses all traces of creative originality. Arguments for the benefits of textual accuracy that one found in the language of stereotyping early in the century had by now been replaced by colder, impersonal images of rote mechanical reproduction.

OWNING ONE'S OWN WORDS: SOJOURNER TRUTH, WILLIAM WELLS
BROWN, AND AFRICAN AMERICAN "STEREOTYPES"

In addition to a growing metaphorical use in literature and everyday language, the material nature of stereotyping and the proliferation of stereotype plates in publishing had immediate relevance to the lives of the group of African American authors and publishers who were able to navigate pathways into print at this time. The writings of the abolitionist movement were rooted in an evangelical culture of morality that was often in tension with the market economy of goods and services. One resulting strategy adopted by reformers was to encourage a form of "evangelical consumerism," different from the charitable practices of the American Bible Society described in chapter 3 and rooted in a competitive publishing marketplace that used its moral center as an incentive to sales and reformist ideas.[37] In addition to tracts and narratives of enslaved individuals, the American Anti-Slavery Society produced annual antislavery almanacs beginning in 1836. The Boston Female Anti-Slavery Society published a literary annual, the *Liberty Bell*, from 1839 to 1858.

Sojourner Truth, who was born enslaved in upstate New York, remained illiterate her entire life. Yet her life story, in the form of a narrative first published in 1850, appeared in several editions during her lifetime, and its success helped to sustain her financially for more than twenty-five years. Truth's success as an author and financial well-being were predicated on her engagement with the creation and selective use of sets of stereotype plates to her works, as much as or more than the printed cartes de visite—photographic cards bearing her likeness—that she also sold to supporters at her many speaking engagements. The first edition of Truth's *Narrative* was published for her on credit in 1850 by an abolitionist printer in Boston, James M. Yerrinton, who also printed William Lloyd Garrison's periodical the *Liberator*. Truth, a free woman since 1826, had little savings and worried about taking on debt together with the considerable risk of having a set of plates made to a book that she was unsure would sell. After its appearance, Truth worked steadily on the abolitionist lecture circuit, eager to pay off the printer's bill and secure some savings of her own. Three years later, the first edition was sold out. As a way of financing a new edition, her friend James Boyle purchased the plates from her, holding them in trust until she would need them again. The plates, while still effectively belonging to Truth, remained in the possession of Boyle, a "spiritualist-physician" whom Truth had known in New York City as early as 1838. Boyle had helped her negotiate her contract with Yerrinton and so was a trusted friend.[38] The second edition was printed in 1853, and Truth continued to sell copies to audiences at her lectures.

Augusta Rohrbach discusses the seeming paradox of Truth's illiteracy, despite her being a published author, by arguing that her presence in the book occurs as both a form of language and a visual presence in the form of the woodcut illustration of the author at the front. Truth's amanuensis Olive Gilbert stated in the narrative that the impression made by Truth on her auditors in creating the book "can never be transmitted to paper . . . till by some Daguerrian act we are able to transfer the look, the gesture, the tones of voice, in connection with the quaint, yet fit expressions used, and the spirit-stirring animation that, at such a time, pervades all she says."[39] For Gilbert, Truth's words were transmitted into the printed books, but her true likeness, unlike Thoreau's vision of the great poet stereotyping nature on the page, could not be captured. There was no technology available for Gilbert, not even a daguerreotype or stereotype plate, that could convey a true likeness of such an animated personality as Truth.

While the first two editions did not include introductions, the 1855 third edition of Truth's *Narrative* included a notable one by Harriet Beecher Stowe, and the book continued to sell well, affording Truth a steady income for many years. In 1875, when she was very ill, friends rallied to her home in Battle Creek, Michigan. Boyle gave her back the plates to her *Narrative* that he had held in trust, and an 1876 edition was brought out, arranged and subsidized by Frances Titus, another friend. This edition was expanded to include one volume of her new work, the *Book of Life*.[40]

Throughout this twenty-five-year period, the stereotype plates to her *Narrative* remained Truth's major piece of literary property, a material text that allowed her autonomy and income. The plates, and the capital represented in them, were first financed on credit to purchase, then lent, and then used as a gift at different times in her life by their shared trustees. Their possession by James Boyle was a practical arrangement struck by Truth in order to see her life story printed and distributed, an investment toward a steady future income where a substantial initial amount was needed to start the publication process. The plates to her *Narrative* represented freedom and the means to acquire stability and a steady income.

As Rohrbach notes, "Unlike Douglass, however, Truth chose to shoulder all the costs of publication herself so that she could control not just the copyright of her book, but also the physical plates from which the book was made.

Owning the stereotype plates meant controlling how many editions were printed.... By owning the plates, authors could license the right to print the book as well as negotiate for the degree of profit from the sales."[41] Truth sold her book for only twenty-five cents a copy and preferred to have copies simply bound in paper wrappers, which was a very different approach from the standard seventy-five cents to $1.25 cost of a cloth-bound narrative sold by the antislavery societies. Truth refused to raise its price, believing that a cheap book would circulate more widely than a more expensive one. As her book was only one source of her income, lectures and signed cartes de visite mutually reinforced each other, her cause, and her livelihood.[42]

William Wells Brown, the first African American novelist (*Clotel*, 1853), had an extensive career as an author in several genres, and like Sojourner Truth he successfully negotiated authorship and the publishing world to his advantage. Born enslaved about 1815 in Lexington, Kentucky, Brown received some early training in the printing trades. He was hired out by his enslaver to work for Elijah P. Lovejoy, the editor of the *St. Louis Times*, at the paper's main office. Lovejoy employed several free and enslaved men at the paper. In subsequent years, Lovejoy became an outspoken abolitionist editor and was killed by a mob that attacked him in Alton, Illinois, in 1843, the only abolitionist to die in the North. When Brown worked for Lovejoy at the *Times* in the 1830s, he ran errands, assisted the owners, and also occasionally operated the press. He wrote in his 1847 *Narrative* about being sent to other newspaper offices to retrieve forms of set type and how he was able to learn the basics of literacy while working in and around the printshop. In his biography of Brown, Ezra Greenspan concludes that he exaggerated the level of literacy he obtained while working in the newspaper office and also suggests that Lovejoy's politics in the early 1830s was far less progressive than his stand on racial equality later on.[43] Lovejoy's death at the hands of proslavery forces more than a decade after these incidents occurred made him into an international martyr for the abolitionist cause and therefore worthy of memorialization by the time Brown's *Narrative* appeared in 1847, four years after Lovejoy's death.

Brown escaped to freedom in 1834 and lived in the Northeast, working for abolitionist and reform causes and becoming a prolific author. When Brown traveled to England and Ireland in 1849 to lecture as part of the antislavery movement and as a chosen delegate to the International Peace Congress in Paris, he carried a second set of stereotype plates to his *Narrative* with him on the ship. Like Frederick Douglass before him in 1845, Brown traveled, immediately upon arrival in Liverpool, to Dublin to have an Irish edition of his

Narrative quickly struck off for sale before his lecture tour. Brown writes in his memoir of his European travel that in addition to the stereotype plates in his luggage, he also took with him "an *Iron Collar* that had been worn by a female slave on the banks of the Mississippi." Arriving at the customs office in Liverpool, the collar became an object of great interest in the customs hall, drawing the attention of the customs inspectors and provoking embarrassment in some of the southerners who arrived on the ship with Brown: "Several of my countrymen who were standing by, were not a little displeased by answers which I gave to questions on the subject of Slavery; but they held their peace. The interest caused by the appearance of the Iron Collar, closed the examination of my luggage."[44]

Literary scholars and historians have placed considerable emphasis on the liberating effect that acquiring literacy had on enslaved people and freedmen, marking an important milestone in their identity. For Brown, traveling with the stereotype plates to his own *Narrative* and with the physical restraints used by his former enslavers meant that his own personhood and story, contained in both his living body as a witness and in his stereotype plates, made a singular journey of testimony and liberation. Jonathan Senchyne writes, "The stereotype plates in Brown's traveling case remind us that producing oneself as a free subject in print and in life is embedded within a set of material textual practices—practices that are (as the double meaning of stereotype suggests) also constitutive in processes of racialization."[45] Brown was intimately connected to the set of plates to his *Narrative* as both a foundation of selfhood and a means of independence and liberation. His body and the embodied words of his *Narrative* as stereotype plates both constitute forms of witness and authority, and on that journey they were inseparable. Like Sojourner Truth's path to print, Brown's stereotype plates represent liberation in the form of economic independence, but they also constitute a greater interconnected path of material narrativity. Brown lent his plates to a printer in Dublin and worked with a publisher in London so they could strike off a European edition of the *Narrative*, which was then sold as he lectured in England, Ireland, Scotland, and France. Brown's successful negotiation of the world of transatlantic and transnational publishing afforded him a degree of agency and independence that set him apart from many of his fellow abolitionist speakers.[46]

While the printing and publishing work of the abolitionist movement has been well documented, locating evidence of the African American presence in the printing trades and publishing industry in the colonial, early national, and antebellum periods is particularly difficult, though recent scholarship is greatly increasing our body of knowledge.[47] Isaiah Thomas, in his *History of Printing in America*, notes several individuals enslaved by eighteenth-century printers in Boston, New Hampshire, and Philadelphia.[48] Sales advertisements for enslaved people in colonial newspapers in northern colonies noted multiple individuals who had been trained as printers.[49]

With the exception of the AME Book Concern, all of the books by African American authors published in the antebellum period were printed in white-owned and -operated printing houses. The printing and publishing houses that were owned by African Americans primarily produced periodicals, beginning in 1827 with John Russwurm and Samuel Cornish's *Freedom's Journal*. Russwurm's printshop in New York City, like those of most of his contemporaries, also did job work for other printers and publishers. One short-lived concern, the John W. Leonard Company in New York City, was founded by a free Black man, James R. W. Leonard, and for two years, from 1855 through 1856, published books exclusively on Freemasonry. Leonard reprinted several core works from the Universal Masonic Library (the standard publications of Anglo-American Freemasonry) and some additional works on masonry before selling his business to a white publisher in 1856. Leonard then worked as a job printer under his own name until at least 1870.[50] Leonard's books, bearing a New York imprint, were printed and bound in Louisville, Kentucky, by at least two different printers and were first stereotyped in New York City by the established stereotyping and electrotyping firm of Holman & Gray.[51] Leonard clearly took advantage of favorable printing costs in Louisville in choosing to ship his New York–cast plates to Kentucky, probably through fellow Masonic connections and networks. The New York jobbing trade, charging more for printing and binding, would not necessarily have been averse to taking on printing jobs from plates owned by a Black publisher.

Leonard's older brother William was also listed as a printer in the New York census of 1850, though no imprints of his own were ever issued under his own name. Richmond believes that he worked for Martin Delany on the *Anti-Slavery Standard* in New York and its successor, the *National Standard*, and may have printed works for the American Anti-Slavery Society but without his name listed.[52]

A second firm, Thomas Hamilton, Sr., published both the *Anglo-African Magazine* and a number of books on Black Africana by African Americans during the Civil War years.[53] It was continued after Hamilton's death by his brother Robert and son William G. Hamilton. They published Robert

Campbell's *Pilgrimage to My Motherland: An Account of a Journey Among the Egbas and Yorubas of Central Africa, in 1859–60*. This book was printed and stereotyped in New York for Hamilton by the white printer and stereotyper John A. Gray. During the Civil War, Hamilton also published two impressions of William Wells Brown's *The Black Man: His Antecedents, His Genius, and His Achievements* (1863), which was first stereotyped at the Boston Stereotype Foundry and printed in New York.[54] Black-owned publishers needed white-owned stereotype firms to cast their plates and white jobbing printers to print their books, and that work could happen in the printing trades in New York at this time.

Despite these gains, and even after the war years, African Americans employed in the printing trades alongside whites, even in the urban North, were never large in number. W. E. B. Du Bois's 1899 study of black employment in Philadelphia notes only three Black job printing shops, ten Black adults who identified as printers, and three male and two female typesetters out of the hundreds of individuals employed in the printing trades in that city.[55]

From its beginnings in the United States in the 1810s, stereotyping represented a technological advance that allowed for wider and potentially more accurate reproduction of material texts. As its use became more widespread, stereotyping became a mechanism for copying that somehow left part of its original essence of hand craft, individual attention, and artisan spirit behind. It became a metaphor for industrialization, together with all the assumptions about dehumanization that accompanied rapid technological change. But, for some authors, stereotyping and stereotypes also became tools of liberation and independence. As authors, publishers, and workers in the printing trades attempted to understand and manage their work in a rapidly changing environment, so too did the public at large identify a convenient metaphor in stereotyping for describing the vague uneasiness in many aspects of everyday life manifested through these changes. In short, stereotyping itself became stereotyped, and we must still work through its consequences in our own uses of the term.

❧ Epilogue
Abraham Hart and Nineteenth-Century Changes in the Printing Trades

Philadelphia publisher Abraham Hart retired from the trade in 1854. His firm, Carey & Hart, run with Mathew Carey's younger son, Edward, had published general-interest titles in Philadelphia since the 1820s. Following Carey's death in 1845, Hart ran the firm alone. In closing the business, he put his entire backlist of stock and a substantial collection of 103 sets of stereotype plates (some with copyrights attached) up for auction at the 1854 Philadelphia trade sale. It was the largest group of plates ever to come onto the market at one time. Advertisements placed by the auctioneers in trade journals such as *Norton's Literary Gazette* and in daily newspapers up and down the East Coast called readers' attention to the upcoming sale, noting, "This is the first Sale of Stereotype Plates, of like magnitude, that has taken place in the United States." Hart's lots of plates filled thirty pages of trade sale catalog copy in addition to the three pages of stereotype plates offered by other consignees. The event was sufficiently newsworthy to receive national press coverage.[1]

Auction lots at the trade sales traditionally came up by publisher in alphabetical order, so when the book offerings of Harper & Brothers were to be sold, James Harper, the cofounder and ex-mayor of New York, addressed the assembled audience. Knowing Abraham Hart's lots would immediately follow his own, he noted:

> It is a painful reflection to me, and I believe it is the same with all of us, that this is the last time we shall be honored by having, as a contributor to these semi-annual sales, our long-tried friend ABRAHAM HART. I most confidently affirm that, from twenty-five years dealing with him, I have never known one more honorable and generous, or more prompt, courteous, and intelligent, than my friend—than our friend—Hart. . . . The name of Hart is more than respected—it is dear to us—because it is an index to its owner's character; because he is earnest, manly, straightforward, not only as a publisher and bookseller in giving character and reputation to the trade, but as a man and a friend; because he is active and hearty in the benevolent associations whose object is to relieve the widow and orphan—the poor and the afflicted.[2]

Harper's remarks met with great applause. Hart was also allowed to address the assembled crowd of bidders when his lots came up. His remarks to Moses Thomas, the Philadelphia auctioneer, were printed in the Philadelphia-based *Godey's Lady's Book*:

> You, sir, were the *first person to introduce me into the book business*, having given me a letter of credit to purchase, at the Boston trade sale, held in 1827, when I was but sixteen years of age, an amount of five thousand dollars, on my own judgment, a confidence which I have remembered to this day; and, two years afterwards, you were instrumental in arranging the partnership for me with the late Edward L. Carey; and now, after twenty-five years of successful business, *you* are about to conduct me out of the trade, by disposing of my stereotype plates; and I must here acknowledge my gratitude to you for those acts of kindness and confidence extended towards a mere boy.[3]

As a smaller group of his final lots of stock came up at the New York trade sale one month later, Hart thanked his many colleagues and fellow publishers, marveling at the growth and expansion of the US printing and publishing industry during his lifetime. The speed and volume with which publishers brought their works to a national marketplace in 1854 was nothing short of miraculous to those who had begun their careers early in the century. Hart noted that the Harper brothers had also started out in business on their own when the printing trades were small and had made their respective firms into large publishing operations that grew along with the trades. He was grateful for James Harper's kind words preceding his lots at the sale and offered reciprocal praise to Harper & Brothers. He noted that Harper & Brothers had brought two hundred thousand items to the trade sale in Philadelphia just three months after the major fire that completely destroyed its printing headquarters, another sign of the speed and agility the American publishing industry had now attained.[4]

Hart's remarks spoke to questions of continuity and stability in the American printing trades, something its practitioners always took special pride in. In the occasionally florid ways in which they described their work at trade sale banquets and other august occasions, their labors were nearly a calling. Printers and publishers in nineteenth-century America believed that they had a mission to create a literate Christian society and to advance American democratic values while engaged in their business.[5] As he stepped into retirement, Hart remembered the confidence shown him at an early age, a reminder to all assembled of the gentlemanly nature of their profession, one that still operated on trust and reputation. The literary property he amassed in the form of plates would now be redistributed to a new, younger group of publishers as he made his exit, prolonging his own influence by proxy as his plates received a second life in the reprint marketplace. Hart entered the printing trades as a young man at the end of the handpress era in the early 1820s and left it, a completely changed industrial publishing world, thirty years later. In 1854, the United States publishing industry was vast and varied. Large publishers competed for a truly national share of the market. Rail networks ensured national distribution methods for printed matter, regardless of weather and season. National periodicals spread news quickly, and smaller regional publishers acquired older stock and secondhand stereotype plates, publishing and selling cheap books to meet ever-increasing consumer demand for printed matter at many different price points.

Hart's lots at the sales went well. His 103 lots of plates sold back to the trade in Philadelphia and brought $55,960. His printed stock at the New York sale one month later brought between $20,000 and $25,000, which was reported by telegraph to newspapers across the country.[6] While Hart's plates were mostly steady sellers (such as his set of Scott's Waverley novels, which brought $4,000), newer plates to works in popular demand, with their copyrights still attached, could potentially command even more significant sums. John P. Jewett & Co. of Boston, despite having a huge success publishing *Uncle Tom's Cabin* in 1852, was hit hard by the Panic of 1857 and forced to mortgage its stereotype plates to it for $10,000.[7]

Other changes in the publishing industry had occurred by midcentury. In the same month as Abraham Hart's final sale of his stock, *Godey's Lady's Book*, the largest-circulation general-interest magazine for women in the United States, announced that "Back numbers of the 'Lady's Book' can be supplied from January, as the work is now stereotyped," offering readers who presumably read a borrowed copy of the journal the opportunity to order their own reprinted back issues without having initially subscribed.[8] Other periodicals had been stereotyped for several decades. The *Family Magazine* was printed simultaneously in New York, Boston, Baltimore, and Cincinnati in 1838 thanks to the multiple copies of stereotype plates made of each issue, which were sent to each city for printing and distribution.[9] *Parley's Magazine*, a children's biweekly, was printed simultaneously in Boston and Maine using multiple sets of stereotype plates beginning in 1834.

The London-based *Penny Magazine*, a product of the Society for the Promotion of Useful Knowledge, was stereotyping issues of its magazine in the mid-1830s and sending sets of plates to the United States for simultaneous printing. It was the first modern journal with a truly global outlook and distribution network. This practice raised concerns from US publishers who opposed an 1838 bill to create an international copyright law. In a petition to Congress, a group of these publishers argued that if such a law were enacted, it would further encourage foreign manufacture and importation of stereotype plates, to the detriment of domestic production. The *Penny Magazine* was targeted by name, the publishers stating that under such an agreement they would be able to send copyrighted plates to the United States to be printed from and could then export them back to Britain when done, depriving US customs of duties, as the import of the plates would effectively cancel out the export.[10] US resistance to an international copyright agreement was so strong that it took until 1891 to reach a workable agreement.

Newspaper publishers created curved stereotype plates to fit their steam-powered rotary presses, which allowed high-speed, high-volume printing of dailies using multiple copies of the same plate on each press. Other innovations to stereotype technology included adding copper facing to both type and plates, using a process similar to electrotyping, to increase durability and lessen the wearing of type and plates over time. By the late 1850s, the majority of newspapers in New York and Boston were printing from copper-faced type and plates. A notice in the *Printer* in 1863 even noted that a London firm was coating its types in silver to better facilitate color printing.[11]

Some earlier attempts to stereotype periodicals were not as successful. William Cobbett, after returning to England following his decade as the fiery journalist and publisher Peter Porcupine in Philadelphia in the 1790s, founded *Cobbett's Register*, an account and transcription of parliamentary speeches. Cobbett sold the paper to Thomas Curson Hansard in 1812, and it continues to be printed and known as *Hansard* today. Beginning in 1817, Cobbett began to have back issues of the *Register* set anew and stereotyped, anticipating a steady demand for back issues, one that never fully materialized.[12] Other initiatives, such as the *Godey's* announcement, were more successful, as the need for back issues could now be met through new impressions from plates instead of from stored printed stock. But the rush to stereotype periodicals also created its own storage problems. *Littell's Living Age* stereotyped each issue of the magazine beginning in the 1840s. By 1854, a newspaper reported that the storehouse for the *Littell's* stereotype plates alone housed upward of one thousand boxes and weighed nearly thirty tons. The proprietors then announced that "they cannot afford to retain so much capital locked up in them even as mere metal; and they accordingly propose to melt them down"— though not, of course, before printing a quantity sufficient to supply a newly announced limited-time offer for back issues.[13]

Abraham Hart left the trade in middle age, choosing to spend his later years focusing on new coal investments in Pennsylvania and working on reform issues in Philadelphia. The trade sales continued until the turn of the century, and several sets of Hart's own plates were resold and printed from by different publishers many decades later.

APPENDIX A

First Uses of Stereotype Plates in the United States, by Date and Location

The following chronological list gives the location and publisher name, followed in parentheses by the name of the foundry that made the plates, where known. Following the list is a key to the foundry names.

1812
Philadelphia, Bible Society at Philadelphia (Rutt)

1813
New York, J. Watts & Co. (Watts)

1814
New York, Collins & Co. (Collins)

1815
Boston, C. Bingham (Collins)
Hartford, Sheldon & Goodwin (Starr)
Newburyport, E. Little & Co. (unknown)
New London, Samuel Green (Starr)
New York, D. & G. Bruce (Bruce)
New York, Isaac Riley (Collins)
New York, Whiting & Watson (Bruce)
Philadelphia, Matthew Carey (Watts, purchased from Collins)
Poughkeepsie, Stockholm & Brownejohn (Collins)

1816
Albany, E. F. Backus (Collins)
Baltimore, Schäffer & Maund (Collins)
Brattleboro, John Holbrook (Collins)
Hartford, Sheldon & Goodrich (Collins)
New York, Auxiliary New-York Bible and Common Prayer Book Society (Bruce)
New York, W. Mercein (Bruce)

154 | Appendix A

New York, New York Bible Society (White)
New York, Smith & Forman (unknown)
New York, T. & J. Swords (Bruce)
Philadelphia, Bennett and Walton (Collins)
Philadelphia, Bible Society at Philadelphia (Rutt)
Philadelphia, Thomas De Silver (Bruce)
Philadelphia, Benjamin Warner (Collins)

1817
Albany, Webster and Skinner (Collins)
Boston, Lincoln and Edmands (Collins)
Bridgeport, CT, L. Lockwood (Collins)
Canandaigua, H. Underhill (Simmons)
Cooperstown, Elihu and Henry Phinney (unknown, possibly Phinney in 1816)
Exeter, NH, E. Little & Co. (unknown)
Georgetown, SC, unknown (Collins)
Hartford, S. G. Goodrich (Collins)
Haverhill, MA, Burrill and Tileston (Collins)
Keene, NH, John Prentiss (unknown, possibly Prentiss)
New York, American Bible Society (Bruce)
New York, American Bible Society (White)
New York, Robert and William A. Bartow (White)
New York, E. M. Blunt and Samuel A. Burtis (unknown)
New York, Henry Durell (unknown)
New York, W. B. Gilley (Collins)
New York, W. B. Gilley (unknown, possibly White)
New York, G. Long (unknown, possibly Long)
New York, M. Swaim & J. Howe (White and Starr)

1818
Baltimore, Joseph Robinson (unknown, possibly Bruce or White)
Boston, West and Richardson (Collins)
Boston, West, Richardson & Lord (Collins)
Boston, R. P. & C. Williams (Collins)
Hartford, Silas Andrus (Starr II)
Hartford, J. & W. Russell (unknown, possibly Starr)
Haverhill, MA, Nathan Burrill (Collins)
Hudson, NY, William E. Norman (unknown, possibly Collins)
Keene, NH, S. A. Morrison & Co. (Collins)
New York, Robert and William A. Bartow (Starr II)

New York, Collins & Hannay (Collins)
New York, Daniel D. Smith (White and Starr)
New York, J. Soule and T. Mason (White)
New York, Charles Starr (Starr II)
Norwich, CT, Russell Hubbard (unknown, possibly Starr)
Philadelphia, W. Fry (Bruce)
Pittsburgh, Cramer and Spear (Collins)
Pittsburgh, R. Patterson & Lambdin (Collins)
Poughkeepsie, Paraclete Potter (Collins)
Rochester, NY, E. Peck and Co. (Starr II)
Troy, NY, Parker and Bliss (unknown)
Utica, William Williams (unknown)
Washington, DC, D. Rapine (Collins)

1819
Exeter, NH, Charles Norris (unknown, possibly White)
Exeter, NH, John I. Williams (Collins)
Lexington, KY, Kentucky Auxiliary Bible Society (Bruce)
New York, Henry I. Megary (Bruce)

Key to Stereotype Foundries

Bruce	D. & G. Bruce, New York
Collins	Collins & Co., New York
Rutt	T. Rutt, Shacklewell, London
Simmons	H. Simmons & Co.
Starr	J. F. and C. Starr, Hartford
Starr II	Charles Starr, New York
Watts	John Watts, New York
White	E. & J. White, New York
White and Starr	E. & J. White and Charles Starr, New York

APPENDIX B

"Directions for Repairing Plates," ca. 1820

This document can be found in the General Agent & Accountant Records, John Nitchie Papers, RG#19.02, box 3, American Bible Society Archives.

1. **The punching block**
Place the plate, solid, between the fixed & moveable plates of brass, placing the letter or word to be taken out even with the notch most suitable to its size. Put a piece of broad cloth on the face of the plate to prevent the letters being injured then put the moveable brass close upon it & punch out the letters inward.

2. **Of repairing**
When any letter in a plate is injured cut it off with a narrow chisel or graver & punch a hole in the plate (according to the directions above) then with a small file cut the hole so that the letter put in may line up with the rest: lay the plate on its face & break the letter off rather below the surface of the plate then observe if the letter is displaced. If it is, it may be put right by prising the metal at the back of the plate to it either at the top, bottom, or sides; when the letter is quite right, put at the back of the plate a small quantity of resin (black resin is the best) then solder it & chisel the solder off smooth. If a battered letter is at the edge of the plate the bevel may be filed away to admit the letter & soldered at the back, and paper reduced to a pulp being placed at the side that the solder may fill up the notch in the bevel, and also to prevent the solder from running to the face of the letter should a letter be battered at the corner of the plate in punching the hole, the corner breaks off, a corner of solder must be put on; in this case paper reduced to a pulp is to be fixed to the plate to preserve a hole sufficiently large for the letter or letters to be put in & the solder must form to the level at the head or bottom of the plate. When the solder has joined take away the pulp & file the hole to the size of the letter to be admitted. Break the letter off at the back & solder it through the solder at the side & end may be filed away to make the plate square. This will require very great care as in soldering the letter the corner is very liable to melt off & the whole will have to be done over again. If a plate is broken in half it may be joined together again with solder by cutting it on each side to admit a sufficient quantity of solder to strengthen it; it will frequently happen when a plate breaks in half that may letters are injured, in this case file the holes for the letters

before you join the plates together (as you cannot with safety punch them through the solder) then put some pulp into the hole or holes to prevent the solder from running in. No more solder should at any time be used than is quite necessary, as there will be danger of melting the plate. In case a plate is so battered that it cannot be repaired, a case of moveable type may be set up & worked with the plates.

3. Imposition & care of the plates

The blocks must be imposed in chases without letters locked up at the end or sides & the proper furniture made up by 2 or 3 bad plates stuck herewith, the plates to be imposed after the blocks are on the press. Never lift the blocks from the press with the plates upon them. After a form is worked off lay the plates in a dry place on their backs. Brush them over directly with a little strong ly[e]; when the ink is sufficiently softened, wash them with clear water with a sponge, keeping the underlays as dry as possible, which with care will last for many Editions.

N.B. in case the dot of an i is broken off, or a full point, the tail of a y or f it may be replaced by a brass pin point, some of which are found herewith—a hole must be made for the point with the fine punch.

APPENDIX C

Inventory of Stereotype Plates Belonging to the American Bible Society, 1829

In February 1829, the standing committee of the managers of the American Bible Society appointed a subcommittee "to report as to what new plates are necessary to be procured and the state of those now owned by the Society." This is the resulting inventory and condition report, which can be found in the minutes of the Standing Committee of the Managers, RG #4.03, 4 March 1829, 87–89, American Bible Society Archives.

1 set in Spanish Octavo. 8000 copies taken and in good order.

1 set in French, duodecimo, gift of Br. For. & BS. 4000 Bibles and 2000 Testaments taken from them, in fair condition.

2 sets Octavo in English Long Primer which have not been used and only one set is corrected.

1 set of the same from which about 57000 copies have been printed these plates are still in good order and the text is considered the most correct of all the plates owned by the Society.

1 set of duodecimo, Brevier type about 87000 copies have been taken from this set since presented to the ABS by the NYBS and also 7000 extra Testaments and it remains in good order.

1 set of duodecimo in English minion located in Lexington Kentucky, no information is before the Committee as to the condition of these plates, but they apprehend they are considerably injured, tho' only 4 Editions have been printed from the knowledge of the Committee comprizing less than 8000 copies.

1 set of the same from which 208,625 copies have been printed. It is worn out and worth no more than the value of the metal.

1 set of the same which is now in constant use. 82,250 copies have already been struck off and about 90,000 copies more may be taken from it—it is in good order.

1 set of duodecimo in nonpareil now in constant use. 79,000 copies have been taken from it already and it will yield about as many more after undergoing the usual repairs.

A set of pocket Bibles Nonpareil & Pearl type. 14000 copies have been printed from this set.

1 set Octavo plates Brevier type received from the Baltimore BS. It rec^d some injury in the transportation but is now being repaired, and an edition will soon be printed from it.

Testaments

A set of Octavo in Pica type from which 24,000 copies have been taken and the plates are but little injured.

A set of Duodecimo in Bourgeois type. 52000 copies have been printed and the plates have been much injured by very coarse hard paper.

A set of same Long Primer type 9000 copies have been taken off and the plates in good condition.

A set of same in Spanish Bourgeois type 17125 copies have been printed and the plates are in good order.

2 sets of English 18mo Brevier type. From these sets about 192,000 have been printed. One set of the plates is worn out and the other in good preservation.

3 sets of Testaments 18mo Nonpareil type. One of these after giving 152,250 copies has been thoroughly repaired. The other two sets have not been used.

NOTES

Introduction

1. Bigelow, *Inaugural Address*, 16–17.
2. Bigelow speaks positively about stereotyping in *Elements of Technology* and describes the process in detail on 66–67.
3. Kasson, *Civilizing the Machine*, 3.
4. Quoted in Meier, "Thomas Jefferson and Democratic Technology," 21.
5. See Fyfe, *Steam-Powered Knowledge*.
6. See, for example, the five-volume *History of the Book in America*; *Cambridge History of the Book in Britain*; *History of the Book in Canada*; and *Oxford History of the Irish Book*. The treatments of stereotyping and other early mechanical innovations in the printing trades in *History of the Book in America* are extremely well done as summaries, but they necessarily lack the depth of treatment for which this book aims.
7. Kubler, a stereotyper himself and the president of the New York–based Certified Dry Mat Corporation, also wrote *A Short History of Stereotyping* (1928); *Historical Treatises, Abstracts, and Papers on Stereotyping* (1936); *Wet Mat Stereotyping in Germany in 1690* (1937); and *The Era of Charles Mahon, Third Earl of Stanhope, Stereotyper* (1938). These histories, while expansive, are also anecdotal and lack standard citations. The only recent scholarly work to take up stereotyping in the United States is Winship, "Printing with Plates." Winship acknowledges that there is much more research to be done on the growth and spread of stereotyping.
8. Peña, "'Slow and Low Progress,'" 915. For an equivalent argument in British cultural studies, see Trentmann, "Materiality in the Future of History."
9. The touchstone anthropological work is Appadurai, *Social Life of Things*. See also Winner, "Do Artifacts Have Politics?" In literary studies, "thing theory" has provided a helpful framework for exploring the meanings people make from objects. See especially B. Brown, "Thing Theory" and *Things*; Ferraris, *Documentality*.
10. Quoted in Despain, *Nineteenth-Century Transatlantic Reprinting*, 2–3. See also Altman, *Silent Film Sound*, 21.
11. Warner, *Letters of the Republic*, 8, 10.
12. Liu, "Imagining the New Media Encounter," 16.

Chapter 1

1. Babbage, *Economy of Machinery and Manufactures*, 112–13.
2. Ibid., 113.
3. See Winship, "Printing with Plates."
4. Carter, "William Ged," 161.
5. See Kubler, *New History of Stereotyping*, 147–59; Nord, *Faith in Reading*.
6. Charlton Hinman's famous study of the Shakespeare folios has shown how both corrected and uncorrected errors somehow made their way into other sheets containing

additional later corrections, making each printed copy of the First Folio essentially unique. See Hinman, *Printing and Proof-Reading*.

7. Abbot, *Harper Establishment*, 43.

8. See Gnirrep, "Standing Type or Stereotype"; Dixon, "Between Script and Specie"; Needham, "Gutenberg and the Catholicon Press"; Argüera y Arcas and Needham, "Computational Analytical Bibliography"; Katz, "Printing the 1460 Catholicon."

9. Gnirrep, "Standing Type or Stereotype." See also Carter and Buday, "Stereotyping by Joseph Athias"; McMullin, "Joseph Athias."

10. For sixteenth-century experiments, see McMurtrie, *Stereotyping in Bavaria*; Woodward, "Evidence for the Use of Stereotyping."

11. Kubler, *New History of Stereotyping*, 39–41.

12. Bishop, *History of American Manufactures*, 212. Many nineteenth-century American industrial histories and printing manuals repeat claims made by the *Encyclopaedia Britannica* and other reference works. See, for example, Coggeshall, *Five Black Arts*.

13. "Invention of Stereotyping," *Family Magazine, or, Monthly Extract of General Knowledge* 5 (1838): 384–85.

14. Carter, "William Ged," 166–68. See also Ged, *Biographical Memoirs*; Mores, *English Typographical Founders*; McMullin, "Cambridge Affair"; and Hillyard, "William Ged."

15. The two works by Sallust were *Belli Catalinarii* and *Jugurthini historiae*. The second book Ged printed was Scougal's *Life of God*, of which there are two separate impressions.

16. Carter, "William Ged," 162. See also Camus, *Histoire et procédés du polytypage*.

17. Horne, *Introduction to the Study of Bibliography*, 744.

18. Kubler, *New History of Stereotyping*, 23.

19. Partington, *Printer's Complete Guide*, 281.

20. Ibid., 282.

21. Bidwell, "Joshua Gilpin and Lord Stanhope's Improvements."

22. Turner, "Andrew Wilson."

23. "Original Paper of the Late Lieut. Gov. Colden"; Dixon, "Between Script and Specie."

24. Moore, *Historical, Biographical, and Miscellaneous Gatherings*, 75.

25. Thomas, *History of Printing in America* (1810), 165.

26. Thomas, *History of Printing in America* (1874), 32.

27. Thomas cites their correspondence, which was published as "New Method of Printing" in the *American Medical and Philosophical Register; or, Annals of Medicine, Natural History, Agriculture, and the Arts* 1 (1810): 439–46. See also Dixon, "Between Script and Specie."

28. Hunnisett, *Engraved on Steel*, 32–34, 329–30.

29. See Winship, "Printing with Plates"; Gaskell, *New Introduction to Bibliography*, 201–6.

30. Brightly, *Method of Founding Stereotype*, 41–60.

31. "Literary and Philosophical Intelligence," *Monthly Magazine* (London) 156, no. 1 (May 1807): 372–73. Wilson's letter to the *Monthly Magazine* itself refuted an assertion made the previous month in an unsigned article asserting that stereotyping was not already widely adopted because only twenty or thirty works in England could justify the expense. See "Varieties, Literary and Philosophical," *Monthly Magazine* (London) 155 (1 April 1807): 264.

32. Turner, introduction to Brightly, *Method of Founding Stereotype*, xiii–xiv.

33. Ibid., vii.

34. Timperley, *Encyclopaedia of Literary and Typographical Anecdote*, 879.

35. Hodgson, *Origin and Progress of Stereotype Printing*, 150–54.

36. Silver, *American Printer*, 96.
37. Van Winkle, *Printer's Guide* (1818), 228.
38. Van Winkle, *Printer's Guide* (1835), 26–27.
39. Quoted in Hansard, *Treatises on Printing and Type-Founding*, 134.
40. Hansard, *Typographia*, 825.
41. Partington, *Printer's Complete Guide*, 284. James Mosley suggests that sandcast copies of woodcuts made by "dabbing" were produced in the eighteenth century and perhaps earlier. See Mosley, "Introduction"; Banham, "Industrialization of the Book."
42. Johnson, *Typographia*, 657. The first American edition of Johnson's book, a one-volume abridgment published four years later, did not include his chapter on stereotyping. See Johnson, *Abridgement of Johnson's Typographia*.
43. Bigelow, *Elements of Technology*, 67.
44. Hazen, *Panorama of Professions and Trades*, 188.
45. Flint et al., *Eighty Years' Progress*, 300–301.
46. *American Dictionary of Printing and Bookmaking*, 527.
47. Silver, *American Printer*, 59. See also *Long-Island (New York) Star*, 23 October 1811; Munsell, *Typographical Miscellany*, 114.
48. Bidwell, "Joshua Gilpin and Lord Stanhope's Improvements," 155; Silver, *American Printer*, 59–61; Silver, *Typefounding in America*, 76–82.
49. Silver, *American Printer*, 60; Silver, *Baltimore Book Trade*, 10. The advertisement appeared in the *Baltimore American*, 6 May 1812, 3.
50. Kubler, *New History of Stereotyping*, 148–49. The *American Dictionary of Printing and Bookmaking* notes that Watts left New York in 1816 for Vienna and set up the first Austrian stereotype foundry (527). Rollo Silver concludes that Watts could not compete with the formidable David and George Bruce and thus chose to sell his business to Collins, their greatest competitor. *American Printer*, 60.
51. Bishop, *History of American Manufactures*, 643.
52. Silver, *American Printer*, 60.
53. Charvat, *Literary Publishing in America*, 19, 84n7.
54. Stern, *Books and Book People*, 6.
55. Crocker, "Reminiscences," 38–40, 49.
56. Silver, *American Printer*, 91–92.
57. "The Complete Coiffeur," *New-York Columbian*, 1 May 1817, 3.
58. *American Dictionary of Printing and Bookmaking*, 351.
59. Ibid., 313.
60. Quoted in Fearon, *Sketches of America*, 37.
61. *American Dictionary of Printing and Bookmaking*, 526.
62. Silver, *American Printer*, 61–62.
63. Silver, *Typefounding in America*, 51.
64. *American Dictionary of Printing and Bookmaking*, 527.
65. Chandler, *Specimen of Ornamental Types* (1820).
66. Quoted in Silver, *Typefounding in America*, 51; Chandler, *Specimen of Ornamental Types* (1822).
67. Quoted in Silver, *Typefounding in America*, 52.
68. *Norton's Literary Gazette*, 1 April 1854, 166.
69. Exman, *Brothers Harper*, 353–62. See also Exman, *House of Harper*, 41. Ironically, the Harpers' fire was started in the fireproof, zinc-lined "camphine room," which was devoted to

cleaning stereotype plates and rollers with the highly flammable substance camphine, a purified form of turpentine.

70. Silver, "Flash of the Comet."
71. Abbot, *Harper Establishment*, 102.
72. Laurie, *Artisans into Workers*, 102.
73. Barnett, "Printers," 243.
74. Laurie, *Artisans into Workers*, 102.
75. See, for example, Boutin, *Catfish in the Bodoni*; Dary, *Red Blood and Black Ink*; Howells and Dearman, *Tramp Printers*.
76. Pretzer, "'Paper Cap and Inky Apron,'" 166.
77. Stevens, *New York Typographical Union No. 6*, 142.
78. Wilentz, *Chants Democratic*, 129.
79. *Boston Courier*, 25 August 1830, 2; Baron, "Questions of Gender."
80. Abbot, *Harper Establishment*.
81. Stott, *Workers in the Metropolis*, 52.
82. Laurie, *Working People of Philadelphia*, 185.
83. Stevens, *New York Typographical Union No. 6*, 108. A long introductory statement to the association's incorporation documents, which carefully states the situation and anxieties of printers in New York at this time, is reprinted in full in the *Bulletin of the Bureau of Labor* 61 (November 1905) (Washington, DC): 896–99. See also Stewart, *Documentary History*.
84. *Proceedings of the Second National Convention of Journeymen Printers*, 8.
85. Mathew Carey, among others, argued successfully against several efforts by American Bible societies to have Congress waive standard importation duties on stereotype plates to scripture imported from England. See "Exemption from Duty," S. Doc. 482 (5 April 1816); and Mathew Carey et al., "Protection to Printers of Books," S. Doc. 572 (26 January 1820).
86. Wilentz, *Chants Democratic*, 112.
87. See J. Jackson, *Treatise on Wood Engraving*; M. Wood, *Blind Memory*.

Chapter 2

1. Green, "From Printer to Publisher," 30.
2. Green, *Mathew Carey*, 10–17.
3. Quoted in Silver, *American Printer*, 90–91; see also Green, "Rise of Book Publishing," 82–83.
4. Gaine had imported the school Bible from Scotland in the early 1790s. See Carey, *Autobiography*, 48; Silver, *American Printer*, 90. The first Bible known to be set in standing type was made by Karl Hildebrand, Baron von Canstein, in Halle in Saxony, beginning around 1710. His Cansteinsche Bibelanstalt was described as a "one-man Bible Society almost a hundred years before such institutions became common everywhere." Quoted in Howsam, *Cheap Bibles*, 75; see also Black, "Printed Bible."
5. Gutjahr, *American Bible*, 26–29.
6. Hills, *English Bible in America*, 15.
7. See, for example, *Philadelphia in 1824*, 111–12. The work was published by Carey, so it is perhaps unsurprising that the printing and publishing industry in Philadelphia is given ample coverage.
8. Mathew Carey, Accounts/Memo Book, 1812, 161–62, Lea & Febiger Records, vol. 16, Historical Society of Pennsylvania (hereafter Lea & Febiger Records). All spelling and

punctuation has been transcribed as written by Carey. See also Remer, *Printers and Men of Capital*, 95–97, 179n63.

9. Kinane, "'Literary Food.'" In addition to subscription agents in the western and southern United States, Carey sent a book agent to Mexico in 1822 for the Spanish-language markets. See Vogeley, *Bookrunner*.

10. Johnson, *Typographia*, 659.

11. Whiting & Watson to Mathew Carey, 19 August 1813, Lea & Febiger Records, box 87.

12. Kubler, *New History of Stereotyping*, 148, 153.

13. D. & G. Bruce to Mathew Carey, 9 April 1814, Lea & Febiger Records, box 88.

14. Green, *Mathew Carey*, 40; Carey, *Autobiography*, 48.

15. Bishop, *History of American Manufactures*, 633–37. As a young man in New York, David Bruce joined a gang of printers and booksellers called the Old Slippers, who clashed with their archrivals, watermen called the White Hallers. He and a friend were once attacked by the Hallers and covered in molasses and sand. See Wilentz, *Chants Democratic*, 56.

16. D. & G. Bruce to Mathew Carey, 15 April 1814, Lea & Febiger Records, box 88.

17. D. & G. Bruce to Mathew Carey, 18 October and 7 November 1814, ibid.

18. Collins & Co. to Mathew Carey, 19 October 1814, ibid.

19. D. & G. Bruce to Mathew Carey, 27 April 1814, ibid.

20. Collins & Co. to Mathew Carey, 26 October 1814, ibid.

21. Mathew Carey to Collins & Co., 24 February 1815, ibid., vol. 28.

22. Collins & Co. to Mathew Carey, 3 March 1815, ibid., box 92.

23. Mathew Carey to Collins & Co., 18 April 1815, ibid., vol. 28.

24. D. & G. Bruce to Mathew Carey, 26 April 1815, ibid., box 92.

25. Mathew Carey to D. & G. Bruce, 29 April 1815, ibid., vol. 28.

26. Collins & Co. to Mathew Carey, 23 February 1815, ibid., box 92.

27. Collins & Co. to Mathew Carey, 26 June 1815, ibid.

28. Collins & Co. to Mathew Carey, 22 August 1815, ibid.

29. Holbrook, *Recollections of a Nonagenarian*, 30.

30. Charvat, *Literary Publishing in America*, 18–20.

31. Whiting & Watson to Mathew Carey, 3 December 1815, Lea & Febiger Records, box 96.

32. This information was conveyed in a letter from Mercein to New York printer and bookseller Thomas Kirk and was kept by Carey. T. & W. Mercein to Thomas Kirk, 15 June 1816, ibid., box 99.

33. Winship, "Printing with Plates," 26.

34. Green, "Rise of Book Publishing," 107.

35. Mathew Carey to D. & G. Bruce, 29 November 1817, Lea & Febiger Records, vol. 32.

36. D. &. G. Bruce to Mathew Carey, 10 December 1817, ibid., box 103.

37. D. &. G. Bruce to Mathew Carey, 4 January 1818, ibid., box 109.

38. Mathew Carey to D. & G. Bruce, 24 November 1818, ibid., vol. 34.

39. Mathew Carey to Collins & Co., 14 February 1817, ibid., vol. 30.

40. Collins & Co. to Mathew Carey, 15 February 1817, ibid., box 103.

41. Collins & Co. to Mathew Carey, 7 November 1817, ibid.

42. Mathew Carey to Collins & Co., 10 November 1817, ibid., vol. 32.

43. Benjamin Collins to Isaac Collins, 26 August 1818, ibid., box 109. Before the standardization of point sizes in the late nineteenth century, typeface sizes had names that were specific to their country of origin. A Pica Bible used roughly twelve-point type and could have been set up as either a quarto or an octavo.

44. Ibid.
45. Mathew Carey to Collins & Co., 27 August 1818, ibid., vol. 34.
46. Collins & Hannay to Mathew Carey, 15 October 1818, ibid., box 109.
47. Collins & Hannay to Mathew Carey, 8 December 1818, ibid.
48. Collins & Hannay to Mathew Carey, 1 May 1819, ibid., box 115.
49. Thomas Kirk to Mathew Carey, 30 January 1819, ibid., box 118.
50. *Holbrook & Fessenden's Cash and Exchange List for 182–* (Brattleboro: Holbrook & Fessenden, 1820), ibid., box 124.
51. D. & G. Bruce to Mathew Carey, 26 August 1820, ibid., box 122.
52. D. & G. Bruce to Mathew Carey, 9 April 1821, ibid., box 131.
53. Mathew Carey to D. & G. Bruce, 17 April 1821, ibid., vol. 38.
54. Mathew Carey to Collins & Hannay, 22 March 1821, ibid., vol. 37.
55. Mathew Carey to Collins & Hannay, 12 June 1821, ibid., vol. 38.
56. Mathew Carey to Collins & Hannay, 18 June 1821, ibid.
57. Collins & Hannay to Mathew Carey, 10 November 1821, ibid., box 131.
58. Mathew Carey to Thomas Kirk, 28 August 1821, ibid., vol. 38.
59. See Bidwell, "Publication of Joel Barlow's *Columbiad*."
60. Thomas Kirk to Mathew Carey, 28 October 1821, Lea & Febiger Records, box 134.
61. Thomas Kirk to Mathew Carey, 27 November 1821, ibid.
62. J. & J. Harper to Mathew Carey, 16 November 1821, ibid., box 133.
63. Everton, *Grand Chorus of Complaint*, 127; Exman, *Brothers Harper*, 20. Exman notes that from an 1830 Harper list of thirty-one available titles, nineteen were stereotype editions. J. C. Derby quotes in his memoir a notice in the *Booksellers' Advertiser* from January 1834 that Harper & Brothers had brought out 234 works in 413 volumes to date, and of them 192 volumes were stereotyped, the plates alone being valued at $75,000. See Derby, *Fifty Years Among Authors*, 94.
64. Mathew Carey to William Collins, 21 January 1822, Lea & Febiger Records, vol. 39.
65. Collins & Co. to Mathew Carey, 8 June 1822, ibid., box 143.
66. William Collins to Mathew Carey, n.d., ibid.

Chapter 3

1. ABS, *Brief View of the Plan and Operations*, 2.
2. ABS, *Annual Reports of the American Bible Society*, 442; minutes of the Standing Committee of the Managers (hereafter Standing Committee Minutes), RG#4.03, 5 March 1829, 97, American Bible Society Archives, Philadelphia (hereafter ABS Archives); ABS, *Brief View of the Plan and Operations*, 4.
3. "What astonishes me in the United States," Tocqueville observed, "is not so much the marvelous grandeur of some undertakings as the innumerable multitude of small ones.... The Americans make immense progress in productive industry, because they all devote themselves to it at once." *Democracy in America*, 156–57.
4. Paulus, "Archibald Alexander," 643; see also Nord, "Evangelical Origins of Mass Media," 19.
5. Nord, *Faith in Reading*, 66–67.
6. C. Brown, *Word in the World*, 46.
7. Fea, *Bible Cause*, 11.
8. The Newark society was officially called "The Bible Society of Coloured People in Newark and Its Vicinity" and was chartered in the summer of 1816. See *Christian Herald*, 21

September 1816, 413. These and later societies would eventually become auxiliaries of the ABS. Joyce, *Black Book Publishers*, 14–17.

9. Nord, "Evangelical Origins of Mass Media." Elias Boudinot wrote in *The Age of Revelation* (1801) that he was shocked to see "children, servants, and the lowest people" tempted into purchasing "thousands of copies of [Paine's] *The Age of Reason* . . . at public auction, in this city [Philadelphia], at a cent and half each." This sight led him to found the New Jersey Bible Society and later organize for a national organization. Boudinot, *Age of Revelation*, 3.

10. Nord, "Benevolent Capital"; Hills, *English Bible in America*, 37.

11. Nord, "Free Grace, Free Books," 250n10; Bible Society of Philadelphia, *Eighth Annual Report*, 3–4.

12. *First Report of the Bible Society*, 6.

13. Simms, *Bible in America*, 162.

14. Steiner, *One Hundred and Ten Years*, 16; Nord, *Faith in Reading*, 51.

15. Nord, *Faith in Reading*, 5.

16. Wosh, "Bibles, Benevolence, and Bureaucracy."

17. C. Brown, *Word in the World*, 28.

18. Nord, *Faith in Reading*, 62. On the market revolution, see Sellers, *Market Revolution*; Stokes and Conway, *Market Revolution in America*.

19. "Review of the Character and Claims of the American Bible Society," *Quarterly Journal of the Methodist Episcopal Church, South* 16, no. 3 (July 1847): 376. While generally lauding their good efforts, the author of this article argued that independent religious publishing organizations like the ABS must ultimately subordinate themselves to church authority as servants, not as allies, in changing times. By 1847, the ABS had long been translating the Bible into foreign languages and sending printed books abroad. Its translations were overseen by a committee of representatives from the major Protestant denominations.

20. C. Brown, *Word in the World*, 52.

21. Quoted in Nord, *Faith in Reading*, 65, and Nord, "Benevolent Books," 230. See also Jay, *Memoir*.

22. Lacy, *Word-Carrying Giant*, 10, 33.

23. Dwight, *Centennial History*, 33.

24. Howsam, *Cheap Bibles*, 79.

25. Paulus, "Archibald Alexander," 653. For market forces and the rise of Methodism in the United States, see Wigger, *Taking Heaven by Storm*; Hatch and Wigger, "Introduction."

26. Minutes of the Board of Managers, RG#4.012, 5 June 1816, 5, ABS Archives (hereafter Board of Managers Minutes).

27. Ibid., 6.

28. Ibid., 6–7.

29. North, "Production and Supply of Scriptures," 1.

30. Board of Managers Minutes, 5 June 1816, 7.

31. Joseph Tarn to John Romeyn, 22 July 1817, Secretary for Domestic Correspondence Records, RG#16.01, John Romeyn Papers, 1816–1819, ABS Archives.

32. Board of Managers Minutes, 15 July 1816, 11.

33. Notices appeared, for example, in the *American Advocate and Kennebec Advertiser* (Hallowell, Maine), *Weekly Recorder* (Chillicothe, Ohio), *Western Monitor* (Lexington, Kentucky), and *Telescope* (Columbia, South Carolina).

34. Board of Managers Minutes, 7 August 1816, 14.

35. Weiss, "Type Founders, Copperplate Printers, Stereotypers," 473.

36. Uniform point sizes for type were not introduced in the United States until the late nineteenth century. Until then, standard type sizes were distinguished by name. Pica was the equivalent of 12-point type; Long Primer, about 10-point; Bourgeois (pronounced "boor-joyce"), about 9-point; Brevier, about 8-point; Minion, about 7-point; Nonpareil, about 6-point; and Pearl, about 5-point.

37. Wright, *Early Bibles in America*, 197–98.

38. Simms, *Bible in America*, 130 (quotation); Wright, *Early Bibles in America*, 333–34; *American Dictionary of Printing and Bookmaking*, 184.

39. Before steam power, Fanshaw used two donkeys to power his first presses. See Derby, *Fifty Years Among Authors*, 652. Fanshaw's rubber rollers were made by Samuel Bingham, an employee of his who went on to found a successful printing roller business. See Bullen, "Oldest Job-Printing Office."

40. Standing Committee Minutes, 5 September 1817, 22.

41. Nord, "Benevolent Books," 231.

42. Paskow, *Dictionary of American Printing and Bookmaking*, 184; Bullen, "Oldest Job-Printing Office."

43. Gibson, *Soldiers of the Word*, 38.

44. Board of Managers Minutes, 6 November 1816, 21.

45. Ibid., 4 December 1816, 28.

46. Joseph Tarn to ABS, 4 October 1817, General Agent and Accountant Records, RG#19.01, John Edward Caldwell Letter Book, 1818–1819, box 1, ABS Archives. Gaskell notes that the first prototype cylinder printing machine was constructed in 1812; the *Times* of London implemented two in November 1814. They were modified in 1816 to print on two sides of the same sheet, making Tarn's letter an early eyewitness account of the new technology. See Gaskell, *New Introduction to Bibliography*, 252.

47. Board of Managers Minutes, 5 March 1817, 43; Standing Committee Minutes, 11 February 1817.

48. The Standing Committee Minutes in the ABS Archives are a rich and underutilized resource documenting the printing, binding, supply sourcing, distribution, and publicity work of the ABS from 1816 onward and deserve greater scholarly attention for the light they shed on the printing trades in New York during this period.

49. Strickland, *History of the American Bible Society*, 46.

50. Standing Committee Minutes, 5 June 1817, 16.

51. Board of Managers Minutes, 7 February 1817, 39.

52. Unlike the family Bible market, which had different retail prices for each type of paper, distinctions in paper quality were not nearly as important to the ABS as obtaining a good price on serviceable paper stock, hence the variety used here.

53. Board of Managers Minutes, 5 March 1817, 44.

54. Ibid., 5 June 1817, 69.

55. "American Bible Society," *Methodist Review* 10, no. 4 (April 1827): 166–68.

56. Fea, "History of the American Bible Society."

57. Board of Managers Minutes, 3 July 1817, 75.

58. ABS, *Annual Reports of the American Bible Society*, 14.

59. See chapter 2 and Makala, "Early History of Stereotyping."

60. Board of Managers Minutes, 22 January 1818, 99, 101.

61. Ibid., 102.

62. Standing Committee Minutes, 16 April 1824, 331.

63. See appendix B.
64. Standing Committee Minutes, 30 October 1818, 92.
65. Ibid., 11 September 1818, 83, and 9 October 1818, 90.
66. Ibid., 19 December 1817, 28.
67. Ibid., 30 December 1817, 35.
68. Barrett, *Old Merchants of New York City*, 380–81.
69. See Norton, *Gospel According to Saint John*.
70. Board of Managers Minutes, 1 October 1818, 144.
71. Ibid., 1 October 1818, 148.
72. Ibid., 21 June 1819, 197.
73. Ibid., 15 July 1819, 201.
74. Ibid., 202.
75. Ibid., 20 July 1820, 282.
76. Ibid., 283.
77. Nord, "Free Grace, Free Books," 256.
78. Lacy, *Word-Carrying Giant*, 40, 44.
79. Standing Committee Minutes, 21 July 1820, 185.
80. Board of Managers Minutes, 3 May 1821, 337; Standing Committee Minutes, 2 March 1821, 214.
81. Board of Managers Minutes, 5 June 1823, 514.
82. Standing Committee Minutes, 17 January 1823, 282.
83. See *Novum Testamentum*; Grellet and Allen, *Lessons for Schools*.
84. Standing Committee Minutes, 23 December 1823, 311.
85. Sizer, *What to Do, and Why*, 76. Sizer was the chief examiner for O. S. and Lorenzo Fowler's phrenological office in New York and wrote this book as a guide to the suitability of various professions to different phrenological types. For printshop compositors, he wrote, rather unfortunately, "The setting of type should be done mainly by men who are not able to knock about in the rough work of life, or by women" (75).
86. Standing Committee Minutes, 13 January 1824, 318.
87. Board of Managers Minutes, 20 November 1823, 543, and 4 December, 1823, 548.
88. John Nitchie to Jedidiah Howe, 5 October 1824, General Agent and Accountant Records, RG#19.01, John Edward Caldwell Letter Book, 1818–1819, box 1, 338, ABS Archives.
89. Jedidiah Howe to John Nitchie, 11 October 1824, ibid., General Correspondence, 1823–1825, box 5.
90. Jedidiah Howe to John Nitchie, 25 March 1825, ibid.
91. The Baltimore Bible was acquired via credit for new books ordered by them. Nitchie directed the secretary in Baltimore to pack the boxes of plates in larger crates and have them made strong and tight "so there may be no shaking of the plates. Let them be carefully stowed in the vessel with a caution against turning them on the side or upside down." See his letter of 7 April 1827, General Agent and Accountant Records, ABS Archives. Despite this attention to detail, Nitchie wrote to Baltimore in January of the following year, once proofs were finally taken from them and examined, that some of the plates had been damaged in shipment.
92. See Hazard, "How Joseph Smith Encountered Printing Plates"; Perry, "Many Bibles of Joseph Smith"; and Gutjahr, "Golden Bible."
93. Standing Committee Minutes, 21 January 1827, unpaginated.
94. North, "Production and Supply of Scriptures," 43.
95. Standing Committee Minutes, 13 October 1827, 15.

96. General Agent and Accountant Records, RG#19.02, General Correspondence, box 5, 1823–1825, ABS Archives.
97. Standing Committee Minutes, 4 March 1829, 89.
98. Nord, "Benevolent Capital," 156.
99. Nord, *Faith in Reading*, 53, 69; Exman, *Brothers Harper*, 17; Bishop, *History of American Manufactures*, 380.
100. Hatch, "Elias Smith," 252.
101. G. Wood, *Empire of Liberty*, 611–12.
102. Nord, "Benevolent Books," 236.
103. C. Brown, *Word in the World*, 51.

Chapter 4

1. Weedon, *Victorian Publishing*, 76.
2. Lehmann-Haupt, *Book in America*, 99–111. See also Green, "Rise of Book Publishing."
3. *Norton's Literary Gazette and Publishers' Circular*, 1 November 1854, 585.
4. See Green, "Rise of Book Publishing," 111–12; Zboray, *Fictive People*, 24–29.
5. Printed trade sale catalogs, often with last-minute supplements, were brought out by their respective auction houses and are a rich resource for understanding the system of book distribution during this period. Catalogs were printed solely for publisher and bookseller use, and there is evidence that they were sometimes used as tickets of admission. See especially the June 1832 Boston trade sale catalog housed at the American Antiquarian Society, the index page of which contains a printed and signed ticket of admission to the sale. As they had a limited distribution and life span, few trade sale catalogs survive.
6. Tryon, "Book Distribution," 223.
7. Nichols, "Literary Fair in the United States." For more on New York publishing in the early nineteenth century, see Smith, *Empire of Print*.
8. Winship, "Getting the Books Out," 11.
9. Kaser, "Origin of the Book Trade Sales."
10. Sheehan, *That Was Publishing*, 150.
11. *Eleventh Trade Sale: June 1838*, copy at the American Antiquarian Society in Worcester, Massachusetts. Charvat writes, "Somewhat later [in the period 1820–50], it happened occasionally that a publisher ordered one or more extra sets of stereotype plates. He would sell a set of these to a bookseller, say in Cincinnati, who would print a new title page bearing his own imprint and that of the original publisher. This, again, was a way of dividing risk, for extra sets of plates, inexpensively cast from the same forms as the first set, were sold at a considerable profit, or were paid for by a charge from each copy printed therefrom." *Literary Publishing in America*, 46. More research needs to be done on the occasions when multiple copies of the same work, from the same plates, appeared for sale in the marketplace.
12. Advertisement for the autumn New York trade sale in *Norton's Literary Advertiser*, 15 July 1851.
13. *Frank Leslie's Illustrated Newspaper*, 5 April 1854, 263.
14. Duyckinck, "Keese-ana," 497.
15. Keese, "Keese-ana," 736.
16. Keese, *John Keese, Wit and Litterateur*, 66.
17. Ibid., 63. See also Derby, *Fifty Years Among Authors*, 659–60.
18. Quoted in Keese, *John Keese, Wit and Litterateur*, 67.

19. *Norton's Literary Advertiser*, 15 July 1851, 54. Using standard accounting practice in this table, the abbreviation "do." stands for "ditto" (i.e., the same as the above line), in these instances meaning the "stereotype plates" or "copyright and stereotype plates" included with each lot.
20. Remer, "Capturing the Bard," 335–36.
21. Winship, "Getting the Books Out," 13.
22. "An Hour at the Book Sales," *Norton's Literary Gazette*, 15 April 1853, 61–62. The three- or four-day sales of the previous decade had grown into nearly two weeks of activity. Sales catalogs from this period often top three hundred pages.
23. Winship, "Getting the Books Out," 6.
24. "The Trade Sale," *Norton's Literary Gazette*, 1 April 1854, 159.
25. Reprinted in ibid.
26. For an excellent introduction to publishers' rhetoric of progress and self-congratulation, see the account of the 1876 American Book Trade Association banquet in Casper, "Introduction."
27. "The Trade Sale," *Norton's Literary Gazette*, 1 April 1854, 160.
28. "Publishers and Publishing in New York," *Norton's Literary Gazette*, 1 April 1854, 165.
29. Sutton, *Western Book Trade*, 266.
30. Ibid., 273.
31. "Correspondence: A Reform Needed in Trade Sales," *American Publisher's Circular*, 1 March 1855, 93–94.
32. See "Harper's Views on the Trade Sales," *American Publisher's Circular and Literary Gazette*, 8 September 1855, together with the editorial response.
33. *American Publishers' Circular and Literary Gazette*, 5 April 1856, 205–6.
34. "City Items: Sale of Stereotype Plates," *New York Daily Tribune*, 21 September 1857, 3.
35. Williams, "Authors and Literary Authorship"; Charvat, *Literary Publishing in America*, 43.
36. *Letters of Herman Melville*, 188n9.
37. Parker, *Herman Melville: A Biography*, 354.
38. *Letters of Herman Melville*, 188–89.
39. "City Items: Sale of Stereotype Plates," *New York Daily Tribune*, 21 September 1857, 3.
40. *Letters of Herman Melville*, 189.
41. Parker, *Herman Melville: A Biography*, 355.
42. Greenspan, *George Palmer Putnam*, 383; Derby, *Fifty Years Among Authors*, 307–8.
43. "City Items: Sale of Stereotype Plates," *New York Daily Tribune*, 21 September 1857, 3.
44. Ibid.
45. Madeleine Stern has written about Derby and Miller in *Books and Book People*. See also Roy, "Cheap Editions, Little Books."
46. Northup, *Twelve Years a Slave* (1859).
47. Northup, *Twelve Years a Slave* (n.d. [not before 1865]).
48. Homestead, *American Women Authors*, 218.
49. Reprinted in the *American Publishers' Circular and Literary Gazette*, 1 November 1862, 115.
50. Derby, *Fifty Years Among Authors*, 392.
51. Kelley, *Private Women, Public Stage*, 173–74. See also Gilpin Faust's introduction to *Macaria*. A pirated New York edition of *Macaria* also appeared. Derby threatened its publisher, Michael Doolady, with prosecution, and Doolady made some amends by providing Wilson

with royalties. An additional Confederate edition of *Macaria* was brought out in Columbia, South Carolina, by Evans & Cogswell.
52. Homestead, *American Women Authors*, 220.
53. *American Publishers' Circular and Literary Gazette*, 1 November 1862, 115.
54. Ibid.
55. Madison, *Book Publishing in America*, 144.
56. Winship, "Distribution and the Trade," 126.
57. *Publishers' Weekly*, 29 January 1876, 112.
58. Ibid., 5 February 1876, 167–68.
59. Similarly, the American Booksellers Association was founded in 1900 to support the interests of independent booksellers. It held its first convention in New York in the spring of 1947 to connect publishers with booksellers. This fair was held annually each spring and was renamed BookExpo America in 1995. BookExpo America was cancelled in 2020 owing to the global COVID-19 pandemic, and its name has now been retired. *Publishers Weekly* filled the void in May 2021 by organizing a new national convention of publishers, authors, and booksellers, the U.S. Book Show, which had a successful inaugural event. A second U.S. Book Show took place online in May 2022.
60. *Publishers' Weekly*, 25 March 1876, 400.
61. Ibid., 4 March 1876, 271–73.
62. Ibid., 285.
63. "The Estate of H. T. Tuckerman," ibid., 1 April 1876, 432.
64. "The Osgood Sale," ibid., 436.
65. Ibid., 437.
66. Ibid.
67. Sheehan, *That Was Publishing*, 158.
68. *Publishers' Weekly*, 19 January 1896, 58–60.

Chapter 5

1. See Matthiessen, *American Renaissance*; Marx, *Machine in the Garden*.
2. Benesh, *Romantic Cyborgs*, 12.
3. See, for example, Johns, *Assault on Progress*; Seltzer, *Bodies and Machines*; Nye, *American Technological Sublime*; Nye, *Narrative and Spaces*; and Heidegger, *Question Concerning Technology*.
4. Poe, "Anastatic Printing," 230. William Blake's process of relief etching, practiced fifty years before Poe's essay and still not entirely understood, is a forerunner of this process.
5. Newbury, *Figuring Authorship*.
6. Twyman, *Lithography, 1800–1850*, 8–11. The first commercially produced book using this process was an edition of La Fontaine's fables published by Renouard in Paris in 1811.
7. Poe, "Anastatic Printing," 231.
8. Clay and Philips, *Secret Location on the Lower East Side*.
9. White, "First (1855) 'Leaves of Grass'"; Myerson, *Walt Whitman*, 17, 25.
10. Whitman to Emerson, August 1856 (transcript added to the 1856 2nd ed. of *Leaves of Grass*, 346), Whitman Archive, http://whitmanarchive.org/published/LG/1856/whole.html.
11. Stern, *Heads and Headlines*, 119.
12. The key book on women's paths to authorship in nineteenth-century America is Kelley, *Private Women, Public Stage*. See also Dowling, *Capital Letters*; Everton, *Grand Chorus of*

Complaint; L. Jackson, *Business of Letters*; McGill, *American Literature and the Culture*; and Newbury, *Figuring Authorship*.

13. Tebbel, *History of Book Publishing*, esp. part 4, "The Rise of Modern Publishing"; McGill, *American Literature and the Culture*.
14. Exman, *House of Harper*, 10.
15. Zboray, *Fictive People*, 10.
16. Winship, "Hawthorne and the 'Scribbling Women,'" 4–5. See also Winship, *American Literary Publishing*, 103–6.
17. Tebbel, *History of Book Publishing*, 211; Charvat, "Longfellow's Income"; Charvat, *Literary Publishing in America*, 43.
18. For an excellent recent study of Melville's material experiences with the publishing industry, see McGettigan, *Herman Melville*.
19. Petroski, *Pencil*, 108–9.
20. *Correspondence of Henry D. Thoreau*, 148n4.
21. Gaskell, *New Introduction to Bibliography*, 206; Abbott, *Harper Establishment*, 67–68, 96–102.
22. Petroski, *Pencil*, 122. See also Walls, *Henry David Thoreau*, 37–40; Harding, *Days of Henry Thoreau*, 261–62.
23. Emerson, *Henry Thoreau as Remembered*, 37.
24. Thompson, "Thoreau on Monadnock."
25. *Correspondence of Henry D. Thoreau*, 245–46. Thoreau is referring to Emerson's "Ode to Beauty," which was printed in the October 1843 issue of the *Dial*.
26. Thoreau, *Week on the Concord and Merrimack Rivers*, 92.
27. Melville uses a similar metaphor in chapter 104 of *Moby-Dick*, "The Fossil Whale," when he calls whale fossils nature's stereotypes: "But not alone has this Leviathan left his pre adamite traces in the stereotype plates of nature, and in limestone and marl bequeathed his ancient bust" (380).
28. Thoreau, *Week on the Concord and Merrimack Rivers*, 274.
29. Ibid., 343.
30. Thoreau, *Walden*, 8.
31. Ibid., 125.
32. Ibid., 318.
33. The term "stereotyping" appears only twice in Thoreau's journal, in 1857. On 13 January 1857, he wrote, "Almost all, perhaps all of our life is, speaking comparatively, a stereotyped despair, i.e. we never at any time realize the full grandeur of our destiny." Later that year, on 2 October, he wrote, "The chief incidents in Minott's life must be more distinct and interesting to him now than immediately after they occurred, for he has recalled and related them so often they are stereotyped in his mind." *Journal of Henry David Thoreau*, 9:217, 10:56.
34. "Letter from a Country Schoolmaster," *Harvard Register* (1828), 133.
35. Stowe, *Dred*, 440.
36. Melville, *Pierre*, 62.
37. Rohrbach, "Profits of Protest," 235.
38. Washington, *Sojourner Truth's America*, 258; Painter, *Sojourner Truth*, 110–11.
39. Rohrbach, "Profits of Protest," 247; *Narrative of Sojourner Truth*, 45.
40. Washington, *Sojourner Truth's America*, 258.
41. Rohrbach, "Profits of Protest," 243.
42. Painter, *Sojourner Truth*, 110–11.

43. Greenspan, *William Wells Brown*, 70–71.
44. W. Brown, *Three Years in Europe*, 6–7. Douglass did not travel with a set of stereotype plates to his *Narrative* but had the text reset in Ireland and then in England. Murray and McKivigan, *Frederick Douglass in Britain and Ireland*, 31–35.
45. Senchyne, *Intimacy of Paper*, 136. See also Senchyne, "Bottles of Ink"; Greenspan, *William Wells Brown*, 192.
46. Like other reform groups, such as the American Sunday School Union and American Bible Society, the American Anti-Slavery Society received gifts of stereotype plates from sister organizations to support its publishing activities. The Boston publisher John P. Jewett and the Fourth Congregational Church in Boston also gave sets of plates to abolitionist tracts to the society. See American Anti-Slavery Society, *Annual Reports*, 189–91.
47. See L. Jackson, "Talking Book." More scholarship is emerging on enslaved and free Black Americans in the printing trades in early America. See Senchyne, "Under Pressure." John Garcia notes the printing work of the freedman Samuel Johnson in Philadelphia and of Charles, "a servant of Samuel Campbell," in New York, both at the turn of the nineteenth century. See Garcia, "Other Samuel Johnson."
48. Thomas, *History of Printing in America* (1874), 130, 133.
49. Richmond, "Afro-American Printers," 25.
50. Ibid., 78.
51. Joyce, *Gatekeepers of Black Culture*, 13; Richmond, "Afro-American Printers." And see, for example, Ashe, *Masonic Manual*.
52. Richmond, "Afro-American Printers," 90–93.
53. For more on the *Anglo-African Magazine*, see chapter 4 in Derrick R. Spires's important recent work, *Practice of Citizenship*.
54. W. Brown, *Black Man*, both 1863 editions.
55. Du Bois, *Philadelphia Negro*, 142. See also Penn, *Afro-American Press*.

Epilogue

1. "Peremptory Sale by M. Thomas & Sons, Philadelphia," *Norton's Literary Gazette*, 15 January 1854, 64; advertisement for M. Thomas & Sons, Auctioneers, *Daily National Intelligencer* (Washington, DC), 30 January 1854; *North American and United States Gazette* (Philadelphia), 9 February 1854.
2. "The Trade Sale," *Norton's Literary Gazette*, 1 April 1854, 159.
3. "Godey's Arm-Chair," *Godey's Lady's Book*, May 1854, 468.
4. "The Trade Sale," *Norton's Literary Gazette*, 1 April 1854, 159.
5. See especially the description of the American Book Trade Association conference at the American Centennial Exhibition of 1876 in Casper, "Introduction," 1–11.
6. "Great Sale of Stereotype Plates," *South Carolinian* (Columbia), 14 March 1854. See also Homestead, "From Periodical to Book"; "The Trade Sale," *Norton's Literary Gazette*, 1 April 1854, 159–60.
7. Parfait, *Publishing History of Uncle Tom's Cabin*, 110. See also Winship, "John Punchard Jewett."
8. "Godey's Arm-Chair," *Godey's Lady's Book*, May 1854, 467. *Godey's* also wrote about manufacturing technologies for its readership, including several articles on how its own magazine issues were produced. See Hinckley, "Day's Ramble" for an excellent illustrated look at the magazine's production facilities, and "Our Printers," *Godey's Lady's Book*, December 1850, 384–85.

9. "Invention of Stereotyping," *Family Magazine, or, Monthly Extract of General Knowledge* 3 (1838): 268–70.

10. "Memorial of the New York Typographical Society Against the Passage of an International Copyright Law," S. Doc. 25-296 (1838).

11. Silver, "Copper-Facing."

12. *Hereford Journal*, 9 April 1817.

13. "Littell's Living Age, No. 532, Has Been Received by the Agents, Merriam & Merrill," *New Hampshire Statesman* (Concord), 5 August 1854.

BIBLIOGRAPHY

A note on manuscript sources: *Publishing Plates* makes use of manuscript collections in two main repositories. The Lea & Febiger Records, 1785–1982, Collection 227B, at the Historical Society of Pennsylvania contain the records of Lea & Febiger's predecessor firms Carey & Lea and Carey & Son, and those of its founder, Mathew Carey, going back to Carey's beginnings as a printer and publisher in the United States. The collection is near-comprehensive: Carey's letter books contain copies of all of his outgoing correspondence, and all incoming correspondence has been preserved, together with the company's business and financial records, along with Carey's personal diary, writings, and other materials. It is a treasure trove for understanding the relationships among printers, publishers, booksellers, typefounders, stereotypers, and authors in the early American Republic.

Equally important to this project are the records of the American Bible Society, a similarly comprehensive collection of documents about the work of the ABS in printing, distributing books, commissioning stereotype plates, and interacting with New York printers, typefounders, stereotypers, binders, and other members of the printing trades throughout the nineteenth century. These records form a rich—and underutilized—repository of printing history sources from this time, especially for the printing trades in New York City, and are worthy of much further study. I examined these records in the ABS's archives and library in New York. The ABS relocated to suburban Philadelphia in 2015.

Sources from both of these repositories are cited primarily in the endnotes.

Abbot, Jacob. *The Harper Establishment; or, How the Story Books Are Made*. 1855. Hamden, CT: Shoe String Press, 1956.
"An Act Requiring the Several Incorporated Banks in This Commonwealth to Adopt the Stereotype Steel Plate in Certain Cases, and for Other Purposes." In *Laws of the Commonwealth of Massachusetts*, 502–4. Boston: Adams and Rhoades, 1808.
Altman, Rick. *Silent Film Sound*. New York: Columbia University Press, 2007.
American Anti-Slavery Society. *Annual Reports of the American Anti-Slavery Society, by the Executive Committee, for the Years Ending May 1, 1857 and May 1, 1858*. New York: The Society, 1859.
American Bible Society (ABS). *Annual Reports of the American Bible Society*. Vol. 1. New York: The Society, 1838.
———. *A Brief View of the Plan and Operations of the American Bible Society, and of Kindred Institutions Throughout the World*. New York: American Bible Society, 1829.

American Dictionary of Printing and Bookmaking. New York: Howard Lockwood & Co., 1894.
Appadurai, Arjun, ed. *The Social Life of Things: Commodities in Cultural Perspective.* Cambridge: Cambridge University Press, 1986.
Argüera y Arcas, Blaise, and Paul Needham. "Computational Analytical Bibliography." In *Proceedings Bibliopolis Conference: The Future History of the Book*, 1–12. The Hague: Koninklijke Bibliotheek, 2002.
Ashe, Jonathan. *The Masonic Manual; or, Lectures on Freemasonry.* New York: J. W. Leonard & Co., American Masonic Agency, 1855.
The Author's Printing and Publishing Assistant. London: Saunders and Otley, 1842.
Babbage, Charles. *On the Economy of Machinery and Manufactures.* 3rd ed., enl. London: Charles Knight, 1833.
Banham, Rob. "The Industrialization of the Book, 1800–1970." In *A Companion to the History of the Book*, edited by Simon Eliot and Jonathan Rose, 273–90. Malden, MA: Blackwell, 2007.
Barnard, John, D. F. MacKenzie, David McKitterick, I. R. Willison, gen. eds. *The Cambridge History of the Book in Britain.* 7 vols. Cambridge: Cambridge University Press, 1999–2019.
Barnett, George E. "The Printers: A Study in Trade Unionism." *American Economic Association Quarterly*, 3rd ser., 10, no. 3 (1909): 3–379.
Baron, Ava. "Questions of Gender: Deskilling and Demasculinization in the U.S. Printing Industry, 1830–1915." *Gender and History* 1, no. 2 (1989): 178–99.
Barrett, Walter. *The Old Merchants of New York City.* 2nd ser. New York: Carleton, 1864.
Benesh, Klaus. *Romantic Cyborgs: Authorship and Technology in the American Renaissance.* Amherst: University of Massachusetts Press, 2002.
Bible Society of Philadelphia. *Eighth Annual Report.* Philadelphia: The Society, 1816.
———. *The First Report of the Bible Society Established in Philadelphia; Read Before the Society at Their Annual Meeting, May 1, 1809.* Philadelphia: Bible Society of Philadelphia, 1809.
Bidwell, John. "Joshua Gilpin and Lord Stanhope's Improvements in Printing." *Papers of the Bibliographical Society of America* 76, no. 2 (1982): 143–58.
———. "The Publication of Joel Barlow's *Columbiad.*" *Proceedings of the American Antiquarian Society* 93, no. 3 (1983): 337–80.
Bigelow, Jacob. *Elements of Technology, Taken Chiefly from a Course of Lectures Delivered at Cambridge, on the Application of the Sciences to the Useful Arts.* Boston: Hilliard, Gray, Little, and Wilkins, 1829.
———. *Inaugural Address, Delivered in the Chapel of the University at Cambridge, December 11, 1816.* Boston: Wells and Lilly, 1817.
Bishop, J. Leander. *A History of American Manufactures from 1608 to 1860.* 3rd ed., rev. and enl. Philadelphia: Edward Young & Co., 1868.
Black, Fiona A., Patricia Lockhart Fleming, Gilles Gallichan, Carol Gerson, Yvan Lamonde, and Jacques Michon, eds. *History of the Book in Canada / Histoire du livre et de l'imprimé au Canada.* 3 vols. Toronto: University of Toronto Press, 2004–7.
Black, M. H. "The Printed Bible." In *The Cambridge History of the Bible*, vol. 3, *The West from the Reformation to the Present Day*, edited by S. L. Greenslade, 408–75. Cambridge: Cambridge University Press, 1963.
Boudinot, Elias. *The Age of Revelation.* Philadelphia: Asbury Dickens, 1801.
Boutin, Otto J. *A Catfish in the Bodoni, and Other Tales from the Golden Age of Tramp Printers.* St. Cloud, MN: North Star Press, 1970.

Brewster, Abel. *The Universal Vitriolic Test, for Producing an Uniform, Safe, and Intelligible Kind of Bank Bills, with an Explanation of Its Importance and Utility*. Hartford: Lincoln & Gleason, 1807.
Brightly, Charles. *The Method of Founding Stereotype, as Practiced by Charles Brightly of Bungay, Suffolk*. Bungay: Printed by C. Brightly, for R. Phillips, Bridge-Street, London, 1809.
Brown, Bill, ed. *Things*. Chicago: University of Chicago Press, 2004.
———. "Thing Theory." *Critical Inquiry* 28 (Autumn 2001): 1–22.
Brown, Candy Gunter. *The Word in the World: Evangelical Writing, Publishing, and Reading in America, 1789–1880*. Chapel Hill: University of North Carolina Press, 2004.
Brown, William Wells. *The Black Man: His Antecedents, His Genius, and His Achievements*. Boston: R. F. Wallcut, 1863. 2nd ed., rev. and enl., New York: Thomas Hamilton, 1863.
———. *Narrative of William W. Brown, a Fugitive Slave*. Boston: Anti-Slavery Society, 1847.
———. *Three Years in Europe; or, Places I Have Seen and People I Have Met*. London: Charles Gilpin; Edinburgh: Oliver and Boyd, 1852.
Bullen, Henry Lewis. "The Oldest Job-Printing Office in New York." *Inland Printer* 50 (1913): 519–21.
Campbell, Robert. *A Pilgrimage to My Motherland: An Account of a Journey Among the Egbas and Yorubas of Central Africa, in 1859–60*. New York: Thomas Hamilton, 1861.
Camus, Armand G. *Histoire et procédés du polytypage et da la stéréotypie*. Paris: Baudouin, l'an X [1801].
Carey, Mathew. *Address to the Booksellers of the United States, from the Booksellers' Company of Philadelphia*. Philadelphia: T. S. Manning, 1813.
———. *Autobiography*. New York: Eugene L. Schwab, 1942.
Carlyle, Thomas. "Signs of the Times." *Edinburgh Review* 49, no. 98 (1829): 439–59.
Carter, Harry, and George Buday. "Stereotyping by Joseph Athias: The Evidence of Nicholas Kris." *Quaerendo* 5, no. 4 (1975): 312–20.
Carter, John. "William Ged and the Invention of Stereotype." *Library*, 5th ser., 15, no. 3 (1960): 161–92.
Casper, Scott E. "Introduction." In *A History of the Book in America*, vol. 3, *The Industrial Book, 1840–1880*, edited by Scott E. Casper, Jeffrey D. Groves, Stephen W. Nissenbaum, and Michael Winship, 1–39. Chapel Hill: University of North Carolina Press, 2007.
Chandler, Adoniram. *Specimen of Ornamental Types and Embellishments, Cast at the Foundry of A. Chandler & Co*. New York: A. Chandler & Co., 1820.
———. *Specimen of Ornamental Types and Printing Ornaments, Cast at the Foundry of A. Chandler & Co*. New York: A. Chandler & Co., 1822.
Charvat, William. *Literary Publishing in America, 1790–1850*. Amherst: University of Massachusetts Press, 1993.
———. "Longfellow's Income from His Writings, 1840–1852." *Papers of the Bibliographical Society of America* 38, no. 1 (1944): 9–21.
Clay, Steven, and Rodney Philips. *A Secret Location on the Lower East Side: Adventures in Writing, 1960–1980*. New York: New York Public Library and Granary Books, 1998.
Coggeshall, William Turner. *Five Black Arts: A Popular Account of the History, Process of Manufacture, and Uses of Printing, Gas-Light, Pottery, Glass, Iron*. Columbus, OH: Follett, Foster and Co., 1861.
Commonwealth of Massachusetts. *Laws of the Commonwealth of Massachusetts, Passed at Several Sessions of the General Court, Holden in Boston*. Boston: Young & Minns, 1806.
Crocker, Uriel. "Reminiscences of His Own Life." In *Memorial of Uriel Crocker*, 24–55. Boston: Privately printed, 1891.

Dary, David. *Red Blood and Black Ink: Journalism in the Old West.* New York: Knopf, 1998.
Derby, J. C. *Fifty Years Among Authors, Books, and Publishers.* New York: G. W. Carleton & Co., 1884.
DeSpain, Jessica. *Nineteenth-Century Transatlantic Reprinting and the Embodied Book.* Burlington, VT: Ashgate, 2014.
Dixon, John. "Between Script and Specie: Cadwallader Colden's Printing Method and the Production of Permanent, Correct Knowledge." *Early American Studies* 8, no. 1 (2010): 75–93.
Dowling, David. *Capital Letters: Authorship in the Antebellum Literary Market.* Iowa City: University of Iowa Press, 2009.
Du Bois, W. E. B. *The Philadelphia Negro.* Philadelphia: University of Pennsylvania Press, 1899.
Duyckinck, Evert. "Keese-ana." *Magazine of American History* 1, no. 8 (1877): 497–502.
Dwight, Henry Otis. *The Centennial History of the American Bible Society.* New York: Macmillan, 1916.
Eleventh Trade Sale: June 1838; Catalogue of Books to Be Sold in Boston, by J. L. Cunningham, at His Auction Rooms. Boston: Munroe and Francis, 1838.
Emerson, Edward Waldo. *Henry Thoreau as Remembered by a Young Friend.* Concord, MA: Thoreau Foundation, 1968.
Evans, Augusta Jane. *Macaria; or, Altars of Sacrifice.* Edited by Drew Gilpin Faust. Baton Rouge: Louisiana State University Press, 1992.
Everton, Michael J. *The Grand Chorus of Complaint: Authors and the Business Ethics of American Publishing.* New York: Oxford University Press, 2011.
Exman, Eugene. *The Brothers Harper: A Unique Partnership and Its Impact on the Cultural Life of America from 1817 to 1853.* New York: Harper & Row, 1965.
———. *The House of Harper: One Hundred and Fifty Years of Publishing.* New York: Harper & Row, 1967.
Faust, Drew Gilpin. Introduction to *Macaria; or, Altars of Sacrifice,* by Augusta Jane Evans, xiii–xxvi. Edited by Drew Gilpin Faust. Baton Rouge: Louisiana State University Press, 1992.
Fea, John. *The Bible Cause: A History of the American Bible Society.* New York: Oxford University Press, 2016.
———. "History of the American Bible Society: An Interview with John Fea." Interview by Jonathan Peterson, 23 May 2016. https://www.biblegateway.com/blog/2016/05/history-of-the-american-bible-society-an-interview-with-john-fea.
Fearon, Henry Bradshaw. *Sketches of America: A Narrative of a Journey of Five Thousand Miles Through the Eastern and Western States of America.* London: Longman, Hurst, Rees, Orme, and Brown, 1819.
Ferraris, Maurizio. *Documentality: Why It Is Necessary to Leave Traces.* New York: Fordham University Press, 2013.
Flint, Charles L., C. F. McKay, Thomas P. Kettell, Frederick B. Perkins, T. Addison Richards, and Henry Barnard. *Eighty Years' Progress of the United States: Showing the Various Channels of Industry and Education.* New York: L. Stebbins, 1861.
Fyfe, Aileen. *Steam-Powered Knowledge: William Chambers and the Business of Publishing, 1820–1860.* Chicago: University of Chicago Press, 2012.
Garcia, John. "The Other Samuel Johnson: African-American Labor in the Vicinity of the Early US Book Trade." *JHI Blog: The Blog of the Journal of the History of Ideas,* April 5, 2017. https://jhiblog.org/2017/04/05/the-other-samuel-johnson-african-american-labor-in-the-vicinity-of-the-early-u-s-book-trade.

Gaskell, Philip. *A New Introduction to Bibliography*. New Castle, DE: Oak Knoll Press, 1995.
Ged, William. *Biographical Memoirs of William Ged: Including a Particular Account of His Progress in the Art of Block-Printing*. London: John Nichols, 1781.
Gibson, John M. *Soldiers of the Word: The Story of the American Bible Society*. New York: Philosophical Library, 1958.
Gnirrep, Kees. "Standing Type or Stereotype in the Seventeenth Century?" *Quaerendo* 27, no. 1 (1997): 19–45.
Green, James N. "From Printer to Publisher: Mathew Carey and the Origins of Nineteenth-Century Book Publishing." In *Getting the Books Out: Papers of the Chicago Conference on the Book in 19th-Century America*, edited by Michael Hackenberg, 26–44. Washington, DC: Library of Congress Center for the Book, 1987.
———. *Mathew Carey: Publisher and Patriot*. Philadelphia: Library Company of Philadelphia, 1985.
———. "The Rise of Book Publishing." In *A History of the Book in America*, vol. 2, *An Extensive Republic: Print, Culture, and Society in the New Nation, 1790–1840*, edited by Robert A. Gross and Mary Kelley, 75–127. Chapel Hill: University of North Carolina Press, 2010.
Greenspan, Ezra. *George Palmer Putnam: Representative American Publisher*. University Park: Penn State University Press, 2000.
———. *William Wells Brown: An African American Life*. New York: W. W. Norton, 2014.
Grellet, Stephen, and William Allen. *Lessons for Schools Taken from the Holy Scriptures, in the Words of the Text*. New-York: Stereotyped for the New-York Free-School Society, 1822.
Gutjahr, Paul C. *An American Bible: A History of the Good Book in the United States, 1777–1880*. Stanford: Stanford University Press, 1999.
———. "The Golden Bible in the Bible's Golden Age: *The Book of Mormon* and Antebellum Print Culture." *ATQ* 12, no. 4 (1998): 275–93.
Hansard, T. C. *Treatises on Printing and Type-Founding*. Edinburgh: Adam and Charles Black, 1841.
———. *Typographia: An Historical Sketch of the Origin and Progress of the Art of Printing*. London: Baldwin, Cradock, and Joy, 1825.
Harding, Walter. *The Days of Henry Thoreau*. New York: Knopf, 1966.
Hatch, Nathan O. "Elias Smith and the Rise of Religious Journalism in the Early Republic." In *Printing and Society in Early America*, edited by William L. Joyce, David D. Hall, Richard D. Brown, and John B. Hench, 250–77. Worcester: American Antiquarian Society, 1983.
Hatch, Nathan O., and John H. Wigger. "Introduction." In *Methodism and the Shaping of American Culture*, edited by Nathan O. Hatch and John H. Wigger, 11–21. Nashville: Abingdon Press, 2001.
Hazard, Sonia. "How Joseph Smith Encountered Printing Plates and Founded Mormonism." *Religion and American Culture: A Journal of Interpretation* 31, no. 2 (2021): 137–92.
Hazen, Edward. *The Panorama of Professions and Trades; or, Every Man's Book*. Philadelphia: Uriah Hunt, 1837.
Heidegger, Martin. *The Question Concerning Technology, and Other Essays*. New York: Harper Perennial Modern Classics, 2013.
Hills, Margaret. *The English Bible in America: A Bibliography of Editions of the Bible and the New Testament Published in America, 1777–1957*. New York: American Bible Society and New York Public Library, 1961.

Hillyard, Brian. "William Ged and the Invention of Stereotype: Another Postscript." *Library* 13, no. 2 (1991): 156–57.
Hinckley, C. T. "A Day's Ramble Through the Mechanical Department of the 'Lady's Book.'" *Godey's Lady's Book*, October 1852, 306–14.
Hinman, Charlton. *The Printing and Proof-Reading of the First Folio of Shakespeare*. Oxford: Clarendon Press, 1963.
Hodgson, Thomas. *An Essay on the Origin and Progress of Stereotype Printing; Including a Description of the Various Processes*. Newcastle, UK: S. Hodgson, 1820.
Holbrook, John C. *Recollections of a Nonagenarian*. Boston: Pilgrim Press, 1897.
The Holy Bible, Containing the Old and New Testaments, Together With the Apocrypha. New York: D. D. Smith, 1820.
The Holy Bible, Containing the Old and New Testaments: Translated Out of the Original Tongues, and with the Former Translations Diligently Compared and Revised. Philadelphia: Stereotyped for the Bible Society by T. Rutt, Shacklewell, London, 1812.
Homestead, Melissa. *American Women Authors and Literary Property, 1822–1869*. Cambridge: Cambridge University Press, 2005.
———. "From Periodical to Book in Her Early Career: E. D. E. N. Southworth's Letters to Abraham Hart." *Legacy: A Journal of American Women Writers* 29, no. 1 (2012): 115–47.
Horne, Thomas Hartwell. *An Introduction to the Study of Bibliography*. Vol. 2. London: G. Woodfall, for T. Cadell and W. Davies, 1814.
Howells, John M., and Marion V. Dearman. *Tramp Printers*. Pacific Grove, CA: Discovery Press, 2003.
Howsam, Leslie. *Cheap Bibles: Nineteenth-Century Publishing and the British and Foreign Bible Society*. Cambridge: Cambridge University Press, 1991.
Hunnisett, Basil. *Engraved on Steel: The History of Picture Production Using Steel Plates*. Burlington, VT: Ashgate, 1998.
Jackson, John. *A Treatise on Wood Engraving, Historical and Practical*. London: C. Knight, 1839.
Jackson, Leon. *The Business of Letters: Authorial Economies in Antebellum America*. Stanford: Stanford University Press, 2008.
———. "The Talking Book and the Talking Book Historian: African American Cultures of Print—The State of the Discipline." *Book History* 13 (2010): 251–309.
Jay, William. *A Memoir on the Subject of a General Bible Society for the United States of America, by a Citizen of the State of New-York*. Burlington, NJ: n.p., 1816.
Johns, J. Adam. *The Assault on Progress: Technology and Time in American Literature*. Tuscaloosa: University of Alabama Press, 2008.
Johnson, John. *An Abridgement of Johnson's Typographia, or The Printer's Instructor*. Boston: C. L. Adams, 1828.
———. *Typographia, or The Printer's Instructor*. Vol. 2. London: Longman, Hurst, Rees, Orme, Brown & Green, 1824.
Joyce, Donald Franklin. *Black Book Publishers in the United States: A Historical Dictionary of the Presses, 1817–1990*. New York: Greenwood Press, 1991.
———. *Gatekeepers of Black Culture: Black-Owned Book Publishing in the United States, 1817–1981*. Westport, CT: Greenwood Press, 1983.
Kaser, David. "The Origin of the Book Trade Sales." *Papers of the Bibliographical Society of America* 50, no. 3 (1956): 296–302.
Kasson, John F. *Civilizing the Machine: Technology and Republican Values in America, 1776–1900*. New York: Grossman, 1976.

Katz, Farley P. "Printing the 1460 Catholicon—Are Slugs the Solution?" *Gutenberg Jahrbuch* 96 (2021): 49–78.
Keese, William L. *John Keese, Wit and Litterateur: A Biographical Memoir*. New York: D. Appleton and Co., 1883.
———. "Keese-ana." *Magazine of American History* 1, no. 12 (1877): 734–39.
Kelley, Mary. *Private Women, Public Stage: Literary Domesticity in Nineteenth-Century America*. New York: Oxford University Press, 1984.
Kinane, Vincent. "'Literary Food' for the American Market: Patrick Byrne's Exports to Mathew Carey." *Proceedings of the American Antiquarian Society* 104, no. 2 (1994): 315–32.
Kubler, George A. *The Era of Charles Mahon, Third Earl of Stanhope, Stereotyper: 1750–1825*. New York: Privately printed, 1938.
———. *Historical Treatises, Abstracts, and Papers on Stereotyping*. New York: J. J. Little & Ives, 1936.
———. *A New History of Stereotyping*. New York: J. J. Little & Ives, 1941.
———. *A Short History of Stereotyping*. New York: The Author, 1928.
———. *Wet Mat Stereotyping in Germany in 1690*. New York: Certified Dry Mat Corporation, 1937.
Lacy, Creighton. *The Word-Carrying Giant: The Growth of the American Bible Society (1816–1966)*. South Pasadena: William Carey Library, 1977.
LaFoy, John B. M. D. *The Complete Coiffeur; or, An Essay on the Art of Adorning Natural, and of Creating Artificial, Beauty*. New York: Stereotyped for the Proprietors, and Sold by All the Principal Booksellers, 1817.
Laurie, Bruce. *Artisans into Workers: Labor in Nineteenth-Century America*. New York: Hill and Wang, 1989.
———. *Working People of Philadelphia, 1800–1850*. Philadelphia: Temple University Press, 1980.
Lehmann-Haupt, Hellmut. *The Book in America: A History of the Making, the Selling, and the Collecting of Books in the United States*. New York: R. R. Bowker, 1939.
Lemprière, John. *A Classical Dictionary: Containing a Copious Amount of All the Proper Names Mentioned in Ancient Authors*. New York: Printed and Published for A. T. Goodrich and William B. Gilley, New-York, Mathew Carey and Edward Earle, Philadelphia, by T. & W. Mercein, 1816.
Liu, Alan. "Imagining the New Media Encounter." In *A Companion to Digital Literary Studies*, edited by Ray Siemens, 3–25. Somerset: John Wiley & Sons, 2013.
Low, Nathaniel. *An Astronomical Diary; or, Almanack, for the Year of Christian Era 1807*. Boston: Munroe & Francis, 1806.
Madison, Charles A. *Book Publishing in America*. New York: McGraw-Hill, 1966.
Makala, Jeffrey. "The Early History of Stereotyping in the United States: Mathew Carey and the Quarto Bible Marketplace." *Papers of the Bibliographical Society of America* 109, no. 4 (2015): 461–89.
———. "Print, Buy, and Sell on Demand: The Secondhand Market in Stereotype Plates in 19th-Century America." Paper given at the annual meeting of the Society for the History of Authorship, Reading, and Publishing (SHARP), 7–10 July 2015, Montreal.
———. "'Spiritual Machinery': The American Bible Society and the Mechanisms of Large-Scale Printing in the Early Nineteenth Century." *Printing History*, new ser., 25 (Winter 2019): 45–66.
Marx, Leo. *The Machine in the Garden: Technology and the Pastoral Ideal in America*. 1964. New York: Oxford University Press, 2000.

Matthiessen, F. O. *American Renaissance: Art and Expression in the Age of Emerson and Whitman*. 1941. New York: Barnes and Noble, 2009.
McGettigan, Katie. *Herman Melville: Modernity and the Material Text*. Durham: University of New Hampshire Press, 2017.
McGill, Meredith. *American Literature and the Culture of Reprinting, 1834–1853*. Philadelphia: University of Pennsylvania Press, 2003.
McMullin, B. J. "The Cambridge Affair: The Ged-Fenner Stereotyping Venture, 1731–3." *Book Collector* 57, no. 2 (2008): 217–46.
———. "Joseph Athias and the Early History of Stereotyping." *Quaerendo* 23, no. 3 (1993): 184–207.
McMurtrie, Douglas C. *Stereotyping in Bavaria in the Sixteenth Century: A Note on the History of Map Printing Processes and of Printer's Platemaking*. New York: Privately printed, 1935.
Meier, Hugo A. "Thomas Jefferson and Democratic Technology." In *Technology in America: A History of Individuals and Ideas*, 2nd ed., edited by Carroll W. Pursell Jr., 17–33. Cambridge: MIT Press, 1990.
Melville, Herman. *The Letters of Herman Melville*. Edited by Merrell R. Davis and William H. Gilman. New Haven: Yale University Press, 1960.
———. *Moby-Dick*. 1851. New York: W. W. Norton, 1967.
———. *Pierre, or The Ambiguities*. 1852. Evanston: Northwestern University Press, 1999.
M'Leod, Alexander. *The Larger Catechism, Agreed upon by the Assembly of Divines at Westminster, with the Assistance of Commissioners from the Church of Scotland, and Received by the Several Presbyterian Churches in America; with the Proofs from the Scripture*. New York: Stereotyped and Printed by J. Watts & Co. for Whiting & Watson, Theological and Classical Booksellers, 1813.
Moore, John W. *Moore's Historical, Biographical, and Miscellaneous Gatherings, in the Form of Disconnected Notes Relative to Printers, Printing, Publishing, and Editing*. Concord, NH: Republican Press Association, 1886.
Mores, Edward Rowe. *A Dissertation upon English Typographical Founders and Foundries*. 1778. Oxford: Oxford Bibliographical Society, 1961.
Mosley, James. "Introduction." In *Ornamented Types: Twenty-Three Alphabets from the Foundry of Louis John Pouchée*, edited by James Mosley. London: I. M. Imprimit, 1993.
Munsell, Joel. *Typographical Miscellany*. Albany: Joel Munsell, 1850.
Murray, Hannah-Rose, and John R. McKivigan. *Frederick Douglass in Britain and Ireland, 1845–1895*. Edinburgh: Edinburgh University Press, 2021.
Murray, Lindley. *English Grammar, Adapted to the Different Classes of Learners, with an Appendix, Containing Rules and Observations for Assisting the More Advanced Students to Write with Perspicuity and Accuracy*. Philadelphia: Printed and sold by Mathew Carey, 1815.
Myerson, Joel. *Walt Whitman: A Descriptive Bibliography*. Pittsburgh: University of Pittsburgh Press, 1993.
Needham, Paul. "Johann Gutenberg and the Catholicon Press." *Papers of the Bibliographical Society of America* 76, no. 4 (1982): 395–456.
Newbury, Michael. *Figuring Authorship in Antebellum America*. Stanford: Stanford University Press, 1997.
The New Testament. New York: Stereotyped and Printed by D. & G. Bruce, 1815.
The New Testament of Our Lord and Saviour Jesus Christ, Newly Translated Out of the Original Greek; And with the Former Translations Diligently Compared and Revised. Philadelphia: Printed and published by Mathew Carey, 1814.

Nichols, Charles L. "The Literary Fair in the United States." In *Bibliographical Essays: A Tribute to Wilberforce Eames*, edited by George Parker Winship, 85–92. 1924. Reprint, Freeport, NY: Books for Libraries Press, 1967.

Nord, David Paul. "Benevolent Books: Printing, Religion, and Reform." In *A History of the Book in America*, vol. 2, *An Extensive Republic: Print, Culture, and Society in the New Nation, 1790–1840*, edited by Robert A. Gross and Mary Kelley, 221–46. Chapel Hill: University of North Carolina Press, 2010.

———. "Benevolent Capital: Financing Evangelical Book Publishing in Early Nineteenth-Century America." In *God and Mammon: Protestants, Money, and the Market, 1790–1860*, edited by Mark A. Noll, 147–70. New York: Oxford University Press, 2002.

———. "The Evangelical Origins of Mass Media in America, 1815–1835." *Journalism Monographs* 88 (May 1984). https://eric.ed.gov/?id=ED245260.

———. *Faith in Reading: Religious Publishing and the Birth of Mass Media in America*. New York: Oxford University Press, 2004.

———. "Free Grace, Free Books, Free Riders: The Economics of Religious Publishing in Early Nineteenth-Century America." *Proceedings of the American Antiquarian Society* 106, no. 2 (1996): 241–72.

North, Eric M. "The Production and Supply of Scriptures: Part I, 1816–1820." ABS Historical Essay #18, 1963, typescript, American Bible Society Archives.

Northup, Solomon. *Twelve Years a Slave: Narrative of Solomon Northup, a Citizen of New-York, Kidnapped in Washington City in 1841, and Rescued in 1853, from a Cotton Plantation Near the Red River, in Louisiana*. New York: C. M. Saxton, 1859.

———. *Twelve Years a Slave: The Thrilling Story of a Free Colored Man, Kidnapped in Washington in 1841, Sold into Slavery, and After a Twelve Years' Bondage, Reclaimed by State Authority from a Cotton Plantation in Louisiana*. Philadelphia: Keystone Publishing Co., n.d. [not before 1865].

Norton, John, trans. *The Gospel According to Saint John: In the Mohawk Language*. New York: Printed for the American Bible Society, D. Fanshaw, Printer, 1818.

Nye, David E. *American Technological Sublime*. Cambridge: MIT Press, 1994.

———. *Narrative and Spaces: Technology and the Construction of American Culture*. New York: Columbia University Press, 1997.

"An Original Paper of the Late Lieut. Gov. Colden, on a New Method of Printing Discovered by Him; Together with an Original Letter from the Late Dr. Franklin, on the Same Subject [...]." In *The American Medical and Philosophical Register; or, Annals of Medicine, Natural History, Agriculture, and the Arts*, 1:439–50, 1814.

Painter, Nell Irvin. *Sojourner Truth: A Life, a Symbol*. New York: W. W. Norton, 1996.

Parfait, Claire. *The Publishing History of "Uncle Tom's Cabin," 1852–2002*. Burlington, VT: Ashgate, 2007.

Parker, Herschel. *Herman Melville: A Biography*. Vol. 2, *1851–1891*. Baltimore: Johns Hopkins University Press, 2002.

Partington, C. F. *The Printer's Complete Guide*. London: Sherwood, Gilbert, and Piper, 1825.

Paulus, Michael J., Jr. "Archibald Alexander and the Use of Books: Theological Education and Print Culture in the Early Republic." *Journal of the Early Republic* 31 (Winter 2011): 639–69.

Peña, Carolyn de la. "'Slow and Low Progress,' or Why American Studies Should Do Technology." *American Quarterly* 58, no. 3 (2006): 915–41.

Penn, Irvine Garland. *The Afro-American Press and Its Editors*. Springfield, MA: Willey and Co., 1891.

The Permanent Stereotype Steel Plate, with Observations on Its Importance, and an Explanation of Its Construction and Uses. Boston: C. Stebbins, 1806.

Perry, Seth. "The Many Bibles of Joseph Smith: Textual, Prophetic, and Scholarly Authority in Early-National Bible Culture." *Journal of the American Academy of Religion* 84, no. 3 (2016): 750–75.

Petroski, Henry. *The Pencil: A History of Design and Circumstance.* New York: Knopf, 2000.

Philadelphia in 1824; or, A Brief Account of the Various Institutions and Public Objects in This Metropolis: Being a Complete Guide for Strangers, and an Useful Compendium for Inhabitants. Philadelphia: H. C. Carey & I. Lea, 1824.

Poe, Edgar Allan. "Anastatic Printing." *Broadway Journal* 1, no. 15 (12 April 1845): 229–31.

Pretzer, William S. "'Of the Paper Cap and Inky Apron': Journeyman Printers." In *A History of the Book in America*, vol. 2, *An Extensive Republic: Print, Culture, and Society in the New Nation, 1790–1840*, edited by Robert A. Gross and Mary Kelley, 160–74. Chapel Hill: University of North Carolina Press, 2010.

Proceedings of the Second National Convention of Journeymen Printers, Held in Baltimore, September 1851. New York: Printed for the National Convention, 1851.

Remer, Rosalind. "Capturing the Bard: An Episode in the American Publication of Shakespeare's Plays, 1822–1851." *Papers of the Bibliographical Society of America* 91, no. 3 (1991): 327–37.

———. *Printers and Men of Capital: Philadelphia Book Publishers in the New Republic.* Philadelphia: University of Pennsylvania Press, 1996.

Richmond, Peggy Jo Zemens. "Afro-American Printers and Book Publishers, 1650–1865." PhD diss., University of Michigan, 1971.

Rohrbach, Augusta. "Profits of Protest: The Market Strategies of Sojourner Truth and Louisa May Alcott." In *Prophets of Protest: Reconsidering the History of American Abolitionism*, edited by Timothy Patrick McCarthy and John Stauffer, 235–55. New York: New Press, 2006.

Roy, Michaël. "Cheap Editions, Little Books, and Handsome Duodecimos: A Book History Approach to Antebellum Slave Narratives." In "African American Print Cultures," edited by Joycelyn Moody and Howard Ramsby II, special issue, *MELUS* 40, no. 3 (2015): 69–93.

Sallust. *Belli Catalinarii et Jugurthini historiae.* Edinburgi: Gulielmus Ged non typis mobilibus, 1739.

Scougal, Henry. *The Life of God in the Soul of Man.* Newcastle, UK: Printed and sold by John White from plates made by William Ged, Edinburgh, 1742.

Sellers, Charles. *The Market Revolution: Jacksonian America, 1815–1840.* New York: Oxford University Press, 1991.

Seltzer, Mark. *Bodies and Machines.* London: Routledge, 2015.

Senchyne, Jonathan. "Bottles of Ink and Reams of Paper: *Clotel*, Racialization, and the Material Culture of Print." In *Early African American Print Culture*, edited by Lara Langer Cohen and Jordan Alexander Stein, 140–60. Philadelphia: University of Pennsylvania Press, 2012.

———. *The Intimacy of Paper in Early and Nineteenth-Century American Literature.* Amherst: University of Massachusetts Press, 2020.

———. "Under Pressure: Reading Material Textuality in the Recovery of Early African American Print Work." *Arizona Quarterly* 75, no. 3 (2019): 109–32.

Sheehan, Daniel. *That Was Publishing: A Chronicle of the Book Trade in the Gilded Age.* Bloomington: Indiana University Press, 1952.

Silver, Rollo. *The American Printer, 1787–1825*. Charlottesville: University Press of Virginia, 1967.
———. *The Baltimore Book Trade, 1800–1825*. New York: New York Public Library, 1953.
———. "Copper-Facing: An Incident in the History of Typefounding." *Library* 29, no. 1 (1974): 103–10.
———. "Flash of the Comet: The Typographical Career of Samuel N. Dickinson." *Studies in Bibliography* 31 (1978): 68–89.
———. *Typefounding in America, 1787–1825*. Charlottesville: University Press of Virginia, 1965.
Simms, P. Marion. *The Bible in America: Versions That Have Played Their Part in the Making of the Republic*. New York: Wilson-Erickson, 1936.
Sizer, Nelson. *What to Do, and Why; And How to Educate Each Man for His Proper Work: Describing Seventy-Five Trades and Professions, and the Talents and Temperaments Required for Each [. . .]*. New York: Edmund C. Fisher & Co., 1874.
Smith, Steven Carl. *An Empire of Print: The New York Publishing Trade in the Early American Republic*. University Park: Penn State University Press, 2017.
Spires, Derrick R. *The Practice of Citizenship: Black Politics and Print Culture in the Early United States*. Philadelphia: University of Pennsylvania Press, 2019.
Steiner, Bernard C. *One Hundred and Ten Years of Bible Society Work in Maryland, 1810–1920*. Baltimore: n.p., 1921.
Stern, Madeleine B. *Books and Book People in 19th-Century America*. New York: R. R. Bowker, 1978.
———. *Heads and Headlines: The Phrenological Fowlers*. Norman: University of Oklahoma Press, 1971.
Stevens, George A. *New York Typographical Union No. 6: Study of a Modern Trade Union and Its Predecessors*. Albany: J. B. Lyon, 1913.
Stewart, Ethelbert. *A Documentary History of the Early Organizations of Printers*. Indianapolis: International Typographical Union, 1907.
Stokes, Melvyn, and Stephen Conway, eds. *The Market Revolution in America: Social, Political, and Religious Expressions, 1800–1880*. Charlottesville: University Press of Virginia, 1996.
Stott, Richard B. *Workers in the Metropolis: Class, Ethnicity, and Youth in Antebellum New York City*. Ithaca: Cornell University Press, 1990.
Stowe, Harriet Beecher. *Dred: A Tale of the Dismal Swamp*. 1856. Boston: Houghton, Mifflin and Co., 1884.
Strickland, William Peter. *History of the American Bible Society, from Its Organization to the Present Time*. New York: Harper & Brothers, 1849.
Sutton, Walter. *The Western Book Trade*. Columbus: Ohio State University Press, 1961.
Tebbel, John. *A History of Book Publishing in the United States*. Vol. 1, *The Creation of an Industry, 1630–1865*. New York: R. R. Bowker, 1972.
Thomas, Isaiah. *The History of Printing in America*. Worcester: Isaiah Thomas, 1810.
———. *The History of Printing in America*. 2nd ed. Albany: Joel Munsell, 1874.
———. *The History of Printing in America, with a Biography of Printers*. 2nd ed. of 1874, with the author's corrections and additions. Reprint, New York: Burt Franklin, 1967.
Thompson, Peter J. "Thoreau on Monadnock: Long on Botany and Philosophy, Short on Geology." *Geological Society of America Abstracts with Programs* 38, no. 7 (2006): 38.
Thoreau, Henry David. *The Correspondence of Henry D. Thoreau*. Vol. 1, *1834–1848*. Edited by Robert N. Hudspeth. Princeton: Princeton University Press, 2013.
———. *The Journal of Henry David Thoreau*. Edited by Bradford Torrey and Francis H. Allen. 15 vols. Salt Lake City: Peregrine Smith, 1984.

---. *Walden, or Life in the Woods*. 1854. Edited by J. Lyndon Shanley. Princeton: Princeton University Press, 1989.
---. *A Week on the Concord and Merrimack Rivers*. 1849. Edited by Carl F. Hovde. Princeton: Princeton University Press, 1980.
Timperley, Charles Henry. *Encyclopaedia of Literary and Typographical Anecdote* [...]. London: Henry G. Bohn, 1842.
Tocqueville, Alexis de. *Democracy in America*. 1835. New York: Vintage Classics, 1990.
Trentmann, Frank. "Materiality in the Future of History: Things, Practices, and Politics." *Journal of British Studies* 48 (April 2009): 283–307.
Truth, Sojourner. *Narrative of Sojourner Truth, a Northern Slave*. Boston: Printed for the Author, 1850.
Tryon, Warren S. "Book Distribution in Mid-Nineteenth Century America: Illustrated by the Publishing Records of Ticknor and Fields, Boston." *Papers of the Bibliographical Society of America* 41, no. 3 (1947): 210–30.
Turner, Michael L. "Andrew Wilson, Lord Stanhope's Stereotype Printer: A Preliminary Report." *Journal of the Printing Historical Society* 9 (1973–74): 22–65.
---. Introduction to *The Method of Founding Stereotype*, by Charles Brightly, and *An Essay on the Origin and Progress of Stereotype Printing*, by Thomas Hodgson. Reprint, New York: Garland, 1982.
Twyman, Michael. *Lithography, 1800–1850: The Techniques of Drawing on Stone in England and France and Their Application in Works of Topology*. New York: Oxford University Press, 1970.
van Winkle, Cornelius. *The Printer's Guide; or, An Introduction to the Art of Printing*. New York: Printed and published for C. S. van Winkle, 1818. 3rd ed., with additions and alterations, New York: White & Hagar, 1835.
Vogeley, Nancy. *The Bookrunner: A History of Inter-American Relations—Print, Politics, and Commerce in the United States and Mexico, 1800–1830*. Philadelphia: American Philosophical Society, 2011.
Walker, John. *An Abridgement of Walker's Critical Pronouncing Dictionary and Expositor of the English Language*. New York: Stereotyped by E. & J. White and C. Starr for D. D. Smith, 1818.
Walls, Laura Dassow. *Henry David Thoreau: A Life*. Chicago: University of Chicago Press, 2017.
Warner, Michael. *The Letters of the Republic: Publication and the Public Sphere in Eighteenth-Century America*. Cambridge: Harvard University Press, 1990.
Washington, Margaret. *Sojourner Truth's America*. Urbana: University of Illinois Press, 2009.
Weedon, Alexis. *Victorian Publishing: The Economics of Book Production for a Mass Market, 1836–1916*. Burlington, VT: Ashgate, 2003.
Weiss, Harry B. "Type Founders, Copperplate Printers, Stereotypers in Early New York City." *Bulletin of the New York Public Library* 55, no. 10 (1951): 471–83.
Welch, Robert, and Brian Walker, gen. eds. *Oxford History of the Irish Book*. 5 vols. New York: Oxford University Press, 2006–11.
White, William. "The First (1855) 'Leaves of Grass': How Many Copies?" *Papers of the Bibliographical Society of America* 57, no. 3 (1963): 352–54.
Wigger, John H. *Taking Heaven by Storm: Methodism and the Rise of Popular Christianity in America*. New York: Oxford University Press, 1998.
Wilentz, Sean. *Chants Democratic: New York City and the Rise of the American Working Class, 1788–1850*. 20th anniversary ed. New York: Oxford University Press, 2004.

Williams, Susan S. "Authors and Literary Authorship." In *A History of the Book in America*, vol. 3, *The Industrial Book, 1840–1880*, edited by Scott E. Casper, Jeffrey D. Groves, Stephen W. Nissenbaum, and Michael Winship, 90–116. Chapel Hill: University of North Carolina Press, 2007.

Wilson, Peter, ed. *Novum Testamentum graecum ad exemplar*. Hartford: Oliver D. Cooke, 1822.

Winner, Langdon. "Do Artifacts Have Politics?" *Daedalus* 109, no. 1 (1980): 121–36.

Winship, Michael. *American Literary Publishing in the Mid-Nineteenth Century: The Business of Ticknor and Fields*. Cambridge: Cambridge University Press, 2002.

———. "Distribution and the Trade." In *A History of the Book in America*, vol. 3, *The Industrial Book, 1840–1880*, edited by Scott E. Casper, Jeffrey D. Groves, Stephen W. Nissenbaum, and Michael Winship, 117–29. Chapel Hill: University of North Carolina Press, 2007.

———. "Getting the Books Out." In *Getting the Books Out: Papers of the Chicago Conference on the Book in 19th-Century America*, edited by Michael Hackenberg, 4–25. Washington, DC: Library of Congress Center for the Book, 1987.

———. "Hawthorne and the 'Scribbling Women': Publishing *The Scarlet Letter* in the Nineteenth-Century United States." *Studies in American Fiction* 29, no. 1 (2001): 3–11.

———. "John Punchard Jewett, Publisher of *Uncle Tom's Cabin*: A Biographical Note with a Preliminary Checklist of His Imprints." In *Roger Eliot Stoddard at Sixty-Five: A Celebration*, edited by Roger Eliot Stoddard, 85–114. New York: Thornwillow Press, 2000.

———. "Printing with Plates in the Nineteenth Century United States." *Printing History* 5, no. 2 (1983): 15–26.

Wood, Gordon S. *Empire of Liberty: A History of the Early Republic, 1789–1815*. New York: Oxford University Press, 1999.

Wood, Marcus. *Blind Memory: Visual Representations of Slavery in England and America, 1780–1865*. New York: Routledge, 2000.

Woodward, David. "Some Evidence for the Use of Stereotyping on Peter Apian's World Map of 1530." *Imago Mundi* 24, no. 1 (1970): 43–48.

Wosh, Peter J. "Bibles, Benevolence, and Bureaucracy: The Changing Nature of Nineteenth Century Religious Records." *American Archivist* 52, no. 2 (1989): 166–78.

Wright, John. *Early Bibles in America: Being A Descriptive Account of Bibles Published in the United States, Mexico, and Canada*. New York: Thomas Whitaker, 1894.

Zboray, Ronald J. *A Fictive People: Antebellum Economic Development and the American Reading Public*. New York: Oxford University Press, 1993.

INDEX

Italicized page references indicate illustrations. Endnotes are referenced with "n" followed by the endnote number.

abolitionism, 121, 141–44, 173n46
Abridgement (Bacon), 111–12
Adams power press, 38
Address to the Booksellers of the United States (Carey), 106
Adoniram Chandler & Co., 33, 92, 95
advances in printing technologies. *See* technological changes and advances
advertisements
 capital investment, 16
 development and spread of stereotyping, 28–29
 enslaved people, 145
 European advances in creating stereotype plates, 44
 Hart sale, 147
 for individual sets of plates, 103–5
 Osgood sale, 125–26
 trade sales, 112–13, 116
 type specimen books, 40
African American authors and publishers, 141–46
African American Bible societies, 70
African Methodist Episcopal Church, 70
Albany, New York, 31, 33, 74
Altman, Rick, 4–5
AME Book Concern, 70
American Anti-Slavery Society, 141, 145
American Bible Society (ABS), 68–101
 assets in stereotype plates, 93
 auxiliary Bible societies, 70–73, 75–78, 80, 82–85, 90–93, 96, 98, 101, 163n85
 Baltimore Bible Society, 92
 bindings, 98–99
 centralization, 84–85
 duodecimo Bibles, 58, 81

 family Bible market, 66
 and Fanshaw, 78–79, 90, 98
 founding of, 70–74
 fundraising, 76
 general supply, 69, 99–101
 headquarters, 85–86
 innovations, 1–2, 12, 15, 79, 97–98
 international publisher, 80–81
 inventory of assets, 68–69, 99–100, 158–59
 joint offer from the New York Bible Society and the New York Auxiliary Bible Society, 78
 Kentucky Bible Society, 79–80, 84–85, 90–92
 New Testaments, 87–95
 octavo Bibles, 81
 Panic of 1819, 89–92
 pocket Bible, 95–96
 publicity and marketing, 83
 resolution, 75–76
 securing stereotype plates, 74–75
 social reforms, 72
 Spanish Bible, 93–95
 stereotype plates management committee, 84
 subscriptions for Bibles, 77–78
 textual accuracy, 81–82, 86–87
 and Wallis, 94–95
American Booksellers' Association, 118, 171n59
American Book Trade Association, 124–25, 128
American Dictionary of Printing and Bookmaking, 32–33
American identity, 130

American mechanical exceptionalism, 3
American Museum (magazine), 41
American Publishers' Circular, 103, 105, 117–18, 123
American Romanticism, 129–30
American Spelling Book (Webster), 43
American Stationers' Company, 109
American Sunday School Union, 72, 100–101
American Tract Society, 72, 79, 89, 100–101
American Universal Geography (Morse), 42
American ways of conduct, 3
anastatic printing, 130–32
"Anastatic Printing" (Poe), 130–32
Anglo-African Magazine, 145
Anglophone printers' manuals, 20
antebellum period, 101, 111, 129, 133, 145
antislavery societies, 141–43
Anti-Slavery Standard, 145
Apocrypha, 48, 52, 60, 74, 76, 87, 99
Appleton & Co., 114–15
apprenticeships, 5, 27, 32, 35–38, 78
assets, 34, 68–69, 86, 88, 93, 96, 118–20
    See also capital investments
Astor House Hotel, 114–15
Astor Place, 124
Athias, Joseph, 16
Atlas (Lavoisne), 65
Auburn, New York, 120–21
auctions, 104–11, 113, 116–20, 124–28, 147–49, 169n5
authorship, 1, 102, 129, 130–33, 143
automated presses, 37
auxiliary Bible societies, 70–73, 80, 82–85, 90–93, 96, 98, 101, 163n85

Babbage, Charles, 10–11, 14–15
Bacon, Mathew, 112
Baltimore, Maryland, 29, 31, 80, 83, 92, 150
Baltimore American (newspaper), 29
Baltimore Bible, 168n91
Baltimore Bible Society, 71, 92, 96
Bangs Brothers, 117, 128
bankruptcies, 15–16, 103, 107, 118–19, 122
Barlow, Joel, 65
Barnett, George, 35–36
Battle Creek, Michigan, 142

Beauties (Irving), 109
Beecher, Lyman, 72
Benesh, Klaus, 130
Bethune, Divie, 74–75
Beulah (Wilson), 122–23
BFBS (British and Foreign Bible Society), 70, 73–76, 80, 84, 88, 96, 100
B. F. Lewis, 82
Bible House, 68–69, 93
Bibles
    Carey's Bible list, 55–56
    coarse Bible, 49, 51, 55, 62
    duodecimo, 43, 48, 58, 77–78, 81, 83–84, 86–89, 97, 99
    family Bibles, 31, 41–67, 77, 82, 85, 95, 135
    and Fanshaw, 68–69, 78–79
    French Bibles, 76, 80, 83, 92
    Gaelic Bibles, 83–84
    general supply, 69, 99–101
    German Bibles, 92, 99
    Minion Bible plates, 80–82, 87–89, 91, 93, 99–100, 167n36
    Nonpareil, 69
    octavo, 29, 48, 74, 76–77, 81–82, 84, 86–89, 92–93, 95–96, 100
    Pica type, 164n43
    pocket Bibles, 77, 95–96
    production and distribution, 78–85, 88–90, 92–93, 96–97, 99–101
    quarto Bibles, 43, 46, 48, 51–55, 60–62, 64, 67, 87, 95–97, 99
    Spanish Bibles, 76, 83, 86–88, 93, 95
    stereotyped illustration blocks, 109
    stereotype woodcuts for, 59
    stereotyping technology, 73
    subscriptions for, 43, 52, 62, 64–65, 77
    textual accuracy, 81–82, 87
    translations of, 83–84, 88, 166n19
    value of, 63, 88, 93
    Welsh Bibles, 83–84
    See also American Bible Society (ABS)
Bible Society of Philadelphia, 73
B. & I. Collins, 88
Bidwell, John, 28
Bigelow, Jacob, 2–3, 27
binding, 52, 82, 90–91, 98–99, 145
Binney & Ronaldson, 32
Bishop, J. Leander, 16–17, 30

B. & J. Collins, 32
black employment in Philadelphia, 146
Black Man, The (Brown), 146
Black-owned publishers, 70, 145–46
Blake, William, 131, 171n4
book fairs, 124–25
Book of Life (Truth), 142
Book of Mormon, 97
book production and distribution
    ABS's goals, 75
    adoption of stereotyping, 11–12
    authorship, 132–33
    of Bibles, 78–85, 88–90, 92–93, 96–97, 99–101
    capital investment, 1
    and Carey, 48–49
    centralization of, 70, 73–74, 76, 80, 84–85, 91, 93
    changes in the publishing industry, 149–50
    costs, 23, 120, 123, 127, 133–34
    domestic production, 39
    electroytyping, 28, 136
    and Fanshaw, 68–69, 89–90
    handpress period, 42
    mass media, 70–71
    rail networks, 149
    secondhand marketplace, 12, 128
    trade regulation, 103, 105–7
    trade sale catalogs, 169n5
    urban centers, 33
book sales, decline in, 118, 125
booksellers, 62–63, 103–4, 106–7, 108–14, 117, 122, 171n59
Booksellers' Exchange and Clearing-House, 124–25
Boston, Massachusetts
    and abolitionists, 141, 173n46
    and the ABS, 83
    Bruces' markets, 30, 48
    enslaved individuals by eighteenth-century printers in, 145
    growth of printing trades in, 103
    periodicals in, 150
    Putnam list of plates, 115
    resistance to using stereotype plates, 31
    stereotype foundries in, 92
    stereotype plate output, 35

Thoreaus' business, 137
trade sales in, 104, 106, 108–9, 169n5
typefounders in, 12
Boston Female Anti-Slavery Society, 141
Boston Stereotype Foundry, 146
Boston Transcript, 113
Boston Type and Stereotype Factory, 136
Boudinot, Elias, 72–73, 79, 88–90, 100
Bourgeois type, 63, 83, 87–89
Boyle, James, 141–42
Bradburn and Doolady, 123
branch production, 76
brass blocks, 50–51
Brattleboro, Vermont, 31, 52, 62
Brightly, Charles, 20–23, 32
Bristol, New Hampshire, 135
British and Foreign Bible Society (BFBS), 70, 73–76, 80, 84, 88, 96, 100
British-produced plates, 48, 112
Brown, Candy Gunter, 72
Brown, William Wells, 143–44, 146
Brown's Bible *Concordance*, 51
Bruce, David, 29–30, 48–51, 57–59, 62–63, 78, 81, 94–95, 162n50
Bruce, George, 30, 48–51, 57–59, 62–63, 78, 81, 94–95, 99, 162n50
Bungay, Suffolk, 20, 32
Burlington Female Auxiliary Bible Society of New Jersey, 77–78
business models, 5

Caldwell, John, 74
Cambridge, 23
Campbell, Robert, 145–46
Campbell & Smith, 121
Camus, Armand Gaston, 17, 23
Canada, 4, 39, 80, 88, 137
Canton, China, 71
capital investments, 1, 15–16, 30, 51, 57, 83, 102–3, 123, 131, 133
Carey, Edward, 147–48
Carey, Henry C., 57, 61, 64, 106, 134
Carey, Mathew, 41–67
    Bible list, 55–56
    commissioning a stereotype family bible, 59–67
    growth and development of printing with plates, 12

importation duties on stereotype plates, 163n85
market for stereotype plates, 46–59
Minion Bible, 82
Murray's *English Grammar*, 29
national marketplace in used sets of plates, 103
Nonpareil Bible, 93
organizing book trades, 105–6
Shakespeare plates, 112
Carey & Hart, 147–51
Carey & Lea, 106, 107
Carey & Son, 46, 51, 66
Carleton, 122
Carlyle, Thomas, 3, 9
Carter, John, 11
casting of a stereotype plates
  Brightly's stereotype process, 20–21
  commercial landscape, 94, 133
  economics of, 44, 48–49
  and Fanshaw, 78
  illustrations of, *21–22*
  increase of, 35
  mass media production and distribution, 71
  Mecom's stereotype process, 19
  newspapers, 28
  process of stereotyping, 10
  from set type, 46
  skill in, 15
  Stanhope's stereotype process, 18–19
  Thomas's stereotype process, 19–20
cast type illustrations and decorations, 24
centralized production and distribution, 70, 73–74, 76, 80, 84–85, 91, 93
certificates of membership from typographical associations, 37
Chandler, Adoniram, 33–34, 92–93, 95
Charless, Joseph, 43
Charleston, South Carolina, 83
  Bible Society, 77–78
Charvat, William, 30, 52
cheap reprint publishers, 107, 121, 125, 128
Cherokee translation, 84
Christianity, 100–101, 149
Cicero, 62–63
Cincinnati, Ohio, 80, 104, 106, 113, 116, 120, 150

Civil War, 122–23, 145–46
Classical Dictionary (Lemprière), 56
cliché, 17, 137–38
Clinton, DeWitt, 72
Clinton Hall, 124
cloth bindings, 98–99
C. M. Saxton, 121
coarse Bibles, 49, 51, 55, 62
Cobbett, William, 42, 151
Cobbett's Register, 151
Colden, Cadwallader, 19–20
Collins, Benjamin, 49–51, 59–62
Collins, Isaac, 49–51, 59–62
Collins, William, 66
Collins & Co., 29–30, 45, 49–55, 59–62, 75, 77, 81–82, 94–95
Collins & Hannay, 32, 59, 64–65, 95
colonial American printing, 19, 144–45
color printing, 150
Columbiad (Barlow), 65
commercial publishing, 2, 73–74, 85, 94, 96, 100
commissioning of plates
  and the ABS, 81, 83–86, 97
  Bible societies, 29–30, 78
  cost of, 15–16, 31
  and Fanshaw, 79
  mark of a well-capitalized firm, 40
  M'Carty and Davis, 112
  multiple sets of plates, 75
  stereotyped editions came from publishers, 31
  stereotype family Bible, 59–67
  and Watts, 29
  widespread adoption of stereotyping, 11–12
Company of Printers of Philadelphia, 105
Complete Coiffeur, The (LaFoy), 31
compositors, 26–27, 35–39, 43
concordances, 51
Confidence Man, The (Melville), 118–19
Congress, 39, 150, 163n85
Connecticut, 30, 79
consignees, 106–13, 147
consolidation, 1, 35, 39, 122
Cooke, Oliver D., 94
Cooper, James Fenimore, 72
Cooperstown, New York, 31, 99

192 | Index

copper-faced type and plates, 150
copperplate illustrations or engravings, 63, 121
copyrights, 15, 45, 57, 102–4, 109, 112–15, 119–20, 122–23, 131, 134, 149–50
Cornish, Samuel, 145
correcting stereotype plates, 26, 61, 81–82, 86–87
costs
    of Bible plates, 48–49, 52, 55, 60–61, 74, 76–77, 100
    of commissioning a set of stereotypes, 15, 31, 64–65
    of imported plates, 39
    of New Testament plates, 56–59
    or printing, 91
    or production, 123–28
    paper stock, 167n52
    standardization of composition prices, 37–38
    of stereotyping process, 19, 22–23
    up-front costs of stereotyping, 32, 44–45
    used sets of plates, 103–5, 108
    See also assets; centralized production and distribution
crisis historiography, 4
Critical Pronouncing Dictionary (Walker), 62
Crocker, Uriel, 31
Crocker & Brewster, 31
Curtis, George Williams, 118–20

damaged plates, 58–59, 66, 92–93
D. Appleton & Co., 114–15
Davis, Thomas, 111–12
Delany, Martin, 145
Delaware translation, 83–84, 90
democratic principles and technological improvement, 2–3, 149
Derby, Henry W., 120
Derby, J. C., 122, 165n63
Derby, Miller and Osgood, 120
Derby, Orton, and Mulligan, 120
Derby and Miller, 120
Derby & Jackson, 122
deskilling of labor, 35–40
Despain, Jessica, 4
D. & G. Bruce

Bibles, 48, 50, 52, 87–88, 93
    corrections of plates, 82
    and Fanshaw, 78
    and Lothian, 32
    repairs to New Testament plates, 57–58
    stereotype plates, 45, 75, 77
    type specimen list from, 24
Dickens series, 127
Dick & Fitzgerald, 120
Didot, 17–20, 24, 29
Digest (Sergeant & Rawle), 112
direct purchase, 108
distress sale, 124
Dix, Edwards & Co., 118–20
domestic production, 39, 150
Downing, Andrew Jackson, 114
Dred: A Tale of the Dismal Swamp (Stowe), 140
Dublin, Ireland, 41, 143–44
Du Bois, W. E. B., 146
Dunbar, Charles, 135
duodecimo Bibles, 43, 48, 58, 77–78, 81, 83–84, 86–89, 97, 99
duodecimo plates, 112, 117, 123, 126
Dutch printers, 16–19, 24
Duyckinck, Evert, 110

E. F. Bakus, 74
E. & J. White, 62, 78
electrotyping, 5, 14, 28, 32, 129, 134, 135–37, 139, 150
Elements of Technology (Bigelow), 3, 27
Elihu White & Co., 24, 74–77, 81–82
Ellen Middleton (Fullerton), 117
Emerson, Ralph Waldo, 132, 137–39
employment, 36, 146
    See also labor practices
England, 18–19, 29, 43–45, 46, 48, 121, 143, 163n85, 173n44
English Grammar (Murray), 29, 31, 49–50, 63
engraved plates, 20
    See also siderography
engravers, 103
Enlightenment and post-Enlightenment reason and progress, 5
enslaved persons, 71, 120, 141, 143–45
Erie Canal, 33

Essay on the Origin and Progress of Stereotype Printing (Hodgson), 23
European commerce in the United States, 33
European immigrants, 37–38
European national model of book trades, 105
European origins of casting plates from set type, 16–20, 44–45
evangelical commissions, 79, 85
evangelical consumerism, 141
evangelization, 70
Evans, John, 97, 99
E. White & Co., 24, 62, 88
exchange of stereotype plates, 42, 46, 49–50, 52, 57–58, 59–60, 103, 105–6, 108, 112, 114, 116
experiments, 16–20, 23

family Bibles, 31, 41–67, 77, 82, 85, 95, 135
Family Magazine, 17, 150
Fanshaw, Daniel, 68–69, 78–79, 82, 86, 88–91, 95, 97–98, 167n39
Fea, John, 83
Female Auxiliary Missionary Society of Bethlehem, Pennsylvania, 90
Fern, Fanny. *See* Willis, Sarah Payson
Fern Leaves from Fanny's Portfolio (Willis), 120–21
Fields, James T., 111, 115–16
fire of December 1853, Harper & Brothers, 34–35, 114, 149, 162n69
Follen, Charles, 103–4
foreign publishers, 45
Forthill Stereotype Foundry, 99
Foulis, Andrew, 17–18
founding convention, ABS, 73, 75–76
foundries. *See* stereotype foundries
Fourdrinier papermaking machine, 79
Fowler and Wells, 133
France, 18–19, 41, 44, 80, 131, 144
Frankfurt book fair, 105–6, 114
Frank Leslie's Illustrated Newspaper, 110
Franklin, Benjamin, 19–20, 41
Freedom's Journal, 145
free markets and deregulation, 105
Freemasonry, 145
French Bibles, 76, 80, 83, 92
Fresh Leaves (Wilson), 123
Fullerton, Georgiana, 117

fundraising, 70, 76, 83, 89, 124
Fyfe, Aileen, 4

Gaelic Bibles, 83–84
Gaine, Hugh, 43, 105–6, 163n4
Gallatin, Albert, 80
Garrison, William Lloyd, 141
Ged, William, 17, 24
General Assembly of the Presbyterian Church, 73
General Convention of the Baptist Church, 73
general supply, 69, 99–101
George Leavitt & Co., 124
Georgia Bible Society, 78
German Bibles, 92, 99
German Grammar (Follen), 103–4, 108
German-language textbooks, 104
German Reader (Follen), 103–4, 108
gifts of stereotype plates, 96, 142, 173n46
Gilbert, Olive, 142
Gilpin, Joshua, 19
Godey's Lady's Book, 148, 150–51
Goldsmith, Oliver, 108, 114
Gospel of Saint John, 88
Grantley Manor (Fullerton), 117
graphite, 13, 135–37
Gray, John A., 146
Great Britain, 23, 32, 71, 96, 98–100, 122, 150
Great Lakes, 33
Greek New Testament, 94–95
Green, James, 42
Greenspan, Ezra, 143
Gutenberg, Johannes, 11, 13, 16
Guthrie, William, 42

Hamilton, Thomas, Sr., 145
Hamilton, William G., 145–46
Hammond Wallis, 93–94
handpresses/handpress period, 12–15, 42, 50, 75, 79, 98
Hansard, 151
Hansard, T. C., 24–26, 151
Harper, James, 147–49
Harper & Brothers
   American Book Trade Association, 125
   auction lots, 147–49
   fire of 1853, 34–35, 114, 149, 162n69

Harper & Brothers *(continued)*
   headquarters, 38
   modernization efforts, 100
   New York Book-Publishers' Association, 113–14, 117
   Osgood sale, 127, 165n63
   reprinted novels, 133–35
   warehousing, 34–35
   and Wilson, 123
Harper's Magazine, 34–35
Hart, Abraham, 115, 147–51
Hartford, Connecticut, 30–31, 92
Harvard Register, 140
Hatch, Nathan, 100
Hawthorne, Nathaniel, 114–15, 134
Hazard, Sonia, 97, 123
Heidegger, Martin, 130
heliotypes, 126
Histoire et procédés du polytypage et de la stéréotypie (Camus), 23
Historical Society of Pennsylvania, 46
History of American Manufactures (Bishop), 17
History of Printing in America (Thomas), 19–20, 145
History of the Roman Republic (Michelet), 117
Hodgson, Thomas, 23
H. O. Houghton & Co., 31
Holbrook & Fessenden, 52, 62
Holman & Gray, 145
Homes of American Authors (Putnam), 114
Horace, 62–63
Houghton, Osgood and Company, 124
Houghton and Mifflin, 124
housing stereotyping plates. *See* warehousing
Howe, Jedidiah, 95–96, 112
Howsam, Leslie, 73
Hubbard, Amos, 79
Hudson & Goodwin, 30
Hunt & Congdon, 126
Hurd & Houghton, 127
Huron tribe, 84

illustrations, 13, 24, 109, 121–22, 142
immigrants, 37, 42
industrialization, 28, 35, 37, 129–30
   See also technological changes and advances
industrial manufacturing, 10–11
Inez (Wilson), 123
innovation(s), 1–3, 17, 19, 23, 27–30, 43, 51, 55, 63, 69–70, 73, 79, 97–99, 101, 106, 110, 150
   See also technological changes and advances
intellectual property, 5, 15, 102
interdenominational evangelical organizations, 101
International Book Company, 121–22
international copyright law, 150
International Peace Congress, 143–44
International Typographical Union, 39
inventory, 68, 87–88, 99, 119, 158–59
investments. *See* capital investments
Ireland, 4, 41–42, 45, 143–44, 173n44
Iroquois nation, 84
Irving, Washington, 109, 119, 134

James, U. P., 116
James R. Osgood & Co., 124–28
Jay, John, 72
Jefferson, Thomas, 3, 70
J. F. and C. Starr, 30–31
J. & J. Harper, 65–66
jobbers, 123–24
job printers, 34, 65, 103
John Childs & Son, 32
John P. Jewett & Co., 149, 173n46
Johnson, John, 27, 45
Johnson, Lawrence, 32
Johnson, Samuel, 173n47
Johnson, S. W., 29
John Thoreau & Co., 135–40
John W. Leonard Company, 145
joint editions, 15–16, 103
journeymen, 36–39

Kasson, John, 3
Keese, John, 110–11
Kentucky Bible Society, 79–80, 84–85, 90–93
Keystone Publishing Company, 121
Kickapoo nation, 84
King James Bible, 82

Kirk, Thomas, 62, 64–65
Kubler, George, 4, 16, 29

labor and shop practices, 2, 5, 12, 27, 35–40
Lafayette, Marquis de, 41
LaFoy, John, 31
Landscape Gardening (Downing), 114
languages in which to print scripture, 83–84, 166n19
Larger Catechism (M'Leod), 29, 46, 47
Laurie, Bruce, 36, 38
Lavoisne, 65
Lea & Febiger Records collection, 46
Lea & Shepard, 127
Leaves of Grass (Whitman), 132
Leavitt & Allen, 114
Leavitt and Company, 110, 116, 124
Leavitt and Delisser, 106–7, 117
Leipzig book fair, 105
Leland, B., 82
Léemprière, John, 56
lending plates, 82, 85, 91, 93, 144
Leonard, James R. W., 145
letterforms, 10, 12–13, 16–17, 131
Lexington, Kentucky, 79–80, 83, 87, 90
Leypoldt & Holt, 104
Liberator, 141
Liberty Bell, 141
Life of Luther (Michelet), 117
Lilly, Wait & Co., 108
liquidation, 15–16, 103, 105, 109, 118–20, 124
literacy, 109, 142–44, 149
Literary and Philosophical Society of Newcastle, 23
literary fairs, 105–6
literary property, 114, 123, 131–32, 142, 149
literary value and authorial interest, 131–32
literary works as a genre, 133–34
Littell's Living Age, 151
Liverpool, England, 23, 143–44
local and regional Bible societies, 70–71, 73, 76, 80, 82–83
local printers, 1–2, 11–12, 16, 42, 103
London Magazine, 24
Longfellow, Henry Wadsworth, 118, 134–35
Long Island Bible Society, 82
Long-Island Star, 28

Long Primer type, 76–77, 81, 88–89, 97, 167n36
Lord, George W., 111
Lothian, George B., 31–32
Louisville, Kentucky, 145
Lovejoy, Elijah P., 143
Lyman & Rawdon, 110

Macaria (Wilson), 122, 170–71n51
machine-made paper, 1, 69, 79
machines
 cylinder presses, 81, 167n46
 Fourdrinier papermaking machine, 79
 and graphite, 135
 handpresses, 12–15, 42, 50, 75, 79, 98
 industrial capitalism, 35–36
 inking device, 79
 mechanical reproduction, 129
 mechanics of the iron printing press, 19
 mechanization of American life, 130
 and modernity, 139
 power press, 28
 spiritual machinery, 72
 swift mechanization, 39
 technological improvement, 3
 uniformity in output, 11
Madison, Charles, 124
mahogany blocks, 50–51
Mahon, Charles, 17–19, 20, 23–24, 27, 28–29
manufacturing
 centered around New York, 33
 of graphite, 135–37
 international copyright law, 150
 swift mechanization, 39
 technological advance, 10–11
 uniformity of output, 10–11
market revolution, 72
Marx, Leo, 130
Maryland, 71
Maryland Bible Society, 93
Massachusetts, 23, 80, 135–37
mass media production and distribution, 70–71
master-apprentice model, 27, 35–38
Mather, George, 97, 99
maturation of American printing trades, 16
M'Carty & Davis, 111–12

Meadville, Pennsylvania, 96
mechanization of American life, 130
Mecom, Benjamin, 19, 20
Melville, Herman, 118–20, 134–35, 140, 172n27
Mémoires de l'Institut, 23
Mental Treasures, 108
Mentz, G. W., 99
Mercein. *See* T. & W. Mercein
metal-stamping process, 17
Methodist Book Concern, 70–71, 100
Methodists, 74
Method of Founding Stereotype, as Practiced by Charles Brightly, The, 20–22
Miami nation, 103
Michelet, Jules, 117
Miller and Co. *See* Miller & Curtis
Miller & Curtis, 118–20
mimeo/xerographic revolution, 132
Minion Bible plates, 80–82, 87–89, 91, 93, 99–100, 167n36
mobility, 52, 102
modernity, 139
Mohawk translation, 83–84, 88
Monthly Magazine, 22, 24–25
Morse, Jedidiah, 42, 72, 100
Mosses from an Old Manse (Hawthorne), 114–15
Mount Monadnock, 137
M. Thomas & Sons, 111
Müller, Johann, 16
multiple sets of plates, 12, 13–15, 24, 28, 34, 48–50, 52, 71, 74–75, 81, 150, 169n11
Munroe, James, 104
Murray, John, 17
Murray, Lindley, 29, 31, 49–50

Napoleonic Wars, 18–19
Narrative (Brown), 143–44
Narrative (Truth), 141–43
national convention of journeyman printers, 1851, 39
national printers' meetings, 38
National Standard, 145
National Typographical Union, 39
Native Americans, 83–84
new advances in printing technology. *See* technological advances

Newark Bible society, 70, 165n8
Newburgh, New York, 82
Newcastle Typographical Society, 23
new economies, 129
New England Tract Society, 100
New Hampshire, 135, 137, 145
New Hampshire Bible Society, 82–83
New Haven Bible Society, 93
New History of Stereotyping (Kubler), 4, 16
new printing technologies. *See* technological advances
newspaper publishers, 12, 28, 33, 36–40, 150
  See also advertisements
New System of Modern Geography (Guthrie), 42
New Testaments, 49–50, 52, 56–59, 63–64, 68, 71, 85–90, 92, 95, 97, 99–100
New York
  and ABS, 69–80
  African Americans authors and publishers, 145–46
  American Booksellers Association convention, 171n59
  associations of printers, 38–39
  Bible printing and publishing, 49, 51–52, 93–94, 97
  book fairs, 125–26
  Bruces' market, 48
  and Carey, 56–57, 61–62, 64–66
  and Fanshaw, 78–79
  journeymen printers, 36–37
  and Kentucky Society, 90–92
  literary fair in, 105–6
  parcel sale, 128
  periodicals, 150
  printing trades in, 103, 163n83, 167n48
  resistance to using stereotype plates, 31
  stereotype foundries in, 30
  stereotype plate production, 12, 28–35, 46
  Thoreaus' business, 137
  trade sales in, 104, 108–10, 112–20, 121, 122–25, 149
  Twelve Years a Slave, 121
  and Wallis, 94–95
New York Auxiliary Bible Society, 78
New York Bible and Common Prayer Book Society, 96–97
New York Bible Society, 71, 78, 82, 84, 86

New York Book-Publishers' Association, 113–17, 124
New-York Columbian, 31
New York Daily Tribune, 118–20
New York Female Auxiliary Bible Society, 75
New-York Free-School Society, 94
New-York Historical Society, 76
New-York Religious Tract Society, 29
New York Tribune, 38, 114, 122
New York Typographical Society, 38–39
Nitchie, John, 95–96, 168n91
nonapprentices, 38
Nonpareil type, 69, 77, 93, 99–100
Nord, David Paul, 69, 71–72
Northup, Solomon, 120–22, 125
Norton's Literary Advertiser, 111–12
Norton's Literary Gazette, 34, 103, 105, 112–13, 115, 116, 147
Notes (Ostervald), 62

octavo Bibles, 29, 48, 74, 76–77, 81–82, 84, 86–89, 92–93, 95–96, 100
Olmstead, James, 82
On the Economy of Machinery and Manufactures (Babbage), 10
Osborn, Joseph, 87
Osgood, James R., 124–28
Ostervald, Jean-Frédéric, 62
ownership transfer, 85, 102
owning plates, 5, 44, 57–59, 62, 71, 75, 103, 143

Paine, Thomas, 70
Palmyra, New York, 97
Panic of 1819, 65, 89–92
Panic of 1837, 37
Panic of 1857, 149
Panic of 1873, 126
papermaking, 73
papier-mâché, 13
parcel sales, 128
Parker, Herschel, 119
Parley's Magazine, 150
Parry & McMillan, 115
Partington, Charles Frederick, 18, 26
Patent Office, 3
Paulus, Michael, 69

Pearl type, 76–77, 167n36
pencil-making industry, 135–37
Pennsylvania, 71, 90, 96, 151
Penny Magazine, 150
periodicals, 12, 33, 40, 133, 145, 150–51
Perkins, Jacob, 20, 23
Peter Porcupine. *See* Cobbett, William
Philadelphia, Pennsylvania
    and ABS, 83
    Bible plates, 48–49
    and Carey, 41–43, 60–63, 66
    changes taking place in typefounding and bookselling, 55
    and Hart, 147–51
    journeymen, 38
    literary fair in, 106
    market for stereotyped New Testaments, 57
    moving books, 52
    and New York, 33
    printing trades in, 103
    resistance to using stereotype plates, 31
    slavery, 163
    stereotype foundries in, 30
    stereotype plate production, 12
    Thoreaus' business, 137, 145
    trade sales in, 104, 108–9, 111–13, 115, 126
    Twelve Years a Slave, 121
Philadelphia Bible Society, 29, 48, 70, 75, 96, 98, 100
Phillips, Sampson, and Co., 103–4
Phinney, Elihu and Henry, 31
Phinney, H. H., 99
Piazza Tales, The (Melville), 118–19
Pica type, 60, 64, 95, 100, 164n43, 167n36
Pickering, William, 98
Pierre (Melville), 140
Pilgrimage to My Motherland (Campbell), 146
Pinckney, Charles Cotesworth, 72
Pittsburgh, Pennsylvania, 32, 80, 90–91, 93
plaster casting method, 13–14, 18, 20, 25
plates. *See* stereotyping/stereotype plates
pocket Bibles, 77, 95–96
Poe, Edgar Allan, 130–32
"Poet, The" (Emerson), 138–39
poetry, 137–39
polytyping, 23

power presses, 1, 12, 28, 36–37, 39, 68–69, 79, 97–98, 133
press feeders, 36, 38
Pretzer, William S., 37
price auctioning, 126
prices. *See* costs
printed stock, 43, 103, 105, 108, 124, 149, 151
Printer, 150
printing trades
    African American presence in, 144–46
    anastic printing, 130–31
    auction sales, 104–7
    capital investments, 15–16
    development of stereotyping in the United States, 28–35
    growth and innovation of, 1–2, 11–12, 103
    and Hart, 147–51
    labor in, 35–40
    market for stereotype plates, 46–55
    Panic of 1873, 126
    power presses, 97–98
    stereotyping experiments, 16–20
    technological changes in, 4–6, 15, 73, 136–37
    trade secrets and techniques of stereotyping, 27–28
    unionization, 38–39
    youth labor, 39
    See also book production and distribution; Carey, Mathew; trade sales; typefounding trade
Printer's Complete Guide (Partington), 18
Printer's Guide, The (van Winkle), 23–24
printshops, 14–15, 33, 36–37, 39, 139, 145
productivity and uniformity, 11
profits, 64–65, 75, 84–85, 102, 104, 108, 131, 134–35
proofreaders, 81–82, 87
Protestant denominations, 71–73, 100, 166n19
Psalms, 62–63
public incorporation of ABS, 85
publicity work, 83, 85, 167n48
Publishers' Weekly, 105, 124–28, 171n59
publisher-to-bookseller sales of printed stock, 105
Putnam, George Palmer, 114, 119, 127
Putnam & Co, 114–15

quarto Bibles, 43, 46, 48, 51–55, 60–62, 64, 67, 87, 95–97, 99

rail networks, 149
Ramage, Adam, 79
Ramage, Mary, 79
Reed, James, 99
reform of the trade sale system, 113, 117, 125, 151
regional biases, 31
regional Bible societies, 70–80, 85
regional booksellers, 104, 113
regional printing and publishing businesses, 1–2, 6, 50, 149
regulation of the printing industry, 103, 106, 117
relief etchings, 131, 171n4
relief woodcuts and wood engravings, 26, 40, 162n41
religious publishing organizations, 12, 70, 73–74, 100, 166n19
    See also American Bible Society (ABS); evangelicals
remaindered book market. *See* secondhand market in stereotype plates
repairs, 57–59, 66, 91, 97, 156–57
    See also proofreaders
republican evangelical movement, 100–101
republicanism, 3
retail sale, 43, 92, 105, 118
    See also trade sales
"Review of the Character and Claims of the American Bible Society," 72
Reynolds, Thomas T., 82
Richmond, Peggy Jo Zemens, 145
Richmond, Virginia, 122
Riker, J. C., 114
Rohrbach, Augusta, 142–43
Roxbury, Massachusetts, 99
royalties, 104, 118, 119, 133, 135, 171n51
rubber inking rollers, 69, 79, 167n39
Russwurm, John, 145
Ruth Hall (Willis), 123

sales. *See* trade sales
Sallust, 17
Samson Low, Son & Co., 121

Scarlet Letter (Hawthorne), 134
scripture. *See* Bibles
secondhand market in stereotype plates, 12, 16, 97, 105, 120, 124–28, 149
Senchyne, Jonathan, 144
Sergeant & Rawle's, 111–12
set type, 10, 13, 16–19, 23, 27, 33–34, 39, 46, 97, 135
Shakespeare, William, 107, 112, 117–18, 160n6
shared profit model, 134
Sheehan, Daniel, 108
Shelby, Isaac, 72
Sheldon & Goodrich, 31
Shield, Francis, 28
siderography, 23
"Signs of the Times" (Carlyle), 3
Sigourney, Lydia, 34–35
Silliman, Benjamin, 30
Silver, Rollo, 23–24, 29–32, 43
single-page plates, 33–34
skilled labor, 35–40
slavery, 120–21, 141–45
Smith, Daniel D., 62, 95–96
Smith, George, 32
Smith, Joseph, 97
Smith & McDougal, 135–37
social reforms, 72
Society for the Promotion of Useful Knowledge, 150
South, 33, 42, 48, 122–23
Spanish Bibles, 76, 83, 86–88, 93, 95
Specimen of Ornamental Type and Printing Ornaments (Chandler), 33–34
Splendid Bible, Carey, 65
standing committee, ABS, 68–69, 80–85, 87–100, 158, 167n48
standing type, 11, 14–15, 42–45, 48–52, 56–58, 66–67, 93
Stanhope, Lord. *See* Mahon, Charles
Starr, Charles, 30–31
steady sellers, 12, 31, 43, 62, 112, 125, 149
steam-powered presses, 33–35, 36–37, 69, 98, 150
Stereotype Company, 30
stereotype woodcuts for Bibles, 59
stereotyping/stereotype plates
and ABS, 73–100, 158–59

African American authors and publishers, 141–46
American Anti-Slavery Society, 173n46
authorship, 129–33
Babbage's six steps, 10–11
and Bigelow, 160n2
commissioning of a family Bible, 59–67
development and spread of in the United States, 28–35
documentation, 20–28
early experiments in, 16–20
enumeration of the costs of, 44–45
first uses of in the United States, 153–55
growing market for, 46–59
and Hart, 147–51
importation duties, 150, 163n85
as innovation, 1
introduction of in United States, 11–16
labor and shop practices, 35–40
in language and literature, 129–46
mass media production and distribution, 70–71
multiple copies of the same work, 12, 13–15, 24, 28, 34, 48–50, 52, 71, 74–75, 81, 150, 169n11
Northrup's *Twelve Years a Slave*, 120–21
scholars in the field of American studies, 4–5, 160n7
stereotype foundries, *18*, *21*, 26, 30–34, 39, 62, 92–94, 103, 153–55, 162n50
and Thoreau, 136–40, 172n33
trade sales, 106–12, 114, 116–19, 123–26
widespread manufacture and trade in, 102–5
Stevens, George, 37
St. Louis Times, 143
Stockholm & Brownejohn, 29
stock images ("cuts"), 40
storage. *See* warehousing
Stowe, Harriet Beecher, 140, 142
subscriptions for Bibles, 43, 52, 62, 64–65, 77
swift mechanization, 39
Syndicate Trading Company, 128

tabletop publishing technologies, 132
Tarn, Joseph, 80–81

technological changes and advances
and ABS, 69–70, 73, 101
American spirit of improvement and interest in, 2–5
authorship, 129–33
and Babbage, 10–11
documentation of, 20–28
and Fanshaw, 79
pencil industry, 136
stereotyping, 146
and Thoreau, 139–40
transformation in print culture, 15
See also innovation(s)
textual accuracy, 62, 81, 87, 107, 131, 140
Thackeray, William Makepeace, 127
Thayer and Eldridge, 133
Thomas, Isaiah, 19–20, 29, 42–43, 52, 93, 103, 145
Thomas, Moses, 148
Thomas & Andrews, 43
Thoreau, Henry, 137–40
Thoreau, Henry David, 130
Thoreau, John, 135–40
Ticknor, Reed and Fields, 114–15
Ticknor and Fields, 106, 134
Tilloch, Alexander, 17–18, 23
Titus, Frances, 142
trade circulars, 52, 53–54, 62, 65
trade journals, 16, 105, 147
trade newspapers, 105
trade regulation, 106
trade sales
advertisements, 104–5
capital investments, 16
catalogs, 105, 107–9, 112, 120, 169n5
Hart's lots of plates, 147–51
organizing, 105–7
plates to *Twelve Years a Slave*, 121
reform of, 124–25, 128
stereotype plates at, 107–20
wartime, 122–24
trade secrets, 27–28, 48
trade unions. *See* International Typographical Union; National Typographical Union
tramp printers, 36
transatlantic system, 12, 112, 144
translating the Bible, 83–84, 88, 166n19

Treadwell, Daniel, 97–98
Truth, Sojourner, 141–43
Tuscarora tribe, 84
Twelve Years a Slave (Northrup), 120–22, 125
Twice Married, 120
T. & W. Mercein, 56–58, 65
typefounding trade
copyright, 45
correction of plates, 82
development and spread of stereotyping in the United States, 29–34
developments in, 10
documentation, 20
experiments, 16–17
labor practices, 39–40
market for stereotype plates, 46–55
in New York, 77, 94–95
secondhand plates, 97
stereotype plates, 12
type specimen books, 24, 40
Typographia (Hansard), 24
Typographia (Johnson), 27, 45
Typographical Association of New York, 38–39
typographical associations, 37–39

United States
adoption of stereotyping, 28–32, 102–5
Bible marketplace, 62–66
Carey's business, 41–59
changes in the publishing industry, 149–50
copyrights, 103–4
documenting technology of stereotyping, 20–28
experiments in printing, 19–20
first uses of stereotype plates in, 153–55
graphic manufacture in, 135–37
labor practices, 35–40
Norton's Literary Advertiser, 111
remaindered book market, 128
sales of stereotype plates in, 126
stereotype plate output, 35
technological advances in, 130
trade sales, 104–20
Twelve Years a Slave stereotype plates, 121

uniform point sizes for type, 167n36
See also American Bible Society (ABS)
Universal Masonic Library, 145
university press at Cambridge, 17, 23
Urban, Francis, 87
urbanization, 35
urban printers and publishers, 33–34, 39
urban typographical associations, 37
used plates, 81, 96–97, 102–5, 107, 108
Utica Bible Society, 80

value
   of Bibles, 63, 88, 93
   literary value, 131–32
   and Melville, 135
   Osgood sale, 127
   of standing plates, 49
   of stereotype plates, 34, 108, 123, 165n63
   of stereotyping, 27
   and trade sales, 120
   worn plates, 125
   See also capital investments; costs
Van der Mey, 16, 19
van Winkle, Cornelius, 23–24, 31
Van Winkle & Wiley, 31
Varick, Richard, 72
Virginia, 71
Volunteer's Journal (newspaper), 41

wages, 36–38
Walden (Thoreau), 130, 139–40
Walker, John, 62
Walker, S., 99
Wallis, Hammond, 93–95
Wallis & Newell, 95
warehousing or storage of plates, 15, 34–35, 42–43, 49, 84–85, 102, 106, 151
Warner, Michael, 5
Washington, Bushrod, 72

Watts, John, 28–32, 44–45, 46, 50, 60–61, 162n50
Webster, Noah, 43
Weedon, Alexis, 102
weekly news magazines, 28
Week on the Concord and Merrimack Rivers, A (Thoreau), 138–40
Welsh Bibles, 83–84
West and Johnston, 122
Western auxiliary societies, 101
Westminster Larger Catechism (M'Leod), 29, 46, 47
White, Elihu, 24, 74–78, 81–82
white-owned stereotype firms, 145–46
Whiting & Watson, 29, 46, 52
Whitman, Walt, 132–33
Whitney, Eli, 30
wholesale prices, 107–8
Wilberforce, William, 70
William D. Allen & Co., 78
Willis, Sarah Payson (Fanny Fern), 120–21
Wilson, Andrew, 19, 22–25, 27, 44–45, 48, 161n31
Wilson, Augusta Evans, 122–23, 170–71n51
Winship, Michael, 134
women, 36–38
Wood, Gordon S., 101
woodblocks, 59
woodcut illustrations, 13, 24, 142
   See also relief woodcuts and wood engravings; stereotype woodcuts for Bibles
Woolsey, William Walton, 88
Wyandot tribe, 84

Yerrinton, James M., 141–42
youth labor, 39

Zboray, Ronald, 133–34

THE PENN STATE SERIES IN THE HISTORY OF THE BOOK
James L. W. West III, *General Editor*

Editorial Board
Robert R. Edwards (Pennsylvania State University)
Paul Eggert (Loyola University Chicago)
Simon Eliot (University of London)
William L. Joyce (Pennsylvania State University)
Beth Luey (Massachusetts Historical Society)
Willa Z. Silverman (Pennsylvania State University)

PREVIOUSLY PUBLISHED TITLES IN THE PENN STATE SERIES IN THE HISTORY OF THE BOOK

Peter Burke, *The Fortunes of the "Courtier": The European Reception of Castiglione's "Cortegiano"* (1996)

Roger Burlingame, *Of Making Many Books: A Hundred Years of Reading, Writing, and Publishing* (1996)

James M. Hutchisson, *The Rise of Sinclair Lewis, 1920–1930* (1996)

Julie Bates Dock, ed., *Charlotte Perkins Gilman's "The Yellow Wall-paper" and the History of Its Publication and Reception: A Critical Edition and Documentary Casebook* (1998)

John Williams, ed., *Imaging the Early Medieval Bible* (1998)

Ezra Greenspan, *George Palmer Putnam: Representative American Publisher* (2000)

James G. Nelson, *Publisher to the Decadents: Leonard Smithers in the Careers of Beardsley, Wilde, Dowson* (2000)

Pamela E. Selwyn, *Everyday Life in the German Book Trade: Friedrich Nicolai as Bookseller and Publisher in the Age of Enlightenment* (2000)

David R. Johnson, *Conrad Richter: A Writer's Life* (2001)

David Finkelstein, *The House of Blackwood: Author-Publisher Relations in the Victorian Era* (2002)

Rodger L. Tarr, ed., *As Ever Yours: The Letters of Max Perkins and Elizabeth Lemmon* (2003)

Randy Robertson, *Censorship and Conflict in Seventeenth-Century England: The Subtle Art of Division* (2009)

Catherine M. Parisian, ed., *The First White House Library: A History and Annotated Catalogue* (2010)

Jane McLeod, *Licensing Loyalty: Printers, Patrons, and the State in Early Modern France* (2011)

Charles Walton, ed., *Into Print: Limits and Legacies of the Enlightenment; Essays in Honor of Robert Darnton* (2011)

James L. W. West III, *Making the Archives Talk: New and Selected Essays in Bibliography, Editing, and Book History* (2012)

John Hruschka, *How Books Came to America: The Rise of the American Book Trade* (2012)

A. Franklin Parks, *William Parks: The Colonial Printer in the Transatlantic World of the Eighteenth Century* (2012)

Roger E. Stoddard, comp., and David R. Whitesell, ed., *A Bibliographic Description of Books and Pamphlets of American Verse Printed from 1610 Through 1820* (2012)

Nancy Cervetti, *S. Weir Mitchell: Philadelphia's Literary Physician* (2012)

Karen Nipps, *Lydia Bailey: A Checklist of Her Imprints* (2013)

Paul Eggert, *Biography of a Book: Henry Lawson's "While the Billy Boils"* (2013)

Allan Westphall, *Books and Religious Devotion: The Redemptive Reading of an Irishman in Nineteenth-Century New England* (2014)

Scott Donaldson, *The Impossible Craft: Literary Biography* (2015)

John Bidwell, *Graphic Passion: Matisse and the Book Arts* (2015)

Peter L. Shillingsburg, *Textuality and Knowledge: Essays* (2017)

Steven Carl Smith, *An Empire of Print: The New York Publishing Trade in the Early American Republic* (2017)

Colm Tóibín, Marc Simpson, and Declan Kiely, *Henry James and American Painting* (2017)

Filipe Carreira da Silva and Mónica Brito Vieira, *The Politics of the Book: A Study on the Materiality of Ideas* (2019)

Colm Tóibín, *One Hundred Years of James Joyce's "Ulysses"* (2022)

Melvyn New and Anthony W. Lee, eds., *Notes on Footnotes: Annotating Eighteenth-Century Literature* (2022)

www.ingramcontent.com/pod-product-compliance
Lightning Source LLC
Chambersburg PA
CBHW022056290426
44109CB00014B/1113